The Life of JOSEPH FIELDING SMITH

Tenth President of The Church of
Jesus Christ of Latter-day Saints

Joseph Fielding Smith, Jr.
and
John J Stewart

Published by
DESERET BOOK COMPANY
Salt Lake City, Utah
1972

Library of Congress Catalog Card No. 72-90344
ISBN Number 0-87747-484-2

LITHOGRAPHED BY

DESERET NEWS PRESS

IN THE UNITED STATES OF AMERICA

Introduction

And blessed are all they who do hunger and thirst after righteousness, for they shall be filled with the Holy Ghost.
(3 Nephi 12:6.)

The words of the hymn, "O prove faithful, O prove faithful to your God and Zion's cause" epitomized the life of President Joseph Fielding Smith. From his early childhood he exhibited a craving thirst for knowledge of gospel principles. He loved to read. "I used to read the books that were prepared for the Primary children and for the Sunday School children in those early days, and I usually had a book in my hands when I was home. . . . One thing that I did from the time I learned to read and write was to study the gospel. I read and committed to memory the Children's Catechism and Primary books in the gospel. Later I read the History of the Church as recorded in the *Millennial Star*. I also read the Bible, the Book of Mormon, the Pearl of Great Price, the Doctrine and Covenants, and other literature that fell into my hands."

His thirst for knowledge never ceased. As a missionary near the turn of the century, he wrote, "It is my desire to improve my mind and talents while I am here, so that I may always be useful for something in life. . . . I want to be right in all things, and nothing gives me more pleasure than to learn something about the gospel, for my desire is to become acquainted with it and gain wisdom."

Truthfully he reported in a recent general conference, "All my life I have studied and pondered the principles of the gospel and sought to live the laws of the Lord. As a result, there has come into my heart a great love for him, and for his work, and for all those who seek to further his purposes in the earth."

His great desire for knowledge placed him as an authority on doctrine almost without equal in the dispensation of the fulness of times. Outside of the Prophet Joseph Smith, few men have given the insight to gospel principles and latter-day revelation as did President Joseph Fielding Smith. How true the words of the patriarch, "You will be gifted to interpret the scriptures above your associates."

President Smith often said that the Lord gave him a testimony of the gospel when he was a child. It is reasonable, then, to understand the words of the patriarch who said, "You have never known the time when you did not believe and feel within your very bones that Joseph Smith was a prophet of God and that his mission was divine."

As a special witness of the Savior, "called and ordained before you came in the flesh as an apostle of the Lord Jesus Christ to represent his work in the earth," President Smith raised his voice unceasingly to the members of the Church and to the people of the world in general to heed the teachings of our Lord and Master. Ordained to the special calling of preaching repentance to the people, he accepted the responsibility and remained true to this commission all the days of his life. Because of his uncompromising defense of the Lord's laws and principles, he was considered by many to be austere. President Smith never compromised with sin, but was quick to forgive and extend a hand of fellowship to a repentant sinner. In truth, no man had greater concern and love for each church member.

To those who knew him President Smith was a man

of great compassion. On the occasion of his eightieth birthday, his brethren over whom he presided in the Council of the Twelve paid tribute, "We who labor in the Council of the Twelve under his leadership have occasion to glimpse the true nobility in his character. . . . We only wish that the entire Church could feel the tenderness of his soul and his great concern over the welfare of the unfortunate and those in distress. He loves all the saints and never ceases to pray for the sinner."

President Smith had great love for his father, Joseph F. Smith, for his grandfather, Hyrum Smith, and for the Prophet Joseph Smith. He honored their names in very deed. How tenderly he spoke of them! He loved his Redeemer with love unfeigned. He delighted in bearing his testimony of the divine mission of the Savior as the Son of God. He was true to every trust, gentle in character, and honorable before all men. His life was one of dedication and devotion to the message of the Master.

From the words of his own testimony: "I know absolutely that Jesus Christ is the only Begotten Son of God, the Redeemer of the world, the Savior of men insofar as they will repent of their sins and accept the gospel. Through his death he redeemed all men and took upon him that sacrifice which would relieve us of our sins that we may not answer for them if we will accept him and be true and faithful to his teachings. . . . My desire is to prove true and faithful to the end."

Joseph Fielding Smith—preacher of righteousness, teacher of doctrine, theologian, scriptorian, apostle, prophet, seer, and revelator—true and faithful! Prophetically the patriarch said, "It is thy privilege to live to a good old age and the will of the Lord that you should become a mighty man in Israel. . . . It shall be thy duty to sit in council with thy brethren and preside among the people. . . . You will indeed stand in the midst of the people a prophet and a revelator to them, for the Lord has blessed you and ordained you to this calling."

It has been a privilege and a rewarding experience for John J Stewart and me to research details of his life and mission and prepare this biography which we sincerely hope will be a fitting tribute to so great a man.

Joseph Fielding Smith, Jr.

Acknowledgment

It is with sincere appreciation that we express our gratitude to the numerous people who have assisted in the production of this biography, too many to mention personally. Special thanks, however, is extended to three sisters of President Smith—Emily S. Walker, Rachel S. Taylor, and Edith S. Patrick—for their numerous contributions; Rubie Egbert, for many years secretary to President Smith; Thomas G. Truitt, and to President Smith's former employees in the Church Historian's Office; to his sons and daughters; mission presidents with whom he traveled while touring missions, general authorities, and other associates who have shared their experiences with him.

John J Stewart
Joseph Fielding Smith, Jr.

Contents

Illustrations

Chapter 1

"If ye labour all your days . . ."

A Prophet in the Space Age

When David O. McKay, president of The Church of Jesus Christ of Latter-day Saints, died in January, 1970, at the age of 96, the Church's Council of Twelve naturally looked to a younger man to succeed him. It unanimously chose Joseph Fielding Smith, then a mere 93 years old!

For a man so old to take on one of the world's most challenging jobs—or, to take on any job at all—struck me as a most singular thing. But in exploring the life of Joseph Fielding Smith, I have discovered a man with a habit of doing the unusual.

For instance, at an age when many men are tucked safely away in a nursing home absorbing liniment, Joseph Fielding Smith took up the hobby of flying in jet planes!

I remember my surprise one day when I called at his office in Salt Lake City. His secretary, Rubie Egbert, said, "Step to the window here and maybe you can see him." Curious, I walked to the window. But all that I could see was a jet streaking through the blue sky high above the Great Salt Lake. Its trail of white vapor clearly marked some steep climbs, loops, dives, rolls and turns. "He's out there fulfilling prophecy," explained his secretary with a chuckle. "Scriptures say that in the last days there will be vapors of smoke in the heavens."

"You mean he's in that plane?" I asked incredulously.

"Oh yes, that's him all right. He's very fond of flying. Says it relaxes him. A friend in the National Guard calls him up and says, 'How about a relaxing?' and up they go. Once they get in the air he often takes over the controls. Flew down to Grand Canyon and back last week, 400 miles an hour!"

I could not resist driving to the airport to be there when he landed. As the two-place T-Bird roared down the runway to a stop, from the rear cockpit, in suit and helmet, climbed this benign old gentleman, then about 80, smiling broadly. "That was wonderful!" he exclaimed. "That's about as close to heaven as I can get just now."

At age 92 he was advanced in the National Guard to the honorary rank of brigadier-general. "But they still didn't want me to fly alone." Later he limited his flying to commercial jetliners. As president of a three-million-member church with a world-wide missionary program, he did travel extensively. "The big planes are not so exciting as the T-Bird, but at my age it's a real comfort to be able to move faster than sound," he said at 95.

One cannot help being impressed with the great *length* of his life. Civil War hero Ulysses S. Grant was in the White House when Joseph Fielding checked into the world in 1876. But more remarkable still, I have found, is the great *depth* and *breadth* of his life. He not only lived life to the fullest each day, but lived totally by his beliefs.

As a Christian clergyman and crusader he had been preaching sermons from the pulpit for 75 years. I don't know how many of these sermons will be remembered. But by his personal life he taught sermons that can never be forgotten.

One day, for instance, a peddler woman called at his home. A daughter answered, but finding no item of interest bought nothing. Learning of it, Joseph Fielding handed his daughter some money and sent her hurrying after the woman. "Buy *something* whether we need it or not," he instructed her. "We must *never* turn anyone in want away from our door!"

From the pulpit he preached sermons on charity.

2

But the one that deeply impresses me he had never even mentioned. It concerns a young newspaper boy, Stanley Dixon. The Smiths already had 11 children. But when Stan was tragically orphaned, Joseph Fielding sought him out and invited him to come into their family. Putting a comforting arm around the sorrowing boy, he assured him that nothing could be quite so nice for the Smiths as to have an even dozen youngsters. Gratefully Stanley Dixon moved in.

The LDS leader preached on the importance of keeping busy. "No one should ever retire. I've known men who announced their retirement, and nature took them at their word!"

But at 95 he was still his own best sermon on non-retirement. I remember early one winter morning driving to Salt Lake City long before daylight. As I turned a corner near Temple Square, the headlight of my car brought into view an elderly man out walking in the cold, snowy air. It was Joseph Fielding. He was up every morning well before 6 o'clock, and put in a heavy day's work. It was a lifelong habit, and one that he also instilled in his children. "People die in bed," he cautioned them. "And so does ambition."

"Somehow it seemed immoral to lie in bed after 6," recalls a son. "Of course, I only tried it once. Father saw to that."

Punctuality was such a habit with him that he always wore two watches, one on each wrist—and kept another two in reserve. He never *rushed* to a meeting to be there on time; he was always there well ahead of time, waiting. Upon arriving in England for a conference in 1971, having made the jet trip so fast, he forgot to reset his watches. In the middle of the night he looked at them. They both said it was 5:30. He was up, dressed, and shaving, before his surprised son, Douglas, awoke and persuaded him to return to bed.

Even in advanced age Joseph Fielding Smith was one of the hardest working men I knew. "How do you manage to get so much done?" I once asked him. "It's in the bag," he said. "In the bag?" I asked. He pointed to a lunch sack. "I'm a brown bagger." For years he carried a sack lunch to his office, so he could keep working through the noon hour. "That gives me an extra 300 hours per year." One day a sister of his called on him at the office and scolded him for not taking a nap after lunch. She cited by name half a dozen of his associates who had long done so. "Yes," he replied, "and where are they today? All dead!"

President Smith was as tough as a keg of railroad spikes. When at 89 years of age he was walking down a flight of steps from his apartment, he slipped, fell, and suffered multiple fractures of his leg. But he was due at a meeting in the Temple a block away. Gritting his teeth, he walked the block, "limping like an old man," attended the meeting, walked home again, and only then, at others' insistence, accepted medical treatment. "The meeting got a little long," he admitted. "But then, most meetings do."

Long meetings were a peeve of his. "Business that can be conducted in two minutes should not take two hours," he insisted. And he especially disliked long, verbose speeches. His own sermons were always short and to the point. He took pride in the fact that he had never imposed on other speakers' time. Once at a church conference he followed on the program a fellow apostle whose exuberant words flowed out in a torrent with never a pause. Reaching the pulpit Joseph Fielding in his whisper-soft voice said, "Whew, I feel as though I had just passed through a tornado!" Conducting another conference session, he was asked to read in his closing remarks a long list of acknowledgments, that would have taken several minutes. He started down the list, suddenly stopped, and announced to a surprised congregation, "I am not going to read all that! We will now have the closing song and prayer."

Despite his love of planes, President Smith's life was one of almost Gandhi-like simplicity. As head of a prosperous church he could have drawn a handsome salary if he had so chosen. He did not. Or as author of two dozen books and head of several business firms he could have been independently wealthy. But he could not have cared less about wealth as such, and any display of it was repugnant to him. "The worth of money is in doing good for others with it." He avoided waste even to the point of saving scraps of string, yet freely gave away thousands of dollars for worthy causes.

One day his book publisher received a rather brusque telephone call from Joseph Fielding that left him speechless. "Why did you send me all that royalty money?" he asked, clearly annoyed. "You know I don't need that money!"

Instead of living in the church-owned Beehive House, the stately mansion that Brigham Young built, he lived in a modest apartment across the street. Instead of riding in the sleek, church-owned, chauffeured Lincoln Continental limousine, he much preferred riding in his compact Hornet. Walking is still better.

He carefully avoided any rich foods or drink; no tea, coffee, liquor, tobacco, drugs, or stimulant in any form. He loved fruits and vegetables, and was a near vegetarian, eating just an occasional piece of meat. Overnight hosts were often surprised when he asked whether instead of anything fancy he might have just his favorite evening meal, a bowl of bread and milk.

The one luxury that he did indulge in was a splendid library, both at home and office. After he was appointed president of the Church he refused to move into the president's office until all of his books had been transferred. Throughout his life he had an insatiable thirst for knowledge, and he could not resist a good book on science, religion, history, geography, sports, or current events. One of his children recalls that ofttimes of an evening when they were studying their school assignments, a textbook would come missing. "If we could find Papa we could find the book. I'm afraid the truth is, our father was sort of a literary packrat."

Although he did not have an opportunity to complete college, Joseph Fielding Smith was possibly the most learned man in a church that emphasizes scholarship. He became not only an apostle of the Church but its official historian and also chairman of the board of trustees of Brigham Young University, the world's largest privately owned school. He saw to it that children have access to good books and music. To help motivate his own youngsters to read good books, he would offer them a cash bonus, from 25 cents to five dollars, for successful completion of a quiz on a particular book.

It was through books that I became personally acquainted with President Smith. From the supervisor of the Church's educational system I learned that he had suggested adoption of a reference book of mine. This led to an interview. With his high ecclesiastical office and busy schedule I had pictured President Smith—then president of the Council of Twelve—as a man with a dictaphone in each hand, two or three telephones on his desk, and a battery of secretaries guarding the doorway.

No such thing. When I arrived at his office his one lone personal secretary, Rubie Egbert, happened to be out for the moment. From the inner office—his door is always left open—I could hear someone busily typing. Shortly the typing stopped, and President Smith himself was inviting me in, into a spacious office lined with books and historic mementos, and in the center of the room a huge desk flanked by a typewriter table. The whole room reflected a man who loved orderliness.

I later learned that he had taught himself typing and had typed many of his own manuscripts. "He will seldom let others do whatever he can do for himself," explained his secretary. I also learned that most of his books had been written in the early morning and late evening at home, to not encroach on his other church duties. I remembered an inscription I once read, "To my little children, without whose help this book could have been written in half the time," and I marveled that a man with a dozen children could ever write two dozen books.

I found Joseph Fielding to be a handsome white-haired man, of medium height and build; quiet, retiring, soft-spoken, even shy, yet friendly. He motioned for me to take an easy chair by his desk. Whatever he had been working on he turned away from, as though he had nothing to do but visit. As a writer I felt pained at interrupting a creative effort, but he was too kind to give any hint of concern.

For an hour or so we talked. His reputation as a Christian scholar I found was well deserved. He might have been a computer housed in flesh and bones. Yet his attitude was that of a student, a seeker after truth, as much as a teacher and authority. That to me was an important living sermon, for a man of his years and stature to be of such humility and of such zest for life as to still be searching after truth, to have a never lagging curiosity about things. "The more we learn the more we realize our ignorance," he assured me. "Only the Lord knows very much. But that's one reason life is infinitely interesting and challenging, because we can keep learning."

When I arose to leave he handed me a gift copy of his latest book, *Answers to Gospel Questions*, compiled from some of his writings by his son Joseph Fielding Jr. "Would you please autograph it for me?" I asked. He did so, in a careful signature, and then he turned and brought from his desk a copy of one of my books, which I did not suppose he even knew of, let alone had. "Now it is your turn to sign," he said, handing the book to me. My signature could have held no possible interest for him. But in his graciousness he invited it. And to a young author that was important.

In the public view President Smith seemed gravely serious. His talks and his writings were all business and no nonsense. As someone said, "He tells it like it is." As Isaiah of old, he considered it his life's chief mission to cry repentance to a wayward generation. And in that sense his pulpit sermons were part of his personal life sermon. Well knowing that *"Repent!"* is never a popular cry, he nevertheless made it his main theme for 75 years. And although he spoke in a soft voice, his words often carried a sting that some listeners found hard to take. Mistakenly they supposed him to be a very stern, cold, unfeeling man.

One Californian made it known that he enjoyed listening to all the church leaders except Joseph Fielding Smith. "He scares the hell out of me!" When the man's complaint reached Joseph Fielding Smith, he clapped his hands in delight. "That is exactly what I want to do, scare hell out of him, then he'll be fit for a better place!"

Refusing to tickle any ears, President Smith said things people do not like to believe, yet know are true, and it bothered them. "He stands up and lets them have it," a friend admitted. One day after speaking on the importance of observing the word of wisdom he was approached by a man who said that for the first time in his life he had enjoyed hearing such a sermon. Pleased, President Smith asked him why the change in his reaction. "Well, for the first time in my life I'm trying to live the word of wisdom!"

Although the Mormon leader had a somber pulpit personality, he also had a quiet sense of humor, a dry wit, as I learned when our paths next crossed. It was at the annual driving of the Golden Spike, celebrating completion of America's first transcontinental railroad. He was guest speaker and I was emcee. At a dinner afterward, a couple in their 60's were sitting near us. The man proudly said to him, "You probably don't remember, but 40 years ago you married my wife to me." President Smith leaned over to the man's wife and gravely asked, "Sister, do you think that you can ever forgive me?"

Modest as well as shy, President Smith disliked being fussed over or made the center of attention. It seemed to embarrass him. Unable to escape the efforts of press reporters and photographers, he sometimes bantered with them a bit, as if to relieve tension. As photographers were taking his picture driving the Golden Spike, and insisting, as photographers typically do, "Just one more!" he suddenly looked up and asked, "Why just *one* more?" As the demand for pictures continued, he said to another, "Apparently I've broken your camera." "Why so?" asked the photographer. "I heard it snap."

On any public occasion there was a clamor for his

autograph. Obligingly he accommodated, though I fancy it was distasteful to him. One young man in rather cavalier fashion thrust a copy of a printed program toward him and said, "As long as you're signing others, how about putting your John Henry on mine?" Quickly he scrawled, "John Henry."

One day President Smith and a daughter were visiting in my home town of Logan. A woman approached them on the temple grounds, studying him carefully, and finally said, "Pardon me, sir, but you look remarkably like President Joseph Fielding Smith!" "I do?" he asked in seeming surprise. "Well, thank you, thank you for the compliment," and tipping his hat walked on. His daughter was astonished. "Father, why didn't you tell her who you are?" "She didn't ask me. Besides, anyone can meet the president of the Church. But to meet someone who looks remarkably like him, that's something she'll never forget!"

Congregations sit up and take notice when the church prophet announced that he could tell them the very day that Jesus Christ will return to the earth. "I did not say that I could tell you the *year*," he reminded them. "But I can tell you the *day*. It will be on the Sabbath day, and people who ought to be in church worshipping will be out sporting or shopping."

But his best sermon on Sabbath observance had to be his own careful keeping of the day. When one of his associates arranged an itinerary that called for their returning from a church meeting in California to Salt Lake City on a Sunday evening, Joseph Fielding Smith advised him to change it to Monday morning—"unless you're coming home without me." And when a supermarket at which he shopped announced it was opening Sundays, President Smith dropped in and bid the manager goodbye. "I will not be back," he said. The manager decided to stay closed Sundays.

Joseph Fielding not only did the unusual, but he did the usual unusually well. He for instance had a way of getting from his employees their best effort. When he hired them he told them, "Remember, you are not working for me. You are working for the Lord, this is his work, and *he* expects your best!" From there they were on their own. Yet he stayed close to them emotionally. They knew he had a sincere interest in them personally, that his door was open to them. As long as his health permitted, he made a habit of walking through the offices every few days, shaking hands and speaking words of appreciation. A lady employee who was having some financial difficulty suddenly found her pay check substantially increased. Gratefully she went in to thank President Smith, but immediately he turned the conversation to other things as though embarrassed to be caught in an act of kindness.

He expected people to be self-reliant, and they knew it. "That is what life is all about," he said, "to develop our potential, and especially to gain self-mastery." He constantly had a flood of mail from men and women seeking advice on personal problems. Frequently his answer was, "Study this out carefully for yourself, and don't be afraid of making a mistake." When a newly appointed general authority of the Church asked him whether there was a manual outlining his duties, President Smith said, "Brother, *you are the manual!*"

Yet, when he ordained bishops of the Church he did give them this much advice, so basic in his thinking: "Remember, everyone has weaknesses, and there are at least two sides to every story. If you err in judgment, be sure you err on the side of love and mercy."

It is in the thoughtful little things of life that the real Joseph Fielding Smith could be seen most clearly. For instance, one day at a church conference in the Mormon Tabernacle on Temple Square a 12-year-old boy, excited to be there for the first time, had come early to be sure to get a seat close to the front. There is always a shortage of seats for the thousands wishing to attend. Just before the meeting began, and when all the seats were taken, an usher asked the boy to give up his seat so that a late arriving United States senator could have it. Meekly the boy complied, and stood in the aisle, disappointed, embarrassed, in tears. From his vantage point on the stand

President Smith noticed the youngster and motioned him to come up. When the boy told him what had happened he said, "That usher had no right to do that to you. But here, you sit by me," and shared his seat with him, in the midst of the apostles of the Church.

One day as he was interviewing a group of young men leaving on two-year missions for the Church, Joseph Fielding noticed a farm boy who had been assigned to eastern Canada. "Son, it's cold up there. Do you have a good warm coat?" "No sir, I haven't." He took the boy across the street to ZCMI department store and bought him the warmest coat in stock.

The day he was sustained in conference as president of the Church a little girl worked her way through the throng after the meeting and reached for his hand. So touched was he by the gesture he stooped down and took the child into his arms. He learned that her name was Venus Hobbs, of Torrance, California, soon to be four years old. On her birthday Venus received a surprise telephone call: Joseph Fielding Smith and his wife calling long distance to sing "Happy Birthday" to her.

President Smith was thrice married and thrice widowed: Only one wife at a time, but all for eternity. From the pulpit he admonished husbands to be loving and devoted to their wives. But the sermon that touches me is his climbing nine blocks up Salt Lake City's steep north avenues to the Latter-day Saint Hospital on a hot July day in 1971 and spending his 95th birthday anniversary sitting at the bedside of his sick wife Jessie. As her condition worsened, he stayed right with her day and night for several weeks keeping an anxious vigil, giving her what comfort and encouragement he could to the end.

Joseph Fielding Smith had his full share of sorrow, losing three wives, and also a soldier son in World War II. But to be courageous and patient in adversity was part of his personal code, and you never heard a word of complaint nor self-pity from him. Only in his private journal was there any expression of the grief that he felt.

The night Jessie died he kneeled in prayer with a

11

son and poured out his heart to God. "It was a beautiful prayer," his son later commented. "There was no bitterness, no venting of grief, only a deep expression of thanks that he had been blessed to have Aunt Jessie, that now she was free from pain, and his gratitude that they would be together again one day."

He was concerned lest his children worry unduly about him now that he was again widowed. A few days after Jessie's death a son was staying with him in his apartment. There was music playing on the radio. Joseph Fielding managed a smile and danced a little jig to the music, to show that his spirit was not vanquished. Upon his return home from a trip a few weeks later, his children had taken care to have the apartment look just like Aunt Jessie would have it for him. "See, Father, it is just the same." "No," he said, "it is not the same. Not the same. But it will have to do."

His tranquil composure reflected the remarkable self-discipline that he had developed through the years, and the absolute faith he had in the eternity of life. Speaking at the funeral of a close associate he said, "Death is not something to be feared. It is simply the final, necessary experience of mortality, and it consists of the transfer of the righteous soul to another sphere, a sphere where the Lord's work still rolls on and where joy and peace reign."

To Latter-day Saints, salvation is a family affair, and Joseph Fielding Smith had been notably successful in family affairs. He was especially wise and fortunate in his choice of wives. All three were talented and devoted, filled with love and adoration for him. The first and second wives, Louie and Ethel, were gracious, dignified, beautiful women, homemakers by choice, ideal mothers, rearing with him an outstanding family.

His third wife, Jessie Ella Evans, was something else. A buxom, jolly, ebullient woman, 26 years younger than he, she was full of fun and tricks, and helped to keep him young. During their 33 years of life together she accompanied him most everywhere, near and far. He in turn helped her do the grocery shopping, dry the supper dishes, and bottle fruit in the fall. He had no qualms about being an apostle with an apron on.

Jessie was a contralto soloist with the famed Mormon Tabernacle Choir, and was much in demand as a singer. Wherever President Smith spoke she sang, and then would insist upon his joining her in a duet. With seeming reluctance he would comply, announcing to the audience, "This is not a *duet*. It's a *do-it!*" Until her fatal illness in 1971 they were still singing do-its, he at age 95. The public loved it. Some of the songs they occasionally sang were of his own composition. In a journal where he recorded them he added a note that he had written them "principally for my own entertainment. . . . I claim no merit as a composer. *Neither do my friends make any such claim for me!*"

There was a direct line of sight between their apartment and his office in the church headquarters building, half a block away. One day as he sat at his desk he received a phone call from Jessie. "Joseph," she demanded, "who is that woman in your office?" "There is no woman in my office," he protested. "Oh, yes, there is!" she insisted. "I have my spy glasses focused on you and I know she's there!" President Smith glanced around his office. Near one wall on a pedestal sits a bust of his great-grandmother, Lucy Mack Smith, mother of the Prophet Joseph Smith. "Jessie, I must confess," he said. "You've caught me cold!" He afterward delighted in telling of his guardian angel with binoculars keeping a close watch over him.

One day the Smiths were standing on the street waiting for me to pick them up in my car. As I came along, Jessie fearing that I had not seen them placed two fingers to her mouth and whistled so loud that any traffic cop might have been envious. If such antics distressed her husband, he never said so. "In his sight Aunt Jessie could do no wrong," commented a son. A good sermon on marriage, it seemed to me.

Joseph Fielding explained, "When President [Heber J.] Grant married us he told me, 'Now, Joseph, kiss your wife.' He said it like he meant it, and I have been doing it ever since." "It couldn't be nicer," Jessie would add. "There's never been a cross word."

One time years ago after he had preached a rather vigorous sermon on the importance of properly governing one's children, an annoyed woman approached two of his little daughters and expressed sympathy for them. "I'll bet your daddy beats you!" The little girls giggled. For the Smith children, life with father was a pops concert. Church assignments frequently took him out of town, but when he got back home it was happy times, from the moment they eagerly met him at the train depot until they sadly bade him farewell again several days hence. He compensated them for the days apart by heaping a double dose of affection upon them when home. With a picnic lunch and a freezer of homemade ice cream they would take the train out to the Great Salt Lake for a swim, or run two shifts of their old Reo automobile up into a nearby canyon—it took two loads to get them all there.

In the evenings there were wondrous tales of places he had been and sights that he had seen! It was like a serialized *Gulliver's Travels.* His one little girl, Julina, became worried lest he be sent on a church assignment to the land of the cannibals, about whom she had read in school. Had he realized her concern he would have assured her that the cannibals had no appetite for Mormon apostles, especially those named Smith!

"When daddy was home it was almost fun to be sick," recalls a daughter. "He would sit for hours at our bedside, telling us stories, peeling oranges for us, playing music on the phonograph, and marching or dancing around the room with a funny hat on his head, anything to entertain us and make us happy. When we were sick in the night, it was daddy who stayed up with us, to ease the burden for mother and help us through the night."

As a boy Joseph Fielding had learned to bake bread and pies. To his youngsters' delight he would occasionally set up shop in the basement of their house and do a mass production of pies, sending the kids off in all directions to fetch this ingredient and that. He made mince meat pies, pumpkin pies, apple pies, cherry pies, lemon cream pies, whatever pies their hearts desired.

Being gone so much, he seldom lost patience with his youngsters, but when he did and scolded them, remembers a daughter, "he would feel so bad about it that we tried to behave ourselves for his sake, to spare him the pain." He developed one standard scolding line, which did not make any sense, and thus was doubly useful. He would look at them closely and say, "You make my tired ache!"

He loved sports, and helped instill this love in his sons. In fact, all five of his sons did exceptionally well in athletics, especially football. Their most enthusiastic fan was their father. Whenever his church assignments permitted, he was at the games cheering for them. He also built a tennis court and a horseshoe diamond in their own backyard. He was long a superb swimmer and for many years was an expert handball player.

Herbert B. Maw, Utah's ex-governor, tells of the day he challenged Joseph Fielding Smith to a game of handball. Maw was 20 years younger. "I thought I would just take it easy on the old gentleman and not beat him too far. Imagine my chagrin when he gave me the trouncing of my life! I thought that I was a good handball player, but I was no competition for him at all."

Each year on his birthday, July 19, his children, grandchildren and great-grandchildren met with him in a family outing in a Salt Lake City park. Gifts were distributed to all the youngsters, and after a picnic lunch there were games of softball. One year as the family patriarch hit a single and raced to first base, he slipped on the wet grass and fell flat on his back. "He landed so hard I was afraid the birthday parties were over," recalls a son. "But he was up in a second and soon tearing on around the bases like Maury Wills!"

Despite his great age President Smith maintained a close rapport with youth. And he showed the same devoted love to grandchildren as he did to his own children, even sitting up nights with them when they were ill. When his son Joseph's wife bore twins, Joseph received a check for $100—when $100 really meant something—together with a note which read, "Joseph, at the time I came into this world babies were considered worth in value about $10 apiece. . . . Knowing that the value of babies has risen with such rapid strides and that this places a burden on fathers, and since I have some interest in the babies that have just arrived, I am enclosing a part of the cost of redeeming them from the clutches of unscrupulous doctors, and hospital charges. . . . With best wishes, Father."

It was in the month that America celebrated the centennial of the Declaration of Independence and the founding of the Republic, that Joseph Fielding Smith was born. Like Hannah, mother of the Prophet Samuel, Joseph Fielding's mother had longed and prayed for a son, and promised to dedicate him to the Lord's service. And like Samuel, young Joseph took the dedication seriously. "He was something special from birth," recalls a proud sister. His father, President Joseph F. Smith, had a fine library, and every spare minute he had from chores young Joseph was studying scriptures and other good books.

Joseph Fielding said his first church assignment was to accompany Brigham Young to the dedication of the St. George Temple in Utah's Dixieland. "Of course, I don't remember it too well," he added with a smile. "I was only one year old then."

Joseph Fielding married first at age 21, but that did not relieve him of the responsibility of filling a foreign mission for his Church. So kissing his bride of one year goodbye he made a lonely journey to England, where he was promptly pelted with garbage by a crowd of ruffians. For two long, lonesome years he labored there, in Robin Hood's country of Nottingham, cooking his own meals, darning his own socks, pressing his own clothes, paying his own keep, walking wherever he went; teaching the gospel to what few would listen. Public speaking was difficult for him, and singing even more so. But in the line of duty he helped organize a quartet, The Sagebrush Singers. "After listening to us sing, people were glad to hear us talk!"

In pleasant contrast to the rudeness he suffered in England as a young missionary was the warm and cordial welcome he received from thousands, including the press, when he returned to conduct a church conference there in August, 1971. BBC even sent a television team to Salt Lake City to do an advance interview with him.

As a young missionary he wrote home to his father in 1899, "It is my desire to improve my mind and talents while I am here, so that I may always be useful for something in life." And that, it seems to me, well expresses the life-long sermon that Joseph Fielding Smith lived. That, and something he said at the 1971 British conference of the Church. Speaking deep from the heart he declared, "Because all men are our brothers, we desire to love and bless and fellowship them."

In Joseph Fielding Smith, youthful at 95, one felt a comforting reassurance that there is something for each of us to look forward to down the road; that while the body eventually grows old, the spirit of man can be eternally young. The secret to it is in his style of Christianity, to live life to the fullest: to love, to learn, to share, to give.

Chapter 2

And Then There Were Eight . . .

His Birth and Ancestry

Joseph Fielding Smith. Joseph Fielding Smith. Quietly, gratefully Julina repeated the name as she snuggled the newborn infant to her breast. So, at last she did have a son! She looked up from her bed at the proud papa, Joseph Fielding Smith Sr. Their eyes met as they silently shared once again the joyous miracle of birth, of life, of parenthood. He leaned over and kissed her tenderly. For ten years they had looked to this moment.

Soon the room was filled with other members of the family anxiously waiting to welcome this newest little one into their happy family circle. There were two other wives, Sarah Ellen and Edna, and seven youngsters, ranging in age from Julina's seven-year-old Mary Sophronia to tiny Heber John, just 16 days old. Sarah Ellen held Heber John in her arms, for he was hers. She also had a five-year-old girl, Leonora, and a three-year-old boy, Joseph Richards. Edna, a younger sister of Julina's, had two little sons at her side, Hyrum Mack, four years old, and Alvin Fielding, not quite two. Edna was four months pregnant and she and the other wives and their husband good naturedly speculated whether hers would also be a boy, her third, or a girl.

Outside it was a hot day—July 19, 1876—but within the thick and shaded walls of the Smith home at 333

Old Joseph F. Smith family home at 333 West First North Street, Salt Lake City, showing some of President Smith's family. Near the poplar tree was a familiar spot for President Joseph Fielding Smith to sit to read the scriptures as a young boy. The house still stands, as of 1972.

West First North in Salt Lake City it seemed tolerably comfortable, and the excitement could not have been greater if this had been the first child rather than the tenth in the family.

It had been agreed between husband and wives that Julina as the oldest and longest married of the three women should have the right to reserve the father's full name, Joseph Fielding, for her firstborn son. Edna had been the first to bear a son, and he was proudly given the name of Hyrum Mack, after his grandfather, the martyred Patriarch to the Church; and to her second son went two other cherished names in the Smith family: Alvin Fielding, Alvin being the Prophet Joseph's and Hyrum's oldest brother, and Fielding being the maiden name of Hyrum's second wife, Mary, the mother of Joseph F. Sarah Ellen was permitted to give her oldest son the name Joseph, coupled with her own maiden name of Richards, and he would be called Richards—and also Richard, Rich, JR, Dick, and Buddy. But to Julina only would be the right of using the two names, Joseph Fielding, together as one.

Julina had given birth to three daughters, and had given the first the feminine form of her husband's name: Mercy Josephine. Next came Mary Sophronia, and then Donette, now three years old. Mercy Josephine, whom her father affectionately called "Dodo," had died before reaching the age of three. Sarah Ellen's firstborn, Sarah Ella, had also died in infancy—just one week old. So that left but seven to greet tiny Joseph Fielding.

For his father, 1876 was indeed a red letter year. Come December Edna did give birth to another son, and they named him Alfred Jason, after Edna's and Julina's father, Alfred Lambson, and after a Smith ancestor, Jason Mack, whose name Joseph Fielding Sr. sometimes used as an alias while on church assignments. Three sons in one year! Sarah Ellen's Heber John, born July 3, on the eve of the centennial anniversary of the signing of the American Declaration of Independence; Julina's Joseph Fielding, on July 19, and Edna's Alfred Jason, on December 13. Life was beautiful.

Sadly, Heber John died when only eight months old, and Alfred Jason when only 15 months old, again plunging the family into sorrow. Fortunately Julina's son of that centennial year survived the rigors of infancy.

Each child in the Smith family was very special— and in time there were 43 of them, plus five adopted ones, for an even four dozen, each warmly loved by affectionate parents. But as all agreed, there was something doubly special about this little one born on July 19, 1876. It was not just that he, of all the 22 boys, got his father's full name. Like Hannah of old, mother of the Prophet Samuel of biblical fame, Julina Smith had greatly longed for and prayed for a son, promising the Lord that if he would so bless her she would do all possible to see that the boy was reared to serve God, to be a credit to the Lord and to his own father. And like Samuel, Joseph Fielding took the agreement between mother and God seriously. When old enough to walk he would walk in his father's footsteps. Like his father he would become a Christian scholar and historian, a missionary, an apostle,

a prophet, seer and revelator, and president of The Church
of Jesus Christ of Latter-day Saints.

If, as the author of Ecclesiastes suggested, "To everything there is a season, and a time to every purpose under
the heaven: a time to be born, and a time to die. . . ."
then perhaps it was more than mere coincidence that
Joseph Fielding Smith was born in the month that America was celebrating the 100th anniversary of the signing
of the Declaration of Independence, and that he was
born in the few-day period between that memorable
July 4th and July 24th, Pioneer Day, when Utahns would
celebrate the 29th anniversary of the arrival of the Mormon pioneers in the Salt Lake Valley.

There was a tragic relationship between those two
dates, the 4th and the 24th of July, the one representing
the founding of a democracy upon the earth, with all
the high hopes and aspirations the founding fathers
held for the infant nation; and the other representing not
just the courage of the Mormon pioneers, but sadly reflecting also the gross failure of the American nation to
live up to those ideals and constitutional guarantees envisioned by the founding fathers. The Mormons, like
many another minority group, had suffered from bigotry,
tyranny, hatred and persecution heaped upon them by a
nation not able or willing to live by the democratic
principles it professed. After suffering nearly two decades of abuse within the confines of the United States
the Mormons had fled into the wilderness of the Rocky
Mountains and Great Basin. It was as George A. Smith,
favorite cousin of the Prophet Joseph and a counselor
to Brigham Young, put it: "The Mormons came to the
Rocky Mountains of their own free will and choice—
because they were compelled to!"

Despite the abusive treatment they had suffered,
the Latter-day Saints clung fast to their belief that the
American democracy had been founded under divine
guidance, as a preliminary step to the restoration of the
gospel and Church of Jesus Christ in their fullness, as
part of the dispensation of the fullness of times, prior

21

to the second coming of the Savior. It grieved them that after a hundred years as a nation the republic had not matured sufficiently to accommodate the rights of all men, regardless of race or religious creed. And so the Mormons had to continue suffering oppression because of their beliefs and practices, particularly at this time the practice of plural marriage.

If the United States government had had its way, Joseph Fielding Smith would never have been born. The Justin Morrill bill passed into law by Congress and signed by President Abraham Lincoln in 1862, in the midst of the Civil War, specifically forbade polygamy and the Supreme Court had upheld the law. Resolutely, Brigham Young and his associates refused to abide by what they considered with good reason to be an unjust, oppressive law enacted as a tool of religious persecution. It was at the specific counsel of President Young, and with the consent of his first wife, Levira Annett Clark Smith, that Joseph Fielding Sr. entered into plural marriage.

He married Julina Lambson, on a beautiful spring day, May 5, 1866, in the Endowment House in Salt Lake City. He was 27 years of age and she was almost 17. Joseph had been working as a clerk in the Church Historian's Office. Church historian then was George A. Smith, an apostle, who had become a sort of foster father to Joseph. The Historian's Office was in his home, and it was there that Joseph met Julina Lambson, a niece of George A. Smith. George's wife, Bathsheba, was a sister of Julina's mother, Melissa Jane Lambson. From the age of nine, Julina had lived with her Uncle George and Aunt Bathsheba, as a matter of family finance and also to afford companionship to Bathsheba's only daughter, who desired a sister.

When Joseph began working there, Julina had become a very beautiful 16-year-old, and he was immediately attracted to her, and she to him. To persons with an eternal view of marriage, a 10-year age difference was of no consequence. Julina fondly recalled this period: "A handsome young man by the name of Joseph F. Smith

Joseph F. Smith when ordained an apostle in The Church of Jesus Christ of Latter-day Saints in 1866.

Julina Lambson Smith soon after her marriage to Joseph F. Smith, May 5, 1866.

President Joseph F. Smith as he appeared in later life.

Julina Lambson Smith as she appeared May 5, 1935.

returned from his third mission and was assisting as a clerk in the Historian's Office. I often saw him and admired him; I thought he was the most handsome and finest man I had ever seen. I didn't think for a moment he had ever really noticed me but later I learned he had watched me for some time and had fallen in love with me. When he proposed marriage, I was somewhat frightened and also happily surprised. I answered him by saying, 'I will not marry anyone unless my Uncle George approves.' Joseph went immediately to Uncle George and asked for my hand. He said, 'Joseph there isn't a young man in the world I would rather give her to.'"

Standing as a witness to their marriage was 25-year-old Levira, whom Joseph had married seven years earlier, in 1859. Levira was his cousin, a daughter of Samuel Harrison Smith, next younger brother of Hyrum and Joseph. In the summer of 1844, five weeks after Hyrum and Joseph were murdered in Carthage Jail, Samuel also gave his life for the gospel cause, dying from results of mob persecution. Levira was then only two years of age, and Joseph but six years of age. In the lonely and difficult years that followed the two cousins grew fond of each other, and their marriage seemed to strengthen and reunite a family that had been torn asunder by persecution and other hardships.

An unfortunate set of circumstances eventually led to Levira's separation from Joseph, in 1867, the year after he married Julina. In a biography of his father, Joseph Fielding offered this explanation: "His first wife, Levira A., due to interference on the part of relatives, and because of the continued absence of her husband in mission fields and in ecclesiastical duties, was drawn away and went to California, having obtained a separation. Enemies of President Smith in later years circulated the report that this separation came because he entered plural marriage. In answer to this charge he said: 'My first wife [Levira] . . . was intimately acquainted from her childhood with the young lady [Julina] who became my second wife, and it was with their [both wives'] full knowledge and consent that I entered into plural marriage, my first wife being present as a witness when I took my second wife, and freely gave her consent thereto. Our associations as a family were pleasant and harmonious. It was not until long after the second marriage that my first wife was drawn from us, not on account of domestic troubles, but for other causes. In eight years of wedded life we had no children. She constantly complained of ill health and was as constantly under a doctor's care. She concluded to go to California for her health and before going procured a separation.' This all occurred previous to 1868. Later Levira A. Smith returned to Utah and then went to St. Louis where she died."

Julina, the second wife, had a similar recollection of the matter: "I made my first home in one room of his [Joseph's] house where another wife was living. She, Levira, was a semi-invalid, and had been ill off and on for a number of years. Her husband had been on two missions, leaving her most of this time with her mother. Levira accepted me and we were dear to each other, but when she learned that Joseph and I were to have a child and told her mother, her mother was upset and said such things as that Joseph would not love her as much any more, etc. With such tales, she filled the girl's mind with suspicions and doubts about the Church and the gospel. Unknown to Joseph and me, Levira went to President Young and expressed her desire for a divorce. She had decided she would prefer going with her mother to another state [California] and another life. This was a very sad experience for both Joseph and me. Some time later I was happily surprised to have a caller. Here was Levira. She said she was on her way through Salt Lake on her way East [to St. Louis, Missouri], but could not go without first seeing me and my baby. We again parted in sadness, but friendly, and my heart surely went out to her."

Levira died December 18, 1888, at age 46, when Joseph Fielding Jr. was 12 years old. But she had separated from the family before there were any children to know her or to be troubled by this domestic rupture. To

Joseph Fielding and his brothers and sisters she was only a name, seldom mentioned.

With Julina's consent, Joseph took a third wife shortly after Levira's departure from the family. On March 1, 1868, he married Sarah Ellen Richards, 17-year-old daughter of the late Willard Richards, a cousin of Brigham Young and a second counselor to him in the presidency of the Church. Willard earlier had been a member of the Council of Twelve and a personal secretary and confidant of the Prophet Joseph. When Brigham Young had suggested that Joseph take another wife, he and Julina had discussed together who it should be and had agreed upon Sarah Ellen, who readily accepted the offer.

Julina's youngest sister, Edna Lambson, became his fourth wife, on New Year's Day, 1871. She was 19 years old. As earlier, it had been a matter of counsel from President Young to enlarge his family, and a mutual decision with Julina as to whom should be asked. These four marriages of his father's had all occurred before Joseph Fielding was born. Two others followed when he was seven years old. On December 6, 1883, his father married Alice Ann Kimball, 25-year-old daughter of the late President Heber C. Kimball, and mother of three youngsters by a previous marriage to David Patten Rich, son of Apostle Charles C. Rich. Five weeks later, on January 13, 1884, Joseph married Mary Taylor Schwartz, 18-year-old daughter of William and Agnes Taylor Schwartz and a niece of President John Taylor, to whom Joseph F. Smith was then serving as a counselor in the Church presidency.

Levira had no children; Julina had 11, four boys and seven girls, plus an adopted son and an adopted daughter; Sarah Ellen had 11 also, four boys and seven girls; Edna had ten, five of each; Alice Ann had seven, five boys and two girls—four of them by Joseph, three boys and one girl, and three by her earlier marriage, two boys and one girl; Mary had seven also, six boys and one girl. That was a total of 43 children by Joseph F. Smith, plus five adopted.

Of these 43, 22 were boys and 21 girls, and of the five adopted, three were boys and two were girls. So sex-wise it was a pretty evenly divided family. Of the 48 children, nine were still living as of October 1, 1972: four of Julina's, including an adopted daughter; one of Sarah Ellen's, one of Edna's, one of Alice Ann's, and two of Mary's.

Joseph Fielding Smith's birth date between Independence Day (July 4) and Pioneer day (July 24) was especially appropriate in that he was born into the most illustrious family in the Church and one of the most substantial families in America; a family distinguished in church history and somewhat in national history by its record of service, sacrifice and leadership in worthy causes. Five of Joseph Fielding's ancestors were Pilgrim passengers on the *Mayflower* which landed near Plymouth Rock, Massachusetts, in 1620, more than a century and half prior to the founding of the American Republic. His direct line of *Smith* ancestors in America goes back to 1638, just 18 years after the *Mayflower* group landed.

His direct line of *Smith* forebears, back to Robert Smith, the first one to come to America, is as follows:

His father, Joseph Fielding Smith Sr. (1838-1918), generally referred to now as Joseph F. Smith, was sixth president of the Church (1901-1918). He is the one and only church president acquainted with all the other nine of the first ten presidents of the Church: He was a nephew of the Prophet Joseph Smith, to whom his father, Hyrum, served as counselor and then assistant president or co-president. He was ordained an apostle by Brigham Young, and served in turn as a counselor to Brigham Young, John Taylor, Wilford Woodruff, and Lorenzo Snow, his predecessors as church president. He was closely associated also with his cousin Heber J. Grant who succeeded him as president of the Church. And it was he who ordained as apostles George Albert Smith, David O. McKay and Joseph Fielding Smith, who became the eighth, ninth and tenth presidents of the Church respectively.

Old site of the home of Robert Smith in Boxford, Mass., first Smith ancestral homesite in America.

Old Smith home, Topsfield, Mass., the birthplace of Joseph Smith, Sr., first patriarch to the Church.

Heber J. Grant, who knew all the other presidents except the Prophet Joseph, stated that Joseph F. was his "ideal" among all the men he had known. Joseph F.'s story is certainly one of the most heroic of any in the Church. He was born in November, 1838, in Far West, Missouri, when the Saints were being driven from Missouri under an extermination order of Governor Lilburn W. Boggs. His father was in prison under a death sentence. When he was but a few days old a mob burst in upon his mother's home and in ransacking the house threw a mattress upon the infant Joseph and left him for dead. Five and a half years later his father and uncle, Hyrum and Joseph, were shot to death in Carthage Jail. Joseph F.'s last glimpse of his father was as he, Joseph, a little five-year-old, stood on the street in Nauvoo, and his father rode up on a horse, leaned over in the saddle, picked him up, kissed him goodbye, set him back down, and rode off to his death in Carthage.

At nine years of age Joseph drove an ox team across the plains and helped his widowed mother, Mary Fielding Smith, establish a home in the Salt Lake Valley. When he was only 13 years old, his mother died, leaving him, his younger sister Martha, and an older half-brother and three older half-sisters orphans. The gross neglect and even abuse that Mary Fielding Smith, widow of the martyred Patriarch, suffered in crossing the plains and making a home in Salt Lake Valley, reflects too vividly the unfortunate gap between gospel teachings and individuals' behavior. It led to her early death, and prompted her son Joseph to emphasize in his ministry the importance of church members truly living the gospel.

At age 15 as a student in Salt Lake City he administered a well deserved whipping to a harsh schoolmaster who had planned to whip his younger sister, Martha, as a disciplinary measure. This resulted in his being expelled from school—the humiliated schoolmaster also dropped out—and he was then called on a mission to Hawaii, at age 15. He filled several missions there, to Great Britain and the eastern United States. At the age of 27 he was ordained an apostle, although there was no opening in the Council of Twelve at the time, and as a counselor to Brigham Young—not first nor second counselor, but a counselor.

Hyrum Smith (1800-1844) father of Joseph Fielding Smith Sr., had an equally illustrious career in the Church. He was the older brother of the Prophet Joseph, nearly six years older, and was one of the first half dozen members of the Church. He was one of the eight witnesses to the Book of Mormon plates and assisted in the first printing of the book. It seems that in the earliest days of the Church he was not as close to the Prophet as some others; at least he did not receive the offices and recognition that others did. But his steadfast loyalty to his younger brother proved particularly beneficial, especially at times when apostasy became rampant even among the leaders. In 1837, on nomination of Sidney Rigdon, Hyrum was sustained as second counselor in the presidency, succeeding Frederick G. Williams, whom the saints in Missouri voted in conference to reject.

By the time Hyrum had returned home to Kirtland after the Missouri visit, his wife Jerusha Barden had died, leaving him with four little children. On advice of Joseph he quickly remarried, choosing Mary Fielding, a recent convert to the Church. A year later she became the mother of Joseph Fielding Smith Sr.

Hyrum's oldest son, John, by his first marriage, would one day become Patriarch to the Church, during the same period that Joseph F. was president. John Smith's descendants continue to occupy the office of church patriarch. So, again in 1970 when Joseph Fielding Smith became tenth president of the Church, Hyrum's direct descendants held both these key offices, those of church president and church patriarch.

In 1841, following the death of their father, the Prophet Joseph released Hyrum from the office of second counselor in the presidency, naming William Law in his place. Then he ordained Hyrum to three other offices: (1) Patriarch to the Church, in place of their father; (2)

Second Elder of the Church, in place of Oliver Cowdery, who had apostatized, and (3) prophet, seer and revelator and assistant president or co-president of the Church, to hold the keys of presidency jointly with the Prophet himself. During the last three years of his life (1841-44) Hyrum was the number two man in the Church, ahead of Sidney Rigdon, Brigham Young or any others. Had he survived the Prophet he would have become the president of the Church. Letters, proclamations and other documents during this period frequently bear the signatures, "Joseph Smith and Hyrum Smith, Presidents of the Church."

So intense was Hyrum's loyalty to Joseph that he chose to die with him in Carthage Jail though the Prophet had urged him to take his family and flee to Cincinnati or elsewhere, that he might live to lead the Church after the Prophet's death. Hyrum's firm reply, from which he would not waiver, was, "Joseph, I will not leave you."

Only once, so far as the church records reveal, did Hyrum ever really oppose the Prophet, or fail to sustain him in a matter, and that was at Nauvoo in 1843: the Prophet sought to have Sidney Rigdon released as his first counselor, for Sidney had rejected plural marriage and other important teachings of the Prophet and was of little use to him in the church leadership. Rigdon got up and pleaded with the people to sustain him in the office, and Hyrum spoke in Rigdon's behalf. Angrily, Joseph, who had already ordained Amasa Lyman to be Rigdon's successor, declared to the congregation, "I have thrown him [Rigdon] off my shoulders and you have again put him on me. You may carry him but I will not!" Rigdon improved somewhat in his behavior, although there was still trouble. Joseph reluctantly accepted him as his running mate when he sought the presidency of the United States in 1844. But after the martyrdom, and his unsuccessful bid to succeed Joseph as head of the Church, Rigdon openly denounced "the Smith brothers" as evil men, adulterers, etc., who had led the Church astray.

Joseph the Prophet, who had seen not only Rigdon

and Cowdery, but many other church leaders, turn against him, grew to appreciate more and more the loyalty of his brother Hyrum. At a time in Kirtland when he was having difficulty with their younger brother William, an apostle, Joseph said, "I could pray in my heart that all my brethren were like unto my beloved brother Hyrum, who possesses the mildness of a lamb, and the integrity of Job, and in short, the meekness and humility of Christ; and I love him with that love that is stronger than death, for I never had occasion to rebuke him, nor he me. . . ."

And the revelation calling Hyrum to be Patriarch, Second Elder, and assistant-President of the Church, declared, "Blessed is my servant Hyrum Smith; for I, the Lord, love him because of the integrity of his heart, and because he loveth that which is right before me, saith the Lord." In this same revelation Hyrum received an unusual promise, the continuing fulfillment of which can be seen today: He was promised of God that his name would "be had in honorable remembrance from generation to generation, forever, and ever." A son and a grandson both became presidents of the Church; another son and grandsons have been patriarchs to the Church; another grandson, Hyrum M. Smith, was an apostle; another, David A., a counselor in the presiding bishopric; and numerous other descendants have held other key Church positions. No other Mormon has been more richly blessed in his posterity than Hyrum Smith.

Joseph Smith Sr. (1771-1840) father of Hyrum and Joseph Smith, was the first Patriarch to the Church. It was to him that young Joseph first mentioned his visitation from the Angel Moroni. At this crucial time in Joseph's life, when a father's confidence and guidance were so important, Joseph Sr. fully sustained him, and urged him to go and do as the angel had directed. Throughout his life he supported his son in his calling, enduring many privations, and eventually giving his life as a martyr, suffering a premature death in Nauvoo as a result of the terrible persecutions inflicted in Missouri and the unhealthy conditions to which he was subjected as a refugee in the Nauvoo area.

Asael Smith (1744-1830), Joseph Smith Sr.'s father, might be considered the first generation Mormon, although he did not actually join the Church, having died just six months after it was organized. But it is in Asael that the several lines of leading families of Smith in the Church converge. He had several sons and daughters. Four sons, Joseph, Asael, Silas and John, joined the Church; two sons, Samuel and Stephen, and one daughter, Sarah Sanford, died before the Church was restored. One son, Jesse, his eldest child, was 62 years old when the Church was restored, and was much opposed to it. In the family history, there is no mention of Asael's three other daughters, Priscilla Waller, Mary Pierce, and Susannah Smith, having joined the Church.

Asael had felt impressed that a prophet would one day arise in his family. "It has been borne in upon my soul that one of my descendants will promulgate a work to revolutionize the world of religious faith," he had declared. Joseph the Prophet recorded in his journal for May 17, 1836, that, "My grandfather, Asael Smith, long ago predicted that there would be a prophet raised up in his family, and my grandfather was fully satisfied that it was fulfilled in me. My grandfather Asael died in East Stockholm, St. Lawrence County, New York, after having the Book of Mormon, and [he] read it nearly through, and he declared that I was the very prophet that he had long known would come in his family. . . . Both Asael Smith and his wife Mary Duty Smith accepted in full the mission of their grandson, Joseph, and rejoiced greatly in the restoration of the gospel before their departure from mortal life." Mary Duty Smith, incidentally, lived to the age of 93, so perhaps President Joseph Fielding Smith inherited the trait of longevity from her.

The youngest of Asael's sons who embraced the gospel was John Smith, who became the first president of the Salt Lake Stake, and also served for a time as Patriarch to the Church until Hyrum's son John was old enough. The first John is frequently referred to in Church history as "Uncle John Smith." His son George Albert Smith became first counselor to Brigham Young in the church presidency. George Albert's son John Henry became second counselor to Joseph F. Smith in the church presidency, and John Henry's son George Albert became the eighth president of the Church.

Asael fought in the American Revolutionary Army. An outspoken critic of sectarian religions of his day, he declined to join any church, but hopefully awaited a restoration of the gospel in its pristine purity.

Asael Smith was not the only American revolutionist who felt a conviction that the true church would one day be restored to the earth. In 1820, the year Asael's grandson, Joseph the Prophet, received his first vision, Thomas Jefferson, author of the American Declaration of Independence and third president of the United States, in denouncing the sectarian priests, declared, "The genuine and simple religion of Jesus will one day be restored, such as it was preached and practiced by Himself. Very soon after His death it became muffled up in mysteries, and has been ever since kept in concealment from the vulgar eye. . . ."

Asael Smith's father, Samuel Smith Jr., (1714-1785) was not only a soldier, though briefly, in the American Revolutionary Army, but according to family tradition he was chairman of the committee of freedom fighters responsible for the so-called Boston Tea Party which precipitated outbreak of the war for independence. (Samuel Adams is generally credited with leadership in that famous act of defiance.) Smith also served as a delegate to the Provincial Congress at Concord, Massachusetts, in 1774-75, just a year before the signing of the Declaration of Independence. Thus he must rightly be regarded as one of the founding fathers of the nation, though in a lesser role than some of the better known leaders of the revolution.

Samuel Smith Jr.'s father, Samuel Smith Sr. (1666-1748)

was a second generation American colonist and a well respected citizen of the Topsfield, Massachusetts area.

Samuel Sr.'s father, Robert Smith (1623-1693) was the first of this Smith line to come to America, from England in 1638, at the age of 15.

Thus the American line of Smiths from Robert to Joseph Fielding Jr. includes eight generations: Robert, Samuel Sr., Samuel Jr., Asael, Joseph Sr., Hyrum, Joseph Fielding Sr., and Joseph Fielding Jr. Three additional generations are presently living: sons, grandsons, and great-grandsons of President Smith.

The women whom these eight men married, who became the mothers of these generations, include the following: *Robert:* Mary French; *Samuel Sr.:* Rebecca Curtis; *Samuel Jr.:* Priscilla Gould; *Asael:* Mary Duty; *Joseph Sr.:* Lucy Mack; *Hyrum:* Jerusha Barden, Mary Fielding, and Catherine Phillips; *Joseph Fielding Sr.:* Levira Annett Clark Smith, Julina Lambson, Sarah Ellen Richards, Edna Lambson, Alice Ann Kimball, and Mary Taylor Schwartz; *Joseph Fielding Jr.:* Louie Emily Shurtliff, Ethel Georgina Reynolds, and Jessie Ella Evans.

His Boyhood Days

It was just a week before Christmas, December 18, 1884, but instead of it being a time of pleasant anticipation and excitement, as it should be for a youngster, it was for eight-year-old Joseph Fielding Smith a dreaded, lonely day.

He along with his several brothers and sisters had sat quietly in the big parlor of the Smith home while his father gave each of them in turn a blessing. His four "aunties"—his father's other wives—each received a departing blessing too. But not his mother, nor his baby sister Julina, ten months old, for they were going with Papa this time, on a long journey far away, for a very long time.

There was a sick and empty feeling in Joseph as he thought about it, though he tried to not think about it at all. His father had been gone so much, away on church assignments and hiding in the underground, that Joseph had become somewhat accustomed to *that*. But now to have his *mother* go too, and not knowing when nor even for sure whether she and Papa would ever be back—it was an overwhelming prospect for a little boy to face. Tears welled up in his eyes, though he tried to fight them down. Papa had told him he must be brave, and be one of the men of the house. He would try. He was a member of the Church now. The previous July, on his birthday, his father had baptized and confirmed him into official membership. So he was big now, and must not cry.

But there were tears in his father's and mother's eyes too as they leaned down and gave him a final hug and kiss goodbye. And then they were gone. Joseph with the other youngsters and the auntie wives stood at the big front window watching with sadness as the horse-drawn sleigh carrying Papa, Mama and baby Julina, glided quietly down the street through the cold and snow. The last thing Joseph could remember of it was his mother leaning out, looking back, waving goodbye once more. And then they were out of sight, and the loneliness set in heavier than Joseph had ever imagined it could. A pall of gloom hung over the once happy house.

That night, his pillow wet with tears, Joseph lay awake thinking back on the many pleasant hours he had spent with his mother, and of those few wonderful

Joseph Fielding Smith as a young child.

Joseph Fielding Smith with his young brothers, David Asael and George Carlos.

occasions when his father could be at home. This was his whole world nearly, this old adobe house, filled with love and with the laughter of many youngsters. Yet, it had not been free of death and sorrow, nor of terror in the night. It was a home of sunlight and shadows.

Joseph Fielding's boyhood could have been much happier had it not been for the malicious meddling of anti-Mormon do-gooders and exploiters in Salt Lake City, in Washington, D.C. and elsewhere in the nation, busy-body men and women who were determined to force the Mormons to discontinue the practice of plural marriage and live in the same social, economic and political patterns as the rest of the country. This they eventually succeeded in doing, but the Mormons strenuously resisted it, fighting for their rights, and the conflict resulted in considerable trial, hardship, and sorrow, which a youngster felt especially keenly. Innocent children, whose only desire was for love and a feeling of security, were the ultimate victims of the anti-Mormon crusades.

Joseph's parents and his father's other wives tried as best they could to shield him and the other children from the threats and oppressions to which the church members were subjected. Frequently, Joseph Fielding's father, along with Brigham Young and other church leaders, was the subject of vicious, vulgar editorial attacks in *The Salt Lake Tribune*, which for many years was one of the most vitriolic and irresponsible newspapers in America. Federal marshals were often prowling around their house, searching for Joseph's father, and interrogating and terrorizing the women and children. "We refused to even tell them our name," President Smith recalled. Yet the constant harassment against the Mormons generally and against the Smith family and other leading families in particular blighted their daily life and was especially difficult for children.

In old age President Smith still had vivid memories of this conflict in his youth, of the dark clouds and shadows that ever lurked around, like a hovering storm that would never quite let the sun shine through and the sky be blue for more than a passing moment. "We lived a very peaceful and happy family except when we became troubled and I became frightened by deputy marshals. In those early days they were always seeking to bring trouble upon the authorities of the Church, and because of those conditions my father was sent away when I was a youth. In the very years when a boy needs the guidance of his parents, both father and mother were in the [Hawaiian] Islands for a number of years."

Recounting his experiences as an authority, President Smith noted, "People will say [to me], 'Well, you ought to be good, having the father to train you that you had.' But, they don't know all the circumstances. My father was a busy man, away from home in those years a good part of his time. In fact, during the years when a boy needs the counsel of his father the most, I had no father, because he was sent away because of difficulties with the government and spent his time with my mother on the Islands of the Pacific, which were called the Sandwich [now Hawaiian] Islands. So during those years when a boy needs his father's help and counsel, I had no father."

Actually, heavy snow and wind storms that made railroad travel impossible across Idaho brought his father and mother and baby Julina back home a few days after they had left for Hawaii that December day in 1884. But a few weeks later the ordeal of parting had to be suffered once more. From the age of eight to the age of 15 Joseph Fielding seldom saw his father, who made but brief visits home. His mother and baby Julina remained in Hawaii for more than two years. While in Hawaii, she gave birth to another baby, Elias Wesley, born at Honolulu.

The necessity of his father being gone so much did have one value perhaps, and that is the youngsters and wives probably held him in even greater esteem, if such were possible, as one naturally does with persons or things to which acquaintance or access is limited. Remembering those choice times when his father was at home, President Smith said, "On such occasions, frequent family meetings were held and he spent his time instructing his children in the principles of the gospel. They one and all rejoiced in his presence and were grateful for the wonderful words of counsel and instruction which he imparted on these occasions in the midst of anxiety. They have never forgotten what they were taught, and the impressions have remained with them and will likely to do so forever. . . . My father was the most tenderhearted man I ever knew. . . . Among my fondest memories are the hours I have spent by his side discussing principles of the gospel and receiving instruction as only he could give it. In this way the foundation for my own knowledge was laid in truth."

He was emotionally hurt once when his father "chastised me with three or four light touches of a buggy whip for a misdeed I had not committed." Years later he reminded his father of it, of the fact his father thought he had lied to him about a matter when really he had not. His father said he did not know that he could remember of any such thing, but when assured by Joseph the incident was real, "Father atoned for this misapplied punishment with these sage and humorously spoken words, 'Oh well, we'll let that apply on some things you got by with when you didn't get punished.'" Despite that incident, he could say of his father, "This man is one in whom I have had more confidence than in anyone else I have known in this world."

Three and a half years following the death of Brigham Young in 1877, Joseph Fielding's father had become second counselor to President John Taylor—the presidency had been reorganized in October, 1880, with the Council of Twelve Apostles serving as the governing body in the interim period. President Taylor's nephew, George Q. Cannon, was first counselor. There was a special bond of comradeship between John Taylor and Joseph F. Smith, because President Taylor had been in Carthage Jail along with Joseph F.'s father Hyrum and the Prophet Joseph when they were murdered. John

Taylor was severely wounded by the same mob, with only Willard Richards escaping serious injury. Also, John Taylor along with Parley P. Pratt had been instrumental in Mary Fielding Smith's conversion to the Church. "I knew President John Taylor," recalled President Joseph Fielding Smith. "I was in his presence on a number of occasions. I was just a youngster, but I remember President John Taylor and being with him. He is a wonderful man. Of course, I was just a young boy during his administration."

Beyond the fact that he was a member of the Church presidency, Joseph F. Smith was especially sought by the U.S. marshals in their anti-polygamy crusade because as an officiator and recorder in the Endowment House he had detailed information and records regarding plural marriage. For this reason President Taylor was especially anxious that President Smith avoid being arrested. As it became increasingly difficult for him to elude the federal officers, he was directed to leave Utah Territory and flee to the Sandwich Islands, where he had spent several years of his youth as a missionary, and where he would now take charge of missionary work, under the alias of J. F. Speight. He sometimes traveled also under the alias of J. Field, a convenient shortening of "Joseph Fielding." Later he would assume the name of Jason Mack, an ancestor. Joseph Fielding's mother, Julina, as the oldest and legal wife, was chosen to accompany him to Hawaii. The other wives and all the children except Julina's baby Julina, called "Ina," would remain in or near Salt Lake City.

The reign of terror which continued against the saints during the absence of Joseph's parents was a frightful thing in the tender years of Joseph Fielding. "Not only was the persecution waged against the authorities of the Church and thousands of other men and women who were deemed violators of the anti-polygamy law, but it followed the innocent children, and scattered families to the four winds," he recalled. "The family of President Smith much of the time while he was away was scattered; his homes were constantly raided by some of the vilest men that ever drew mortal breath. Inmates and attendants [family members] were grossly insulted, and defenseless children intimidated. Nothing was considered sacred from the morbid gaze and indecent acts of men who had been given power to search and seize, and who frequently did both without warrant of law. Bedrooms were forcibly entered while the inmates were in peaceful slumber. Women were insulted, not having the privilege of properly clothing themselves, and in that condition forced to stand before these fiends and answer their indecent and vulgar questions. Frequently these 'guardians of the law' were staggering under the influence of liquor, and giving vent to vulgar blasphemies."

Come twilight the blinds were drawn down over the windows to keep the peeping tom marshals from looking in the house. And in the dim light of coal oil lamps the children were assigned the task of cutting strips of old cloth and braiding them for rag rugs. The evenings became long and tiring with such confinement, but the wives did not feel it safe to let their children out. Aunt Sarah recalled that while her husband and Julina and baby were in Hawaii, "Julina's five older children were left with Edna and me. This was known as the underground time. We had to watch the children constantly and keep ourselves out of society. We were under a strain all the time and had to keep alert for fear deputies were sneaking about trying to find Joseph."

Such was the American concept of justice forced upon the Mormons under terms of a series of infamous bills passed into law by Congress. "It was always the case that the most severe criticism and the greatest bitterness shown against the Latter-day Saints for the practice of plural marriage, has come from those who were themselves guilty of the grossest immoral practices," declared President Joseph Fielding Smith. Apparently, there was a concentration of such men in the halls of Congress, and the most vindictive of them against the

Mormons often were the Vermonters. President George Q. Cannon, who served as Utah's territorial delegate to Congress, observed that while the state of Vermont had produced several of the Church's leaders, including Joseph and Hyrum Smith, Brigham Young, Erastus Snow, Heber C. Kimball and others, it had also produced some of the Church's most vicious enemies, including Senators Justin Morrill, George F. Edmunds, and Luke P. Poland, Representative Dudley Chase Haskell, President Chester Arthur, and other political opportunists, who had authored, co-sponsored, signed, or otherwise promoted the hateful anti-polygamy laws.

"How remarkable it is, is it not," commented President Cannon, "that we should have received so many blessings through men born in the Green Mountain state [Vermont], and that our chief enemies, apparently stirred up by the adversary to destroy the work which their fellow citizens, men born upon the same soil, were the means in the hands of God, of establishing—that they, Vermonters also, should be stirred up to seek for its destruction."

Mr. Morrill, while still in the House of Representatives, had gotten the first bill through in 1862, and President Abraham Lincoln, whom the Mormons had slighted in Illinois politics years before, had signed it, outlawing the practice of plural marriage in Utah. In 1874 the tougher Poland bill was passed, and in 1882 Senator Edmunds pushed through an even stiffer bill, and President Arthur had signed it into law.

Under the Edmunds law polygamy and cohabitation were punishable by a fine of up to $500 or by imprisonment up to five years, or both. Men and women living in polygamy forfeited their rights of citizenship, including the right to vote and the right to hold public office. Anyone who even believed in the doctrine of plural marriage, though not living it, was barred from jury service. The crass hypocrisy of Senator Edmunds and other congressmen who supported the bill can readily be seen in the wording of its test oath that must be taken by Mormons before they were allowed to vote: "I do not live or co-habit with more than one woman *in the marriage rela-tionship.*" If you wished to keep a mistress or two, or patronize prostitutes, or indulge in other forms of adultery or sex perversion, there was no problem. But if you chose to live in an honorable polygamous marriage relationship you forfeited your rights as an American citizen and sub-jected yourself to fines and imprisonment! Such was the justice the federal government imposed upon the Mor-mons. Under the terms of Edmunds' bill, Utah was over-run with hundreds of political appointees: commissioners, judges, marshals, et al, who with few exceptions were, morally speaking, the scum of the earth. Indeed this political pork barrel of federal jobs seems to have been a major motive behind the enactment of the law. Fortu-nately, some of the marshals and other federal officers felt sympathy for the Mormons and thus took a re-laxed view of their jobs. But they were the exception.

President Joseph F. Smith's response to this political boondoggling bill was to marry two more wives, Alice Ann Kimball, on December 6, 1883, and Mary Taylor Schwartz, on January 13, 1884—and to continue eluding the marshals seeking him. His feelings were well ex-pressed in a note penned to members of his family at that time: "Uncle Elias Smith and Aunt Susan E. Smith were subpoenaed this morning. I am said to be in great demand! I often feel wrathy and perhaps never more so than now, but I will not express my wrath, for it would be inadequate to the occasion. I rely upon the promise that God has made—'Vengeance is mine and I will repay!' Retribution will come upon the heads of this whole nation, and especially on the immediate enemies of the Latter-day Saints. I cannot conceive of anything more contemptible or more execrable than the present and continued attempts of the federal officials to blast the peace and break up the sacred relations of husbands and wives, parents and children! What business is it of theirs if I and my family are happy in the relation of plural marriage? Have I wronged anyone? Have I or my family interfered with the rights of others? Is anybody injured? According to their own theory no one is injured except it may be those who practice plural marriage themselves. Then why not let those who are injured complain and seek liberation and redress? . . ."

President John Taylor, as prophet, seer and revelator, emphatically stated that the Supreme Court had no right to uphold these unconstitutional laws enacted against plural marriage even though it had done so for two decades, and would continue to do so. Upon passage of the Edmunds' law, President Taylor declared: "When the Constitution of the United States was framed and adopted, those high contracting parties did positively agree that they would not interfere with religious affairs. Now, if our marital relations are not religious, what is? This ordinance of marriage was a direct revelation to us, through Joseph Smith, the prophet. . . . This is a revelation from God and a command to his people, and therefore it is my religion. I do not believe that the Supreme Court of the United States has any right to interfere with my religious views, and in doing it they are violating their most sacred obligations. . . ."

The basic controversy really was Mormon vs. anti-Mormon economic and political control in Utah Territory. Brigham Young and his associates in church leadership were attempting to establish the Kingdom of God upon the earth, and felt the need of giving leadership in economic and political as well as theological affairs. Having been driven into the Rocky Mountain wilderness and having settled this area, they felt with good reason that they should be allowed the freedom of developing the Great Basin commonwealth in harmony with their own ideas of government. But Gentiles and apostate Mormons objected to the Church's domination in secular affairs, and polygamy made a good whipping boy by which the anti-Church forces were able to further arouse public sentiment against an already unpopular and persecuted people. This issue was exploited to the fullest possible extent without due regard for the constitutional rights of the Mormons, nor for the tender feelings and the love in family relationships.

Had the Mormons been allowed their constitutional rights of freedom of religion, Joseph Fielding's childhood might have been something approaching a heaven on earth, so great was the love and harmony in his father's family. "It would be difficult to find in any part of the world any family where the members manifested greater love and solicitude for each other than in the family of President Joseph F. Smith," wrote Joseph Fielding. "No father ever at any age of the world, we feel confident in saying, had a greater love for wife or wives and children, and was more earnestly concerned for their welfare. . . . Out in the world, where marriage is looked upon too frequently merely as a contract, which on the slightest provocation may be broken; where families are constantly racked by disunity, and where, through the action of the divorce courts, children are deprived of the most sacred right of loving parental affection, there is a general feeling that a family such as that of President Smith's could only be a family of discord and jealous strife and hatred. To the contrary, there was and is no monogamist family which could be more united. To the astonishment of the unbelieving world, the wives loved each other dearly. In times of sickness they tenderly waited upon and nursed each other. When death invaded one of the homes and a child was taken, all wept and mourned together with sincere grief. . . . Two of the wives [Julina and Edna] were skilled and licensed practitioners in obstetrics, and brought many babies into the world. They waited upon each other and upon the other wives, and when babies came all rejoiced equally with the mother.

"The children recognized each other as brothers and sisters, full-fledged not as half, as they would be considered in the world. They defended each and stood by each other no matter which branch of the family was theirs. Nor was this condition peculiar to the family of President Smith. It was a condition found in most of the plural homes, for these homes were governed in the spirit of love with a foundation in righteousness, not the lust of the flesh which prevails so generally in the world. It was because the outside world judged the 'Mormon' people by their own corrupt standards that they failed to understand the true condition which prevailed in 'Mormon' homes. . . . Joseph F. Smith loved his wives and children with a holy love that is seldom seen, never surpassed. Like Job of old, he prayed for them night and day and asked the Lord to keep them pure and undefiled in the path of righteousness. . . ."

This feeling of love and harmony that Joseph experienced as a youngster in a plural family is also attested to by the five wives who lived together. In autobiographical statements made in their later years they fondly recalled the happiness they had enjoyed together even through years of poverty and persecution. "Levira accepted me and we were dear to each other," remembered Julina, adding her regret that Levira later became estranged from the family. "Sarah and I lived together sharing the home duties and also our husband." Julina's daughter Mary, called Mamie, and Sarah's daughter Leonora, called Nonie, "were almost like twins. We often dressed them alike and they were loving little sisters." When Julina's sister Edna also became Joseph's wife, Julina noted that the three women "loved each other and worked together."

Sarah remembered that "when Joseph proposed marriage I was sure I would rather be his wife than to marry any single man I had ever met." Sarah liked to sew and Julina and Edna preferred to cook, so, "often dividing the chores to our likings, we got along beautifully."

Julina's next younger sister, Melissa, married Albert Davis. Her youngest sister, Edna, recalled, "I used to get lonesome now that my two older sisters were married, so I spent quite a good deal of time at Julina's helping tend the babies, etc. This is where I became acquainted with my brother-in-law Joseph. When he proposed marriage to me I was thrilled for I had seen how kind and wonderful he was. After the marriage ceremony I moved into the same home, having my own bedroom, but sharing all else with Julina and Sarah. . . . We shared the chores and learned to love each other and the babies. My first child was Joseph's first son and naturally I was thrilled. I wanted to give him his father's name, but Papa would not consent. He said this name was to go to Julina's son. So we named our baby Hyrum Mack. . . . I also studied obstetrics and delivered many babies. I very often assisted Julina in bringing some of Papa's babies into the world."

These three wives, Julina, Sarah and Edna, who felt so close to each other, found it a bit difficult to accept the last two wives, Alice and Mary. Part of the difficulty perhaps lay in the fact that they were not consulted on the choice. "We were not too happy at first when we received news that Joseph was to take as his fourth [actually fifth] wife, a widow [actually a divorcee, Alice Kimball] with three children," remembered Edna. "We already had 13 living children in the family. Then just one month later our husband was told to take his fifth [actually sixth] wife. Again we could have had misgivings, for the young lady [Mary Schwartz] he chose was known as one of the prettiest girls in the valley." But, Edna added, "of course in time we all made adjustments and learned to accept other changes and more responsibilities."

"My first marriage was not a happy one," recalled Alice, "so naturally I was a little apprehensive at first marrying into a family where there were some children older than mine and some near the ages of my own three. But, as Edna has said, adjustments were made so we could be accepted." At the time of her second marriage Alice had a daughter six years old and twin sons two years old. She found great happiness in the Smith family. Mrs. Zula Cole, a niece of her first husband, remembered Alice as "a very beautiful woman."

Mary, whom Edna said was "known as one of the prettiest girls in the valley," was a niece of President John Taylor. "During my teenage years my mother was housekeeper for her brother in the Gardo House. I helped with the housekeeping, and often acted as waitress to the general authorities when they ate lunch with the president. It was at this time that I became acquainted with Joseph F. Smith, who was a counselor to President Taylor. . . . I was 19 [actually 18] years old when Joseph F. proposed marriage to me. I was indeed thrilled for I realized he was one of the finest young men in the city. We were married just one month after his marriage to Alice Kimball, on January 13, 1884. I was only four years older than Julina's eldest daughter Mamie. I married into a large family, all of whom accepted me and whom I learned to love—especially Mamie. I have often said she was the most angelic person I have ever known."

The world in which Joseph Fielding spent his boyhood had little resemblance to the world in which he has lived his years as church president. Salt Lake City was a town of approximately 20,000 persons, with dirt and dusty roads. Horses and buggies were the chief mode of transportation. Railroads were gradually built through some parts of Utah, following completion of America's first transcontinental railroad at Promontory, in 1869, just seven years before Joseph's birth. The Salt Lake Temple was still under construction, since 1853.

The first Mormon temple in Utah was completed in 1877 at St. George, Utah's Dixieland, where Brigham Young had a winter home. "My first church assignment," said President Smith, with a twinkle in his eye, "was to accompany Brigham Young to the dedication of the St. George Temple. Of course, I don't remember that assignment too well, for I was just one year old then." He was in fact just nine months old. It was as a babe in arms that he had gone with his parents to St. George, to attend this significant event. The April general conference of the Church was held in St. George that year, with the dedication of the temple as a key event. On the second day of the conference Joseph F. Smith was called to preside over the European missions of the Church, with headquarters at Liverpool, England. This was the second time he had received that assignment, the first being three years earlier, in 1874. He had left all three wives home then and was gone for a year and a half. Now he took Sarah Ellen and their four-year-old son Joseph Richards with him. Their baby son Heber John had died in March. "Nonie [Sarah's six-year-old daughter] stayed with me," recalled Julina. "I had a fine baby boy, Joseph Fielding, only nine months old, and Aunt Edna had Alvin, a little over two years, and little Alfred, only four months old. Now again we had to struggle. Edna and I took turns cooking at the Endowment House to earn enough money to supplement our income and balance our diet. [Both Julina and Edna also continued their work as midwives]. This mission was cut shorter than expected by the death of President Brigham Young in August, 1877 [four months after Joseph F.'s call]. This was a sad event, but it brought Joseph home to his family."

In that same year, 1877, John D. Lee was executed—shot into his coffin at Mountain Meadows by federal troops violating the constitution—for complicity in the Mountain Meadows massacre 20 years earlier.

As a member of a large family with limited means Joseph Fielding as a boy spent considerable time in helping with farm and household chores. His father owned a farm in Taylorsville, where Joseph assisted with the irrigating and harvesting of hay and in caring for livestock. He herded cows near the Jordan River, and on a hot summer day occasionally took time for a swim in its murky waters. One day when he and his brothers were herding and got hungry, they bought a loaf of bread from a neighboring farm woman. But upon slicing the bread they discovered it was full of flies. That ruined their appetites.

Two of his most vivid recollections of his youthful days on the farm were of two accidents he suffered: "I had an unfortunate thing happen to me one time, when I fell and broke a leg. That wasn't my fault. My brother [his oldest brother, Hyrum M.] and I were coming in with a load of hay. It was the last load and we did not want to go back again. And we built up what was really two loads. When we went in with what was to be the pay-our-tithing load, I was swept off the top because there was a bar across [the top of] the gate [to the tithing yard] and I fell and broke a leg. Well, that was my carelessness. . . ."

The other accident also involved a load of hay. He and his younger brother, George, were on the way in from the field and had stopped near a canal to let the horses have a drink. When the horses were watered, Joseph said, "George, you stand at the horses' head and hold their bridles while I climb up and take the reins." George either did not hear him or failed to obey, for instead of standing at the horses' head he walked around to the back of the wagon. Something frightened the horses, causing them to bolt down the embankment of the canal. Joseph was thrown from the hay load onto the double tree between the horses. For a moment he thought the end had come, but finally managed to get clear of both horses and wagon. A passing farmer helped them get the horses and wagon out of the canal.

It was Joseph's duty, along with that of his brothers and sisters, to help care for a vegetable garden, a flock of chickens, some cows and horses, all at the home place on First North Street. Carrots, turnips, string beans, peas, and other vegetables were grown in the garden, harvested and eaten fresh or canned for winter use. There were several fruit trees and three long rows of Concord grapes—which made a good hiding place for nighttime games, especially when the grapes were ripe. The flock of chickens kept the family in eggs, and afforded an occasional Sunday chicken dinner. Three cows were required to supply the family's milk needs. And a few horses were kept for transportation.

With his father gone from home so much of the time, Joseph Fielding as his mother's oldest son assumed more responsibilities than he might have done under more favorable circumstances. Like his father before him he spent much of his childhood doing the work of an adult. These experiences did, however, help him gain sound judgment, a sense of responsibility, and other traits useful in his life's mission as a leader in the Church. He unwittingly inherited one job earlier than he need have, when in boyish pride he secretly milked one of the family cows to prove that he was capable of doing it, and thus was assigned the job permanently.

Joseph's brothers nearest his age and with whom he did most of his work and play were Aunt Edna's two oldest boys, Hyrum, four years older, and Alvin, two years older; Aunt Sarah's oldest, Joseph Richards, three years older, and his own mother's next two sons, David, three years younger, and George, five years younger; also, Aunt Alice's twin sons by her previous marriage, Heber and Charles, five years younger. So, while there were no brothers his exact age, there were seven brothers within five years of his age. He and Joseph Richards would later become fellow missionaries to England; and he and Hyrum would later be members of the Council of Twelve Apostles; David, a counselor in the presiding bishopric of the Church; Alvin, and also a younger brother, Andrew K., co-workers with him in the Church Historian's Office.

When his mother returned from the Hawaiian Islands, Joseph was ten years old, and it was at that tender age that he began assisting her in her professional duties as a licensed midwife or obstetrician. Joseph's job was that of stable boy and buggy driver. At all hours of the day or night, when the call came for his mother's services, Joseph was to hitch up the faithful mare "Old Meg" to the buggy and drive his mother to the home of the confinement case. Here he might wait while she delivered the baby, or, if his mother thought the wait would be too long, she would send him home with instructions on when to return for her. And how fortunate the mothers of Salt Lake City were to have her services. "I brought nearly 1,000 babies into the world, and, not to brag at all, I never lost a mother nor a baby in my practice. I often gave this service free, and sometimes received as much as five or six dollars. This included going daily for five or six days caring for the mother and child."

In the daytime and summertime Joseph's assignment

was not too unpleasant a one for a ten-year-old youngster. But in the nighttime and wintertime it was very unpleasant. To have to turn out in the darkness of the night or the cold of the winter, or both, and hitch up the horse and drive for several blocks or miles and maybe wait for several hours, was no light chore for a mere lad. There was no electricity. In the night he had to light a kerosene lantern, grope his way through the dark into the barnyard, find and corner Old Meg, persuade her she ought to cooperate, stand on a box to get the harness on her and the bit into her mouth, and then get her hooked up to the buggy, before the night's journey even began. Then he had to drive along dirt roads, often muddy and rutted, with but an occasional dim street lamp to light the way. Sometimes they traveled through rain, sleet or snow, or bitter cold wind, in a well ventilated buggy. And then upon reaching the house of the expectant mother, he had what often seemed an endless wait.

"Sometimes I nearly froze to death. I marveled that so many babies were born in the middle of the night, especially on cold winter nights. I fervently wished that mothers might time things a little better."

Old Meg, the third member of the obstetrics team, was a dependable mare. She was not the mischief maker that another mare, "Junie," was. Joseph's father had bought Junie from George Q. Cannon, fellow counselor in the Church presidency. "Junie was one of the most intelligent animals I ever saw. She seemed almost human in her ability. I could not keep her locked in the barn because she would continually undo the strap on the door of her stall. I used to put the strap connected to the half-door of the stall over the top of the post, but she would simply lift it off with her nose and teeth. Then she would go out in the yard.

"There was a water tap in the yard used for filling the water trough for our animals. Junie would turn this on with her teeth and then leave the water running. My father would get after me because I couldn't keep that horse in the barn. She never ran away; she just turned on the water and then walked around the yard or over the lawn or through the garden. In the middle of the night, I would hear the water running and then I would have to get up and shut it off and lock Junie up again.

"My father suggested that the horse seemed smarter than I was. One day he decided that he would lock her in so that she could not get out. He took the strap that usually looped over the top of the post and buckled it around the post and under a crossbar, and then he said, 'Young lady, let's see you get out of there now!' My father and I left the barn and started to walk back to the house; and before we reached it, Junie was at our side, somewhat to my delight. I could not refrain from suggesting to Father that I was not the only one whose head compared unfavorably with the mare's."

Baseball was Joseph's chief sport as a youngster. He was a member of the Latter-day Saint Sixteenth Ward in the Salt Lake Stake. There was a school in each ward, and each school had a baseball team. "Our chief 'enemies' were the boys of the Fifteenth Ward, which adjoined the Sixteenth Ward, to which I belonged," he recalls. One of these "enemies" in the Fifteenth Ward was George Q. Morris, who later became a fellow member of the Council of Twelve. They also competed with a Catholic school.

Joseph occasionally went fishing, but cared not at all for hunting, perhaps because his father had persuaded him that it was morally wrong to kill for pleasure. One day, however, some of his brothers and friends coaxed him into going rabbit hunting. Reluctantly he shot a rabbit, heard it cry out like a baby, as wounded rabbits often will, was sick at heart, dropped his gun and has never used one since. Like his father, he taught that it is wrong to kill for pleasure.

Christmas held excitement for youngsters then as it does now, even though there was no dazzle of bright lights, and gift-giving was very limited, because there was neither tradition nor money for the extravagance common today. A book or a magazine subscription, and an orange or a few nuts, that was the extent of gifts to Joseph Fielding as a boy. Each year over a period of years he got one additional volume toward completion of a set of Chatterbox books. Nor did he always get a gift of any kind. Being in a large family in times of poverty and persecution did not make for easy gift giving. "I—we all— were on foot and of necessity tugging away with all our might to keep body and soul together," recalled his father of a certain Christmas season during Joseph's early boyhood. "Under these spiritless conditions, one day just before Christmas, I left the old home with feelings I cannot describe. I wanted to do something for my chicks. I wanted something to please them, and to mark the Christmas day from all other days. But not a cent to do it with. I walked up and down Main Street, looking into the store windows, into Amussens' jewelry store, into every store everywhere, and then slunk out of sight of humanity and sat down and wept like a child, until my poured-out grief relieved my aching heart; and after a while returned home, as empty as when I left."

But for Joseph and his brothers and sisters it was still a special day. "In those early days the only good times that I remember having and that I looked forward to were Christmas, Thanksgiving day, and the 4th and 24th of July. These days stood out, especially the 4th and 24th and Thanksgiving day, because on these days we had ice cream. Ice cream was something scarce. It was a rare and wonderful treat. The making of ice artificially was something that was not done in my boyhood days. The ice had to be cut in the wintertime in great blocks of frozen ice on the ponds, and then placed in the ice warehouses and covered with sawdust, and thus it was preserved through the summer months. We could afford to buy it, from the tithing office, only two or three times a year. . . . We did not have ice to keep our milk from going sour until I was older, and then . . . we bought just so much ice every other day from the ice man, and he got it out of the great bed of ice that had been placed under sawdust and kept for that purpose."

Busy as he was with farm and household chores and

assisting his mother in her midwifery, Joseph Fielding nevertheless tended to his studies, both at home and in school. From his earliest years the study he liked best was the gospel. Having a testimony of the gospel, he had a natural inclination as a child to increase his knowledge and understanding of it. "I was born with a testimony of the gospel. . . . I do not remember a time when I did not have full confidence in the mission of the Prophet Joseph Smith and in the teachings and guidance of my parents." This statement is endorsed in a blessing given to him in 1913 by Patriarch Joseph D. Smith.

Both his father and mother were careful to see that he was well taught in the gospel and in church history. He was ordained in turn to the office of deacon, teacher and priest in the Aaronic Priesthood as he reached the required ages for these offices. "I was trained at my mother's knee to love the Prophet Joseph Smith and to love my Redeemer. . . . I am grateful for the training that I received and I tried to follow the counsel that was given to me by my father. But I must not give him all the credit. I think a good part of it, a very great part of it, should go to my mother whose knee I used to sit by as a little child and listen to her stories about the pioneers. My mother deserves a great deal of credit so far as I am concerned because she used to teach me and put in my hands, when I was old enough to read, things that I could understand. She taught me to pray . . . to be true and faithful to my covenants and obligations, to attend to my duties as a deacon and as a teacher . . . and later as a priest. . . . I had a mother who saw to it that I did read, and I loved to read. I used to read the books that were prepared for the Primary children and for Sunday School children in those early days, and I usually had a book in my hands when I was home. . . . One thing that I did from the time I learned to read and write was to study the gospel. I read and committed to memory the Children's Catechism and Primary books in the gospel. Later I read the History of the Church as recorded in the *Millennial Star.* I also read the Bible, the Book of Mormon, the Pearl of Great Price, the Doctrine and Covenants and other literature which fell into my hands. I learned at a very early day that God lives. He gave me a testimony when I was a child and I have tried to be obedient, always with some measure of success."

His father, hard pressed for money, was able to buy a defective copy of the Book of Mormon at a reduced rate—there was a faulty sequence in its pages. He gave this copy to Joseph when eight years of age, as he became officially a member of the Church. "When I was a small boy, too young to hold the Aaronic Priesthood, my father placed a copy of the Book of Mormon in my hands with the request that I read it. I received this Nephite record with thanksgiving and applied myself to the task which had been assigned to me. There are certain passages that have been stamped upon my mind and I have never forgotten them." By the time he was ten years old he had read the Book of Mormon through not just once but twice. His brothers remembered of his hurrying to get through his chores as quickly as possible, and sometimes even leaving a ball game early, and secluding himself in the hayloft or in the shade of a tree to get back to his reading of the book.

When he was a youngster, Salt Lake City also comprised Salt Lake Latter-day Saint Stake, with 19 wards, being numbered consecutively from the southeast corner to the northwest corner of the city. "There was a school in each of the wards of Salt Lake City at that time. . . . I went to school in Primary days and on until I was in my teens in the old Sixteenth Ward meeting house which was then one of the district school buildings also. Our home was just across the street from what later became the University of Utah [first known as University of Deseret] and which later became the West High School [first known as Salt Lake High School]. . . . Later in my life, I attended school at the Latter-day Saints College [earlier known as the Salt Lake Stake Academy] in the Social Hall on State Street, or just off State Street, on what is now called Social Hall Avenue. There's a street that runs through now where the school house existed. [This is where Utah's television stations are located.] The building was used for all kinds of purposes: theatrical performances and regular meetings, as well as part of the Latter-day Saints College. Later in years, I attended the same school but it was located on First North Street, one block east of where I was born. . . . [This is the present site of Horace Mann Junior High School.] There I spent my school days until I was married."

During the two years his mother was in Hawaii with his father, Aunt Sarah and Aunt Edna looked after him and Julina's other children. Joseph and his brothers and sisters were also especially fond of Uncle Albert and Aunt Melissa Davis who lived on a farm west of the Jordan River. In the absence of his own father, Joseph sometimes looked to Uncle Albert for counsel and friendship. The Davises, however, also spent some time in Hawaii while Joseph's folks were there. Another person who had a good influence upon him in his childhood was his father's Aunt Mercy Rachel Fielding Thompson, sister of Mary Fielding Smith and widow of Robert B. Thompson, the Prophet Joseph's personal secretary who died at Nauvoo in 1840. Aunt Mercy lived in the same block as Joseph. His father helped look after her needs. "I never knew my Grandmother Mary Fielding Smith. She died shortly after coming to the valleys of the mountains, long before I was born. I have always regretted that, because she was one of the most noble women who ever lived. But I did know her good sister, Aunt Mercy Thompson, and as a boy I used to go and visit her in her home and sit at her knee, where she told me stories about the Prophet Joseph Smith, and oh, how grateful I am for that experience."

When Joseph's mother Julina left home in January, 1885, taking baby "Ina" with her, and accompanied her husband to Hawaii, she expected to be gone only a few weeks. "I left my five other little children with Edna and Sarah. We watched for news on each boat that came from America, expecting our release. Time went on. My baby

Wesley was born, and time still went on. After two years I was so homesick we decided I would leave and go to my little ones at home. Joseph [her husband] wept when we [she and her two babies] left. He was as homesick as I was." For Joseph Fielding and his brothers and sisters, the return of their mother from Hawaii, in March of 1887, was a joyous day. It was as though she had brought with her all the warmth and sunshine of the south sea islands.

Sadly, it seemed as though their father would be away indefinitely, but President John Taylor became very ill and sent for Joseph F. Smith to return home. Thus it was that Joseph's eleventh birthday anniversary proved one of the happiest of his life, for just the evening before, on July 18, 1887, secret word reached the Smith home that their husband and father, "Papa," was back in Utah, and was just a few miles north of Salt Lake City, at President Taylor's hideaway house, the residence of Thomas F. Roueche in Davis County. Although Joseph did not get to see his father that day nor the next, it was the finest of birthday gifts to know that he was once again close by, for of all persons in the world Joseph was probably fondest of his father. President Taylor died a week later, July 25, 1887, so Papa stayed in Utah for several weeks.

Passage of the vicious Edmunds-Tucker anti-polygamy bill in this same year, 1887, and the harshness with which it was enforced, made life increasingly difficult for the Smith family, as well as for other polygamous families. This bill, which President Grover Cleveland allowed to become law without his signature, disincorporated the Church and authorized the government to confiscate church property. It allowed women to testify against their husbands in court, it disinherited children of polygamous marriages, and in several other particulars heaped further abuse upon the Mormons.

Joseph Fielding's parents and the auntie wives courageously defied this unconstitutional law. The disdain that they felt for this latest threat to their family was demonstrated the following year, 1888, when four of the wives gave birth to babies. Joseph Fielding was then 12 years old, and happily received ordination to the Aaronic Priesthood and the office of a deacon. Again he witnessed the joy that comes into a family living in harmony with gospel principles, as he saw the mothers help one another and share in the happiness of the newborn infants. Mary, the youngest wife, remembered, "My first child, John, was born in Julina's home. She was my doctor and was eight months pregnant with Emily at the time. The very next day, August 21, she delivered Edna with [of] her daughter Emma. Emily arrived September 11. Sarah's Frank was four months old, and Edna, Julina, and I all had new babies about the same time. Mine, being my first, was just a little special—that is, to me!" It was in this same year that President Joseph F. Smith's first wife, Levira, died, at St. Louis, Missouri, December 18, 1888.

Under relentless persecution by federal government agents, the Church finally capitulated in 1890. At the October conference, when Joseph Fielding was 14 years old, President Wilford Woodruff issued an official declaration calling upon the Church to suspend the practice of plural marriage. This statement, commonly referred to as the Manifesto, put an end to the general practice of marrying additional wives. There remained some question as to whether polygamists might continue with church sanction to live with wives they already had. The objective was to get the government off the Church's back, and whatever was necessary to accomplish that was to be done. President Woodruff and some others discontinued living with all but one wife and family, while still giving financial support to the others. Even the anti-Mormon government officials and others were divided in their opinions on this point, some feeling it was not reasonable to ask polygamists to give up their present wives, while others insisted they must. The law continued in effect, prohibiting plural marriage and cohabitation.

Most of the anti-Mormons obviously were disappointed that the Church had surrendered its rights and renounced the practice of plural marriage, for this robbed them of their pretext for persecuting the Mormons. And in fact, even after the Manifesto was issued, the persecution continued, so vindictive were the Church's enemies.

Joseph F. Smith petitioned for and was granted amnesty in September, 1891, by President Benjamin Harrison. This meant he could now walk the streets without fear of arrest. It was a relief to him and his family, but it was short lived, for, to his credit, he refused to give up his plural wives and families, and so the government was soon after him again. Thirteen children were born to his wives after the Manifesto was issued. "I am one of the bad boys," he told a congressional committee in 1904 at the Reed Smoot hearings in Washington, D.C. To continue living in plural marriage Joseph F. Smith found it expedient to disperse his families, placing each wife in a different home.

"In 1892 I moved with my two little sons to Franklin, Idaho," recalled Mary Schwartz Smith. "This was underground time and Joseph was in hiding most of this time. When we moved back [to Salt Lake City] we lived on South Ninth East. These were all lean years as far as money was concerned. We had to learn many lessons in economy and self-reliance, and many a time we would skimp on our own food in order to have a special dinner when Papa came to visit us."

Sarah, Edna, and Alice moved into separate homes also, leaving only Julina and her youngsters, including Joseph Fielding, in the original Smith home at 333 West First North. But these other three wives' houses were all within the same block, so it was still possible to continue the close association much as they had enjoyed under one roof. Mary later moved to a house on North Temple Street between Main and State Streets, where the new Latter-day Saints Church Office Building is located. Still later Mary and her youngsters moved to the Smith family farm in Taylorsville, immediately south of Salt Lake City, the farm where Joseph Fielding and his brothers had often labored. "I have always loved company," noted Mary. "The pleasure of preparing for others seemed to outweigh the extra work. When any of the family came out to the farm I always tried to have something extra so they would have a desire to come again." If only Papa could have been home more. . . .

The year 1893, the year he became 17 years of age, was a red letter year for Joseph, for two reasons: First, because the Salt Lake Temple was completed and dedicated, after 40 years in the building. Through his youth Joseph had watched with keen interest the daily progress in construction on this magnificent edifice. He had seen the last of the huge granite stones brought in by railroad cars from the rock quarry in Little Cottonwood Canyon, 18 miles to the southeast; had seen the majestic spires finally take shape. The building foreman himself could hardly have kept a closer check on its progress than did young Joseph. But it had seemed agonizingly slow to him. "I used to wonder whether I would ever live long enough to see the temple completed." But finally came that wonderful day when the temple was completed and dedicated, the first dedicatory ceremonies being on April 6, 1893, with the dedicatory prayer offered by President Wilford Wodruff, and the rousing "Hosanna! Hosanna!" shout given by the assembled congregations. To Joseph, who attended the first dedication, it was one of the most thrilling of all days. It was exactly 40 years since work on the temple had started.

A second notable event in Joseph's life that year was his journey in late summer to the World's Fair in Chicago. The Mormon Tabernacle Choir had been invited to compete at the fair, and the Church presidency made a point of being there. President Woodruff, then 86 years old, invited his counselors and some members of their families to join him in a special train caravan to the fair. Joseph was among the fortunate ones his father invited to go along on the trip. It would be the first time he had traveled any great distance from Utah, and the anticipation of taking such a train ride was thrilling indeed. In his late eighties President Joseph Fielding fondly recalled this journey, and also remembered some impressions of President Woodruff:

"I was well acquainted with President Woodruff and the members of his family. I had the privilege of accompanying my father and President Woodruff to the World's Fair in Chicago in 1893 and we rode in a Pullman car from Salt Lake City to Chicago. I had the privilege of sitting in the state room or the room that was given to President Woodruff, and listened to his counsel and advice. Of course, I was just a youngster, and in company with his son and one of his daughters, and someone else, I don't remember just who now, we went out on the platform. We could do it then. The platform was all open at the back of the train, and we went out on the back of the train to eat some watermelons, so we could throw the pieces away, and when we came in we got a scolding. We were told that if that train had gone with speed around a curve we could have been swept off, which was absolutely true, and I remember that very keenly. And so we got scolded by President Woodruff."

Despite the scolding, Joseph had some pleasant memories of President Woodruff: "I was in his presence, of course, a number of times and became acquainted with him. I will have to tell you a story on him: It was in his day when they built Saltair, and the water then came well up under the pavilion, about four or five feet —they would not have built it there if water was not there. Now the water is a long way out and the pavilion is high and dry. But out traveling on the lake, President Woodruff, who was rather impetuous, said, 'Which way are we going?' He was answered, 'We are going directly west!' 'Then which way is east?' I remember that! But, he was a wonderful man, a man of inspiration. He had the guidance of the Holy Spirit, like the brethren before him. He was faithful and true, constant in his love for the Prophet Joseph Smith. I almost grew up with members of his family. . . .

"I was not too well acquainted with President Lorenzo Snow. He was a rather austere man. I was in his presence a great number of times, however. But, let me say to you, so far as integrity is concerned, and faithfulness and loyalty to the Church, these brethren who have gone on ahead of us were loyal and true to the Gospel of Jesus Christ. There was not one of them that would not have laid down his life if it had been necessary. They loved the truth."

Such were the examples and the influences in the boyhood of Joseph Fielding Smith.

Chapter 4

Life, Liberty, and the Happiness of Pursuit

Young Manhood and Marriage

It was a late summer evening in Salt Lake City, in the year of 1894. Joseph Fielding Smith, 18 years of age, had just completed another day of heavy work as a cash boy in the wholesale grocery department in the basement of the Zion's Cooperative Mercantile Institution, at Main and South Temple Streets. He flexed his shoulders, took a deep breath, tried to stand up straight. It was not easy. The hours were long, the work was exhausting, and the pay was pitifully meager. "I worked like a work horse all day long and was tired out when night came, carrying sacks of flour and sacks of sugar and hams and bacons on my back. I weighed 150 pounds, but I thought nothing of picking up a 200-pound sack and putting it on my shoulders. I was a very foolish fellow, because ever since that time my shoulders have been just a little out of kilter. The right one got a little more 'treatment' than the left."

But jobs were not easy to find and his family needed all the financial support it could get, from him and his brothers old enough to work. So Joseph felt fortunate to have this job despite the strenuous working conditions and low pay. The daily physical workout might even be good for him in the long run, if it did not kill him first.

And now, as was his habit, he stopped by the candy counter and bought a sack of hardtack to take home to

Mama and to his younger brothers and sisters. He found pleasure in seeing the little ones' joy at this frequent treat.

It was almost a six-block walk to the family home, at 333 West First North. At the end of a day of heavy work it seemed twice that far, but there was one nice thing about it, his route took him past the recently completed temple. He never grew tired of looking at that magnificent structure, its spires reaching up toward the heavens. The gold and red sky of sunset behind it gave the temple an ethereal appearance that was particularly appealing.

Joseph Fielding Smith at age 19, Oct. 26, 1895.

As Joseph rounded the corner on North Temple Street and headed west down along City Creek, he delighted in the sound of the water rippling along over the rocks. He also noted there was a touch of fall in the air now as dusk settled in on the valley. He would have to remember and wear his jacket to work in the morning. Walking along he pulled from his shirt pocket a small copy of the New Testament that he carried with him constantly, reading it during his noon break and while going to and from work, and in fact whenever he had opportunity. He opened it to his marker in the Book of Acts, Chapter 3, and read a few verses, but the light had grown dim, for the days were getting shorter, a thing he disliked, and it was a strain on his eyes to read, especially while walking. So he put the book back in his pocket. His eyes were not too strong anyway, and it would not do to unnecessarily strain them. There was a lot of reading to get done in the days and years ahead. Instead of reading the rest of the way home he would mentally run through some scriptures that he was trying to commit to memory. Matthew, Chapter 11, "Come unto me, all ye that labour and are heavy laden, and I will give you rest. Take my yoke upon you, and learn of me; for I am meek and lowly in heart; and ye shall find rest unto your souls. For my yoke is easy, and my burden light. . . ."

As Joseph turned in at the gate of the Smith home, he suddenly became aware of the sound of piano music coming from the house, a favorite hymn, "Sweet Hour of Prayer." But who was playing it? He stopped and listened carefully a moment. There was a difference in the way individuals played and he had not heard the piano played this way before: a very fine, soft touch, whoever it was at the keyboard. Then he remembered something he had forgotten: Mama had mentioned that morning as he was leaving for work that this might be the day Louie Shurtliff, a young woman from Ogden, would be moving into their home, to stay there while attending school across the street at the University of Utah (now West High School). Might that be she at the piano?

University building where Louie Shurtliff and David O. McKay attended college in their youth. The school was located on property now occupied by West High School across the street from the old Smith family home.

Joseph took a quick inspection look down his front, brushed some dirt off his trouser leg, straightened his shirt collar, walked up the steps, his heart strangely beating just a bit faster. As he stepped onto the porch the front door flew open and two little pig-tailed girls in cotton plaid dresses rushed excitedly out to meet him and jumped into his arms: six-year-old Emily and three-year-old Rachel.

"Guess who's here!" exclaimed Emily, her eyes sparkling with excitement.

"Who?" asked Joseph.

"Louie! Her name is Louie! That's her playing the piano! And boy, is she pretty! Come see for yourself!"

Joseph had met Louie a time or two before. Their fathers had been friends since boyhood days in Nauvoo, and now again especially in church leadership, with Joseph's father a counselor in the church presidency and Louie's father, Lewis Warren Shurtliff, the president of Weber Stake in Ogden. When President Smith learned that President Shurtliff's daughter wished to attend college in Salt Lake City, he invited her to live at Julina's house where it would be convenient for her. Joseph had always had the most profound respect for his father's wisdom. With that invitation to Louie, his respect became even more profound.

Now, somewhat hesitantly, Joseph walked on into the house, with Emily and Rachel each tugging at a hand, eagerly leading him through the entrance hallway and into the parlor. There sitting at the piano was a girl of exquisite beauty, with long flowing brown hair. As Joseph entered the room she stopped playing and turned to greet him. Their eyes met, and Joseph's chemistry changed from inorganic to organic.

"Hello," said Louie, getting up from the piano with a smile.

"You—you play very beautifully," said Joseph. What he wanted to say was, "You *are* very beautiful." She was in fact the most beautiful girl he fancied he had ever seen. "Mama said you were coming."

"I hope you won't mind my living here," said Louie. She suddenly no longer felt homesick. No, Joseph allowed he would not mind her living there.

During those next three years Joseph had the handiest courting arrangement any young man ever enjoyed— and he did enjoy it. Somehow he managed to walk home from the ZCMI just a little faster in the evenings. The sacks of candy he brought home got larger, and the variety got better. Along with hardtack there were mints and chocolates, taffy and fudge and an occasional English toffee. It was a regular bonanza for Julina's other youngsters: David, 15; George, 13; Ina, 10; Wesley, eight; Emily, Rachel, and eight-month-old baby Edith, who was the darling of all the family.

Even David with the exceeding wisdom of a 15-year-

Scene in old ZCMI Department Store where Joseph Fielding Smith worked when a young man.

old could only partially understand the change that he saw come over Joseph, who had never shown any real interest in girls before Louie. Yet, Joseph was in no hurry to get married. He had a mission to fill for the Church before he could think seriously of marriage. His oldest brother Hyrum, Edna's son, was getting married in a few weeks, to Ida Bowman. But Hyrum had filled his mission, in England, so it was all right for him to go ahead now and marry. That was the proper order of things, of course. His father had filled a four-year mission from the age of 15 to 19 in Hawaii. Already Joseph was behind him on that score. Here he was 18, nearly as old as his father was when he had completed his first mission, and still he had not even begun his. But he would, of course. There must be no thought of marriage until after a mission. No thought. . . .

After being held to the inferior category of a territory and denied statehood by a prejudiced nation for nearly half a century, Utah finally attained it on January 4, 1896, entering the Union as the forty-fifth state. Ceremonies were conducted in the Salt Lake Mormon Tabernacle. Heber M. Wells became the first governor. He was a son of Daniel H. Wells, who had served on the Nauvoo City Council with Joseph Smith, later joined the Church and subsequently became the first mayor of Salt Lake City and a counselor to Brigham Young in the church presidency. Brigham H. Roberts, a general authority of the Church, in 1896 was elected as Utah's representative to the United States Congress, then was denied his seat because he was a polygamist. But with Utah's statehood, the federal government did at least return to the Church the property it had confiscated in 1887 under the Edmunds-Tucker law, or some of it anyway.

Two weeks after Utah's statehood ceremony, Joseph had an important meeting of a personal nature. At 19 and a half years of age he decided it was time he received a patriarchal blessing, to give him further guidance and direction in his life. He made an appointment with his father's older brother, John Smith, the presiding patriarch to the Church. It was on January 19 that Patriarch Smith placed his hands upon Joseph's head and gave him a blessing that was both comforting and challenging to him:

> Joseph Fielding Smith Jr., by the authority of the Priesthood I bear, I place my hands upon thy head and pronounce and seal a blessing upon thee as the spirit shall direct.
> Thou art numbered among the sons of Zion, of whom much is expected. Thy name is written in the Lamb's Book of Life and shall be registered in the chronicles of thy fathers with thy brethren.
> It is thy privilege to live to a good old age and the will of the Lord that you should become a mighty man in Israel. Therefore, I say unto thee, reflect often upon the past, present, and future, and thou shalt realize that the hand of the Lord has been and is over thee for good, and that thy life has been preserved for a wise purpose. Thou shalt realize also that thou hast much to do in order to complete thy mission upon the earth.
> It shall be thy duty to sit in counsel with thy brethren and to preside among the people. It shall be thy duty also to travel much at home and abroad, by land and water, laboring in the ministry. And I say unto thee, hold up thy head, lift up thy voice without fear or favor, as the Spirit of the Lord shall direct, and the blessings of the Lord shall rest upon thee. His spirit shall direct thy mind and give thee word and

sentiment, that thou shalt confound the wisdom of the wicked and set at naught the counsels of the unjust.

Thou shalt have power over thine enemies and peace shall be in thy circle. It shall be thy duty to be a peacemaker wheresoever thou shalt sojourn, and so long as thou art in the discharge of duty no power shall prevail against thee. Thou shalt find friends among strangers.

Therefore, I say unto thee, remember that there is a God in Israel in whom we should trust. Remember also that he will reward according to merit, and it shall be well with thee.

Thou art of Ephraim and entitled to the blessings of Abraham, Isaac, and Jacob, with the gifts and privileges promised unto the fathers in Israel among whom thou shalt be remembered. Therefore, let thy faith fail not, strive to inform thy mind and be prepared for events to come, and remember the instructions of thy parents, and honor the Priesthood, and the blessings of the Lord shall be with thee, and thy guardian angel will direct thy course.

Thou shalt lay hands upon the sick and they shall recover, for this shall be one of thy gifts received through prayer and faith.

This blessing I seal upon thee in the name of Jesus Christ, and I seal thee up unto eternal life to come forth in the morning of the first resurrection, a savior in thy father's house, even so, Amen.

Future events would bear witness to the fulfillment of the blessing.

Joseph's formal education had closed with two years of study at the Latter-day Saint College. His father had a large family to support, and maintaining a separate house for each wife was no easy financial task. Joseph was glad to work to help. He also tended to some of the household duties, helping with the ironing, and mixing the bread at night and putting it into pans for baking in the early morning before leaving for ZCMI.

As for Louie, getting a college degree seemed the most important consideration in her life just then. It would give her a sense of achievement and security, and prepare her to teach in the elementary grades. She had already graduated from the Weber Stake Academy, of which her father was a founder. At the university she would take a three-year course for a teaching certificate. Louie was a tall, shapely girl. She was slightly taller than Joseph, who was five-foot-nine. She was also a month older than he, having been born June 16, 1876.

Joseph and Louie found they had much in common. They were both devoted to the gospel, both enjoyed reading and studying good books, especially the scriptures, and both enjoyed good music, and the out-of-doors. Louie liked playing the piano, and Joseph enjoyed sitting by her and listening to her play. She tried to get him to sing with her, but he claimed to have no voice for singing. They attended Sacrament Service, Sunday School and MIA classes and socials together. Joseph taught a Sunday School class. Envious eyes were cast at Louie by other girls in the Sixteenth Ward, who had failed to attract Joseph's attention. Besides the MIA dances and other socials, Joseph occasionally took Louie to a performance at the Salt Lake Theater, located on the corner of First South and State Streets where the Mountain States Telephone Company office now stands.

Joseph would slip sacks of candy into Louie's bedroom. Later she would share it with him and the youngsters as she and Joseph studied together in the big dining room or at the kitchen table. Although Joseph was not in school he took considerable interest in Louie's studies. Wes, Ina, Emily, Rachel, and baby Edith vied for their attention in the evening. Louie was always very sweet and helpful with the Smith children. Typically it is easier to be pleasant with someone else's brothers and sisters than with one's own, and Louie had completely won the hearts of the Smith youngsters. But sometimes their interest took the form of spying on Joseph and Louie, and then Joseph would send them off to bed—if Mama was out on a maternity case or visiting over at Aunt Edna's house or somewhere else. Or if they got too noisy chasing through the house, he would hustle them off to bed to get things a bit quieter for studying. The children did not care for that at all, and seven-year-old Emily began including in her prayers a request that the Lord call Joseph on a mission, so that he could no longer send them off to bed early.

Come summertimes (in 1895 and again in 1896) Louie returned to her parents in Ogden. Those were lonely summers, for both Louie and Joseph. Ogden and Salt Lake City were not just an hour's drive or less apart as they are today. Travel was slow, difficult, and by train expensive. Once or twice Joseph rode a bicycle the hundred-mile round-trip to visit her. That should convince her of his true love, for the roads were dirt and rutted and difficult for bike riding. It was the closest thing available to slaying a dragon. Louie also made an occasional visit to Salt Lake, sometimes bringing her little brother Frank with her.

On September 8, 1896, approximately the time Louie started her third and final year of school in Salt Lake City, Joseph was ordained an elder in the Melchizedek Priesthood by Charles Seal. His elder's certificate is signed by Z. C. Mitchell, president, and Frederick A. Fish, secretary, of the Sixth Quorum of Elders, Salt Lake Stake of Zion. Two days later he received his endowments in the Salt Lake Temple. It was an impressive experience, seeing the inside of that inspiring edifice and participating in the sacred ceremony. Nor could he help but look to the day when he and Louie would be going to the temple together to be married for an eternity.

Near the end of Louie's final school year in Salt Lake City, there were serious thoughts of marriage passing through two heads. Joseph was rather torn between the idea of marrying or first going on a mission. His father had married at the age of 20, which Joseph was now. Surely that must be a good age. But then his father had filled a mission before that, and Joseph had not. What was this thing called love anyway, that it could dissolve resolves and put to flight determination?

Come the spring of 1897 Louie Shurtliff was a candidate for graduation from the university. She was one of 52 who would be getting either a diploma or certificate. The graduation was to be conducted in the Salt Lake Theater, Wednesday morning, June 7. For the commencement exercises Louie's parents gave her a beautiful white brocaded satin gown with a lacy stand-up collar. Sitting proudly in the audience to watch her graduate was Joseph Fielding Smith, along with her parents and family, and his.

It was easy to wish that he too might have been among the graduates, but there were other ways to get a good education in life, and hard work was one of them. Giving the valedictory address was a friend from Taylorsville, Milton Bennion. David Oman McKay of Huntsville was one of the graduates.

Now that Louie had graduated and would no longer have occasion to be living in Salt Lake City at the Smith home, would she leave his life as suddenly as she had come into it, wondered Joseph. The future seemed highly uncertain to the young couple on that spring commencement day. Joseph would be expected to fill a mission for the Church, and wished to do so, of course. How soon he might be called was a question. Louie was uncertain as to what she wished to do or could do. Maybe make a career of teaching school. As they strolled hand in hand on that night after her graduation, one thing was certain, they loved each other deeply, and they placed hope in the old saying that "love finds a way."

It took another year of courtship for Joseph to get the job done, from her graduation day in the spring of 1897 to the spring of 1898. But it was a pleasant chore—life, liberty, and the happiness of pursuit. Louie moved back to Ogden, helping her father as a clerk at his store and doing some teaching. Joseph got to Ogden as frequently as possible and Louie to Salt Lake City, on weekend visits. "When she finished and graduated from her school," recalled President Smith, "I did not permit her to go home and stay there, but I persuaded her to change her place of residence, and on the 26th day of April, 1898, we went to the Salt Lake Temple and were married for time and all eternity by my father, President Joseph F. Smith." Four days prior to their marriage they went through the temple for her endowments. For her wedding Louie wore the same beautiful dress she had worn at commencement exercises a year earlier. Joseph bought a wedding ring for his bride and a new suit for himself. April 26 was a delightful spring day, the air balmy and invigorating. It seemed to Joseph and Louie that heaven was upon earth. Louie

Louie Shurtliff, first wife of Joseph Fielding Smith, depicted as a child, teenager, and in her later life.

Louie Shurtliff in her wedding dress which she also wore at her commencement exercises.

Smith. Mrs. Joseph Fielding Smith. They liked the sound of her new name.

Then it was back to work at the ZCMI for Joseph. It was still the same back-breaking labor of hauling hams, bacons, sacks of sugar and flour. But Louie was a wonderfully good back rubber. They continued making their home at Mama Julina's house, occupying the northwest corner room. Finances did not permit their building or buying a house of their own immediately. But Papa and Mama Smith designated one of the empty lots in the Smith block to be theirs whenever they were ready to build. It would be just around the corner to the east and south. They began saving their pennies and nickles toward that day, buying shares of stock in a building society. Life was beautiful.

President Wilford Woodruff, to whom Joseph's father served as second counselor, died at San Francisco,

September 2, 1898, four-and-a-half months after Joseph and Louie's marriage. President Woodruff was 91 years old, the greatest age any Church leader had yet attained. What would it be like to live to be 91 years old, wondered Joseph. Having been a close friend with some of President Woodruff's youngsters, and having made a trip to the Chicago Fair five years earlier with the Woodruffs, Joseph had felt a particular fondness for him, among the church leaders he knew.

Eleven days later Lorenzo Snow was sustained as president of the Church. This time schedule was a departure from the past: previously there had been a lengthy waiting period from the death of one president to the ordaining of the next. After the death of Joseph Smith, Brigham Young waited three and a half years to become president; John Taylor waited more than three years; Wilford Woodruff waited nearly two years. At the age of 84 Lorenzo Snow could not afford to wait, nor was there any need of it. George Q. Cannon was again chosen as first counselor, and Joseph's father as second. These two men had now been counselors in turn to Presidents Taylor, Woodruff and Snow.

In October, 1898, half a year after their marriage, Joseph was appointed as a board member in the Salt Lake Stake YMMIA and was set apart by two members of the stake presidency, Angus M. Cannon, president, and Joseph E. Taylor, counselor, and by Richard R. Lyman, president of the stake YMMIA. Louie helped him in his assignments, attending the various MIA functions with him. It was a happy year for the young couple. Louie was a favorite with the Smith family, with Papa Joseph and Mama Julina, with Joseph's brothers and sisters and with his father's other wives, all of whom welcomed her into the family. Louie had something very special in common with those five older women, Julina, Sarah, Edna, Alice and Mary: they each bore the name of Mrs. Joseph Fielding Smith.

It was fun for Joseph and Louie to hitch up the team of horses to the buggy and drive out to the family farm at

Taylorsville, or up Little Cottonwood Canyon for a picnic. Occasionally they would take a train ride to Ogden to visit with Louie's folks and family.

Louie was the oldest of her mother's children. She had three younger brothers, John, Luman, and Frank. Another brother, William, had died at age two. Louie had been born in Plain City, west of Ogden, where her father served as bishop before becoming Weber Stake president. By his first wife, Louisa Catherine Smith, her father had two sons and two daughters, Laura, Louis, Haskell and Louisa. So Louie really came midway in the family. Although three and a half years older than President Joseph F. Smith, her father had not entered plural marriage. His first wife, who had married him when only 14 years old, died in 1866 at the age of 22. The next year he took a mission to England. After being a widower for nearly six years he married again in 1872, choosing Emily Wainwright, a 19-year-old English girl. Four years later her first child was born. They named her Louie Emily, in memory of the first wife as well as the second. She also went by "Louie Emyla," but mostly just by "Louie."

It was in March, 1899, that Joseph received the word which he and Louie had been half expecting through their several months of marriage: a mission call! "I was called on March 17, 1899, to go on a mission to Great Britain, being called by President Lorenzo Snow. I had been interviewed for a mission by Franklin D. Richards [president of the Council of Twelve Apostles] who asked me where I'd like to go. I told him I had no choice particularly, only to go where I was sent. But he said, 'You must have some place where you would prefer to go to.' I said, 'Well, I'd prefer to go to Germany.' So they sent me to England!"

It is a bit surprising that Joseph did not voice a preference for Hawaii, where his father had filled a number of missions, and where his mother had also lived. But England it was, the land where many of his forebears and those of his wife had lived. The assignment to England gave him an opportunity to do some family genealogical research. Joseph would not be going to England alone.

One of his older brothers, Joseph Richards, Sarah's son, was also called on a mission to England at the same time; also, a neighbor boy, William Armstrong. It would be Joseph Richards' second trip there. That was a comforting thought, to have an older brother and a neighbor going along. They were given two months to get ready to leave, in May.

It was of course with mixed emotions that Joseph and Louie accepted his call. They were agreed that it was the right thing, and an opportunity for him. Still, it was difficult to say goodbye for two years after just one year of marriage. But at least they would be able to spend their first wedding anniversary together before he had to go. As the day for his mission departure grew ever closer, each day together became more precious to them. It caused an ache in the heart just to think of his leaving. They both hoped that Louie might become pregnant. They both desired children, and for her to have a baby would be a real comfort to her in his absence. But in this hope and expectation they were disappointed.

To prepare to leave on his mission there were many things to be done. Joseph and his parents urged Louie to continue living at Julina's in Salt Lake City. But she decided the loneliness of separation could be best endured if she were back in Ogden with her own parents and family. She would work for her father and help support Joseph in his mission. So one of the last minute chores was to move her wardrobe and a few pieces of furniture up to her parents' home. Papa and Mama Smith sought to assure her that her room at Julina's would be kept ready for her any time she chose to come back, either to live or just to visit.

From the Department of State Joseph had to obtain a passport, permitting his passage abroad for two years. This document, dated April 22, 1899, gives a brief physical description of him: Age 22 years; height five-feet-nine-inches; forehead high; eyes bluish grey; nose sharp; mouth small; chin round; hair brown; complexion light; face long. It was hardly a flattering or adequate description of an unusually handsome young man. His signature on the document was "Jos. F. Smith Jr." For many years, in fact, he signed as Joseph F. Jr. rather than as Joseph Fielding Smith.

Departure date was set for Saturday, May 13, by train via Ogden and points east. On May 12 Joseph Fielding, Joseph Richards, and William Armstrong and others were blessed and set apart as missionaries and also ordained to the office of Seventy, the Smith brothers by their father. President Smith and two members of the Council of the Twelve, George Teasdale and Heber J. Grant, also instructed them in missionary work, reviewing with them what would be expected of them and warning them of the problems and challenges they must face. England was not an easy mission field. There was considerable hostility to the Church there as in most parts of the world; so much so that it was legally libelous to falsely accuse a person of being a Mormon! Each of the boys also received a missionary certificate to carry.

The certificate depicts the all-seeing eye of God and carries the caption: Holiness to the Lord/Missionary Certificate. "This certifies that the bearer Elder Joseph F. Smith Jr. is in full faith and fellowship with The Church of Jesus Christ of Latter-day Saints and by the General Authorities of said Church has been duly appointed a Mission to Great Britain to Preach the Gospel and administer in all the Ordinances thereof pertaining to his office.

"And we invite all men to give heed to his Teachings and Counsels as a man of God, sent to open to them the door of Life and Salvation—and to assist him in his travels, in whatsoever things he may need.

"And we pray God, The Eternal Father, to bless Elder Smith and all who receive him and minister to his comfort, with the blessings of Heaven and Earth, for time and all eternity, in the name of Jesus Christ, Amen.

"Signed at Salt Lake City, Utah, May 12th, 1899, in behalf of said Church. Lorenzo Snow, George Q. Cannon, Jos. F. Smith, First Presidency."

Saturday, the departure day, Joseph and Louie

walkèd up town in the morning and purchased several items he would need for his journey. One item was a three-and-a-half-by-six-inch notebook with a leather snap-on cover, in which he that day began keeping a personal journal, a practice he followed with some regularity the rest of his life. They also bought some stationery and envelopes and promised to write frequent letters to each other.

Saturday afternoon they carefully packed his trunk, and Louie, Mama Julina, Mama Sarah, sisters and aunties joined in preparing some cookies and other treats for Joseph and Richards to take on the train with them.

Farewells are never pleasant nor easy. They decided it would be less painful to say goodbye at home than at the train depot. Although it was a beautiful spring day, yet in the heart it seemed like mid-winter. It brought back to Joseph vivid memories of that awful December day when as a boy eight years old he had said a tearful goodbye to Papa and Mama and baby Ina as they left for Hawaii. But now it was he who was leaving. Being left behind as a child had been terrible, but leaving others behind now was just as hard. Just as hard.

"I'll go where you want me to go, dear Lord, o'er mountain or plain or sea . . ." Two long years, or more. Twenty-four months at least. A hundred and four weeks. Seven hundred and thirty days. An endless number of hours and minutes. An eternity of time. How would it ever pass? "He that loveth father and mother more than me is not worthy of me, and he that loveth son or daughter more than me is not worthy of me. And he that taketh not his cross, and followeth after me, is not worthy of me. . . ."

Joseph's sister Emily, now nine years old, felt so guilty that she had prayed him into a mission—so that he would not send her and the other children off to bed early —that after dinner Saturday afternoon, when it came time for him to say goodbye, she ran over to Aunt Mamie's house and hid in a closet until after Joseph had left for the depot so that she would not have to face him. He searched in vain for her.

Louie tried to be brave, tried not to let Joseph see her cry. But it was hard to conceal red eyes. And Joseph was already so homesick just at the thought of leaving that he did not feel much like talking with anyone.

The first entry in his journal reads, "Saturday May 13, 1899: I went up town and purchased some articles to take with me on the way to England. Packed my trunk in the afternoon and got all ready to leave. At six o'clock told all the folks goodbye and left for the depot with feelings that I never felt before, because I was never away from home more than one month in my life, and to think of going away for two years or more causes very peculiar feelings to take possession of me."

There was a lump in Joseph's throat as he paused at the front door of the old home on First North Street and kissed each of his loved ones goodbye: Mama, Papa, brothers and sisters, aunties, and last of all, Louie. "Goodbye Louie, my precious. God bless you and keep you safe for me." Then he turned and walked down the path to the street, met Richards, and proceeded on to the depot. There must be no turning back, no looking back, no giving way to emotions.

Chapter 5

"I'll go where you want me to go,
dear Lord . . ."

Mission to England

It was a long and wretched night, riding across the high windswept plateau country of Wyoming, in a chair car that was crowded, dirty, stinky and noisy. The air was bad, filled with stale tobacco smoke and the accumulated filth of a train car that seemed to have not been cleaned since Columbus discovered America. It was a steady uphill climb from Ogden into Wyoming and the train moved tediously slow. There was a fierce cold wind, rocking the cars more than usual. The constant swaying motion of the train, which under more favorable circumstances might have lulled a passenger to sleep, was but another nightmarish irritant.

With his legs and feet cramped into too small a space between seats, Joseph tried to get into a position that would be somewhat comfortable. He leaned his head sometimes this way and sometimes the other. He crouched over and he straightened up. He slumped to the left and slumped to the right, trying to get some sleep. But it was no use. Train chairs were foolproof, guaranteed to be uncomfortable no matter how you sat in them. "We could not sleep, for the car was so crowded and we were cramped in our seats and there was great confusion." And each miserable passing hour took him farther and farther away from home—from Louie and Papa and Mama, from brothers and sisters, from the home and valley he loved, from all that was dear and meaningful to him in life.

Ironic it was, thought Joseph, that his father and other pioneers in making their westward trek across this same country, by covered wagon, seeking their home in the valley of the mountains, could progress only at snail's pace, a few miles a day at most, when they would like to have gone much, much faster. But now the speed of the train could carry him away from the valley, from all that was precious to him, at a speed several times as great. Difficult though their trek had been, at least the pioneers had the advantage of being out in the open, breathing pure air. Joseph's lungs and head were soon clogged with tobacco smoke, being blown at him it seemed from every direction on the car, by men who apparently cared neither for their own health and comfort nor for that of anyone else in the car. There were even little children and babies on the train being subjected to the stink of it. There was no danger of Indian attack on the train, as the pioneers sometimes suffered. But there was the poison of the Indians' gift to the white man: the tobacco smoke.

Joseph felt like walking up and down the isle declaring aloud a verse of scripture: "Behold, verily, thus saith the Lord unto you: In consequence of evils and designs which do and will exist in the hearts of conspiring men in the last days I have warned you, and forewarn you, by giving unto you this Word of Wisdom by revelation . . . tobacco is not for the body, neither for the belly, and is not good for man . . ."!

For another 73 years Joseph Fielding Smith would travel on trains and other public conveyances on church assignments, and would be plagued by the nauseating smell of tobacco smoke, one of the banes of his life, a thing he could never quite get used to, part of the price he must pay to be in the Lord's service. "A dirty, filthy habit!" he labeled it; one of the curses of mankind.

Joseph tried to think upon more pleasant subjects. He tried to picture Louie in her sweetness and beauty. He tried to recount those last few precious hours with her.

Saying goodbye to a wife of one year was not easy. His father had done the same thing back in 1860, leaving his beloved Levira, bride of one year, to take a two-year mission to England. If his father could do it, he could do it, and there was comfort in the thought.

Despite the farewells spoken at the family home, quite a large crowd had gathered at the depot to see him and the other missionaries off. The train had pulled out at 6:40, as the sun was setting. It was the last glorious sunset over the Great Salt Lake that he would see for more than two years, and he had watched it rather steadily as the train rolled north toward Ogden to meet the transcontinental Union Pacific train. Fred Williams, a fellow missionary, had climbed aboard at Kaysville, and President Lewis W. Shurtliff, Joseph's father-in-law, "met me half way to Ogden and rode up to Ogden with us." It was a thoughtful gesture and appreciated. Lewis Shurtliff also knew the sorrow of saying goodbye to a wife, for his first wife had died in her early twenties, and the next year, 1867, Lewis had taken a mission to England, leaving four little children behind. No doubt things had changed in England in the 30 years since he had been there, but there were still some names of persons and places and other details to share with Joseph, and some fatherly advice and comfort to offer. Of most importance he wished to assure Joseph of Louie's safekeeping while they were separated. . . .

Fortunately at Cheyenne, Wyoming, late Sunday afternoon, Joseph and his companions were able to transfer to a cleaner car and "I washed myself for the first time since leaving home for I had not had a chance before then, there being no water on the car we were on." Switching trains at Omaha and again at Chicago and parting with their missionary companions, Joseph and his brother Richards traveled via Buffalo, New York, so they could take a sidetrip to Niagara Falls, which proved a delightful experience. "It is the greatest sight that I ever saw," wrote Joseph in his journal after a four-hour visit. "When we got there we hired a hack which took us to all principle points on both the U.S. and Canadian sides. There are very many schemes to get a man's money from him, but we did very well as the entire trip cost us less than four dollars each." His brief touchdown on Canadian soil was "the first time that I ever was out of my native country."

Reaching New York City on Thursday they were met by a missionary friend, Howard Garrett. "The first thing I did when I reached here was to take a good bath. . . . I feel like a new man now." Two days of sightseeing gave Joseph and his companions, these country boys from Utah, including several other missionaries who joined them there, a whole new dimension of the world. "Saw the largest building in N.Y. [30 stories] but do not know its name." In his most ecstatic daydream he could hardly have imagined that one day as head of the Church he would be sponsoring construction of a building 31 stories high in his own native Salt Lake City.

Joseph and Richards were enthralled by the ships. They spent several hours in the Brooklyn Navy Yard where they boarded half a dozen boats and saw several others, also watched ships sailing into the harbor near South Ferry Park, and on the Hudson River. They viewed the Statue of Liberty, rode an elevated railroad to Harlem Heights for a visit to Grant's Tomb, rode a ferry, walked through Central Park, visited a wax museum, and marveled that 20 cars passed them in one minute's time as they stood on Brooklyn Bridge. In 1899 New York City already had the making of a traffic jam!

Their ship, the Belgian liner *Pennland,* was leaving from Philadelphia, on Sunday, May 21. Joseph and Richards spent Saturday visiting such historic sites in Philadelphia as Independence Square, the Liberty Bell, Carpenter Hall where the first Continental Congress met, saw the signatures of George Washington, Patrick Henry, and of the signers of the Declaration of Independence: John Hancock, Thomas Jefferson, et al. To a person with a keen interest in history, the Philadelphia visits had a great appeal. But the most pleasant part of the brief stay in Philadelphia was receipt of a letter from Louie. "It was a very agreeable surprise to me to receive a letter from home as I did not expect one until I reached Liverpool."

The anticipation of crossing the ocean must have been exciting for the youthful missionaries. Richards as a four-year-old had accompanied his parents to England and had some slim memories of that voyage. But to Joseph and the several other missionaries who had joined them in Philadelphia the experience was a new one— and one they soon found disappointing. Of the missionary group of 19 Joseph was one of only five that did not get seasick. Poor Richards was nauseous during most of the 13-day voyage and wished he had stayed home. The first night or two out, Joseph sat up late looking at the stars from the vantage point of the ocean. He and the other missionaries distributed Church tracts to some of the other passengers. "We hope they will read them," he noted in his journal. The missionaries also conducted a Sunday service, inviting other passengers to attend. Joseph was one of two speakers, and noted a mixed response from the non-Mormon audience as he reviewed the history of the Church and the persecutions the Mormons had suffered.

Other, faster ships passed the *Pennland* with such ease that Joseph became disgusted with the slowness of the Belgian liner. He felt somewhat comforted when the *Pennland* finally passed another ship. "It is good to think that we can move faster than *some things*," he confided to his journal, "even if it is not very much faster. It has taken about six hours for us to lose sight of her, while the *St. Louis* left us in the same way in about one and one half hours." Several glimpses of fish, a whale and an iceberg helped to break the monotony of the ship voyage. But the first sight of Ireland at mid-morning Friday, June 2, was a welcome one. A day later they docked at Liverpool, England, where they received their mission assignments. To their keen disappointment, Joseph and Richards were separated, assigned to different conferences, Richards being sent to Leeds, where their oldest brother Hyrum had earlier labored, and Joseph to Nottingham, in central England.

Joseph Fielding and his older brother, Richards, as they appeared as young missionaries in England, 1899-1901.

The three-hour train trip to Nottingham Sunday evening was a lonely one for Joseph. "The railroads in this country are so different from those in our own country that a person must keep his wits about him. I traveled alone, in a strange land, and among a strange people, where I would have little or no sympathy if I were known. My thoughts were continually turning towards home." It did not help his morale any when he arrived at the conference mission home only to find it locked and nobody there to greet him, everyone being off to church services. "I placed my trunk and grip in the doorway and walked up and down the street where I could watch them [his trunk and grip]." Passersby eyed him with both curiosity and disdain, associating him as they did with the Mormon mission house. A crowd of rude little boys in the neighborhood apparently was a self-appointed welcoming committee for Mormon missionaries. "Many small boys who were in the street when I came eyed me with curiosity and sang a parody on one of our mountain hymns for my own personal benefit. If I approached them they would run from me, which amused me as much as I amused them." To the English the name "Mormon" was synonymous with "polygamist," and the boys' line of song was "Chase me, girls, to Salt Lake City, where the Mormons have no pity!" It was an hour before the missionaries returned to the house from their Sunday services and rescued Joseph from this harassment.

Fortunately Monday dawned "a nice clear day for this land"—where it was cold and rainy or overcast most of the time. Joseph's spirits picked up a little as he became acquainted with other missionaries and got somewhat oriented in the famous Robin Hood city that was to be his headquarters for the next two years. George Ruff of Coalville, Utah, president of the Nottingham conference of the English mission, was away when Joseph got there, "so I do not know what is to be done with me." In company with another elder, George F. Ashley, Joseph spent his first day buying a hat and some writing paper and envelopes, and visiting "the Arboretum Park for a short time where they keep all kinds of birds and I know not what all," a spot he returned to quite often.

It was on Tuesday, June 6, that he actually started in his missionary endeavors. "This has been a very important day in my short life. I came from my home less than a month ago for the purpose of preaching the gospel of our Lord. . . . I have been out tracting today and delivered 25 tracts. It is the first of this kind of work that I ever tried to do and it did not come to me very easy." That night he and two others conducted a street meeting. It was the first he had "ever stood on a street to preach the gospel of Christ. I bore my testimony to the world for the first time today, but will be able to do so better. With the help of the Lord I shall do his will as I was called to do." The street meetings generally proved of little value and were often canceled because of rain, holidays, or no attendance. After a year he reported to Louie, "We have not been able to do much this month in the open air because of the rain. This is a very poor place for open air work at best, as we can only go in some out-of-the-way place to hold meetings and then to talk to lamp posts and dirty youngsters who never saw a bathtub nor heard of an article called soap."

At times the mission became almost a traumatic experience for him as he daily faced the frustration of having a message of vital importance to deliver to a people who seemed totally indifferent to what he had to say. By the end of his first week of proselyting he confided to his journal that in England "the honest in heart have nearly all received the gospel. The blood of Israel has almost all been gathered. Those who are there do not care for the truth." Two years later he was still of the same opinion only more so. Despite diligent labors he did not make one convert, did not have opportunity to perform one baptism, although he did confirm one convert. It was enough to discourage the stoutest heart. He had heard of the days when the gospel was first introduced in England, when converts came in by the hundreds, sometimes by whole congregations. That was 60 years earlier. Times had indeed changed. Most of the few people there who were members of the Church were so apathetic toward it that it was sometimes necessary to cancel Sunday meeting for lack of attendance.

One Sunday he and a companion walked four miles to the neighboring town of Arnold to conduct a Sunday School, but only four little girls came. And in the city of Derby a few months later he noted that "most of the saints in this branch are rather lukewarm as to their duties in the Church, which makes much unnecessary work for us as traveling elders. They do not seem to have the gospel at heart as they should have or as the saints used to have. The reason things are so is strange, but I believe the best blood of Israel has long since been gathered out of this land."

He once told his son Joseph that conditions were so bad and the people so disinterested that he reached a frame of mind where he thought that he could not continue. One night he lay awake thinking of the need to work for passage home.

The futility of his efforts was the worst aspect of his missionary life. But there were other elements of gloom: the gnawing homesickness, the atrocious English weather —day after day of rain, cold, gray skies, the animosity of the people toward Mormons, and the dirty living quarters to which he was often subjected. Joseph had been reared in a home where cleanliness was next to godliness. A typical journal entry reads:

"This morning I got up early as I am on the committee preparing breakfast this week. Learned a passage of scripture as our custom requires each day. I took a bath and changed my clothing. I am covered from head to foot with bites from some kind of insect or something. The quarters we occupy are not the cleanest in the world. Many of the customs of the people are very far behind the times, and not as cleanly as they at home. . . . I went through the cupboard this morning and tried hard to straighten it up a little for it was in a terrible condition. After I had thrown away a large number of tin cans, etc., and emptied a dozen or more papers of mush into one and after throwing many other papers away and cleaning a few dishes that were covered with dirt and grease, the place looked somewhat respectable. . . . We elders do most of our own kitchen work. . . ."

It seems that much of his time was spent in kitchen duty, perhaps because he had learned at home to cook well. About midway in his mission his mother wrote to him, "I am sorry you are back in the kitchen again. I do not think I will ever teach another boy to cook. You made a mistake. You should have spoiled everything you tried to cook."

In her letters Louie a number of times expressed concern over Joseph's getting an adequate diet. About a month after his arrival he wrote her, "I eat very well . . . , but I will not know what a good meal is by the time I am ready to come home. We have the same thing every day of the week and every week of the year. The elders speak of it as the one mush, one meat, and one jam. Every morning we have mush made from graham flour, never a change, for the law is as strict as that of the Medes and Persians. For dinner we have meat that has been dead many days, and for tea ham and canned tomatoes or some lettuce. But I do not starve by any means. I can eat plenty." He especially missed having Utah strawberries and peaches. After two weeks of English food he confided to his journal, "I have had to eat things since I have been here that would turn almost any Utahn's stomach." But he got used to it by and by and it did not seem so bad.

For a time Joseph specialized in cooking beans. "I taught them [the other elders] some things that they did not know. One was that navy beans were very good. You could eat them boiled or in soup. I went to the store one day to get some navy beans. . . . The man reached down off the shelf a one-pound package and handed it to me. I said, 'I don't want just one pound; I want eight or ten pounds.' He looked at me in astonishment. He went to his shelf, looked up, and he took down eight one-pound packages and said, 'This is all I've got.' I took the eight packages home. We lived on beans boiled and bean soup. You don't know how good it is if you haven't tried it!" One day, however, he placed a pan of beans in water on the coal stove to cook and when he came back some time later found the beans all over the stove.

The all-bean menu was improved upon at times. "You know we are doing our own work now," he wrote to Louie in November, 1900. "We buy in for ourselves and cook for ourselves, so we have just what we want and plenty of it. We are not starving ourselves now. We live almost entirely on vegetables and fruit. We seldom see meat unless we get a piece to make soup with. . . . All the elders here say they never felt better in their lives. I feel well, and I think the way we are living has a great deal to do with it."

Louie, Mama Julina, and Joseph's sisters sometimes sent, via missionaries traveling to England, cakes, cookies or other special treats to him. Once while laboring in the city of Derby, 12 miles from Nottingham, he received word that a package of books and clothes had arrived for him at conference headquarters. He and his companion, Stephen W. Walker, took the four-hour walk to Nottingham to pick them up, and after staying overnight started again for their apartment in Derby. "This morning Brother Walker and I left Nottingham for Derby carrying our bundles with us. They weighed altogether about thirty pounds. The snow made it very bad under foot and increased the difficulty of walking. When we reached home I was surprised to find a large fruit cake in my bundle which I thought contained only books, and on the way in I had used the bundle as a seat while we ate our lunch. But the cake tasted just as good for all that, and ten times better because it was made by my sister at home. . . ."

Joseph and his companions walked nearly everywhere they went, just occasionally taking a train ride for longer trips or if there was some particular hurry. It was not uncommon for them to walk up to 20 miles a day. This particular day as he carried his bundle to Derby, in March, 1900, he "suffered somewhat from water blisters on my feet due to the walk and the dampness."

Generally in tracting from door to door, Joseph was unsuccessful in getting the people even to talk with him. Sometimes they would slam a door in his face, occasionally they would accept a tract and even show a touch of friendliness, but usually it was just a what-the-hell-do-you-want glare and silence.

Typical of the comments he placed in his journal was this: "I visited 81 houses with tracts but could not get the people to talk." And this, "I tracted Uttoxeter New Road again today for the third time, but found it somewhat difficult to get the people to talk. One or two tracts were refused and one door was slammed in my face. In tracting I find it very difficult to get the people to talk either for or against us. Most of them are silent unless it is to say 'Good afternoon.' "

This frustration of being unable generally to get people even to talk to him he noted in a letter to Louie: "We always feel good when we can get someone to talk to us even if they do have no good or kind word for us. It is when we cannot get anyone to speak that we feel our time is thrown away. I would rather have someone accuse us of almost anything so long as he will talk than to have them keep as mum as oysters. If they will talk even if they do so with the spirit of Satan we can defend ourselves and ofttimes set them right, for many of those who speak against us thank us when they hear our side of the story and admit that they have been deceived.

"I met a lady today who said she had no use for the 'Mormonites' as she did not believe as they did. I told her I knew she did not or I would not be there. I wanted to know what it was about their doctrines she did not agree with. 'Well,' she said, 'they believe in having more than one wife.' I told her that we did not teach nor practice polygamy. The only way to meet those people is to ask them if they believe the Bible and when they say yes you can soon make them wriggle. They harp on that question [polygamy] no matter what you say until you silence them with the scriptures. . . . I drove her from one point to another until she began to abuse our people and tell me how wicked they are, etc. When she got through I spoke to her in such a way that she became ashamed of herself and began to beg my pardon without telling me so in that many words. I left her a Morgan tract #1 and told her I would call again."

The cold shoulder treatment day after day begins to get to a person after awhile, and it seemed good to occasionally have someone take time to heap abuse upon him. Such a one was a certain lady whom he encountered shortly after he began his missionary work:

"Last week when I was out tracting," he wrote Louie, "I went to the house of a Catholic lady who gave me a thorough roasting. She could not say anything mean enough about the 'Mormons' as she called us. She said they were the vilest people on the earth. Brigham Young was the twin brother of Henry the Eighth. It was useless for me to say anything, but I did bear my testimony. She said I did not look like there was very much sin in me and I had better leave the Church, for I was deceived. I often meet such people and often meet with those who are not willing to hear me."

Joseph declared in a letter to Louie that the reason the people would not receive the gospel was "because their deeds are evil and they love darkness rather than light. There are many in this nation who know the gospel is true that we teach, but they have not the moral courage to come out of the world and embrace it. There is a young man here named Sykes who calls to see us every week. He is a Methodist but is very friendly to us. We have forced him to admit that his church is not the church that is recognized in the heavens. He admits that all are without the gospel unless we have it, and he knows that we have it, but he is afraid that he will lose the goodwill of his friends and he would fail in his business. But there is no man who has left father or mother or wife, etc., who shall not receive his reward both in this life and life eternal. Mark X:29. I hope I may always be found faithful and willing to do the will of my Father in Heaven. . . ."

Judging from his journal entries the aspect of his mission that Joseph enjoyed most was the occasional opportunity he had of engaging someone in a serious gospel discussion, whether the person was friendly or antagonistic. He and his companion Stephen Walker, who by then had succeeded George Ruff as conference president, became embroiled one day in a rather heated debate with their landlord, a Mr. Blood, who quizzed them about their belief in the Bible.

". . . I was somewhat backward at first about speaking and only did so when I saw it was certainly necessary. Mr. Blood said that we should not believe differently from anyone else in our *foundation* although we might in church government. But we drew the line at this, and by request of President Walker I took the argument off his hands. I told Mr. Blood that one good reason we did not have the *foundation* that others had was because we built upon the foundation of revelation and the everlasting gospel of the kingdom; that we taught that God could reveal to man his mind and will today as much as he ever did, and it would be unto us scripture. This idea horrified him and he began to take me in hand as a youth whose knowledge of the scriptures had been sadly neglected and perverted, to ever think of such an idea. And to clinch his argument he told me the curse John pronounced upon all who 'shall add unto these things' which God had revealed. I asked him what John referred to and he said 'the Bible.' 'Then if John meant the Bible, he himself must be very guilty of breaking the commandment of God,' I said. When I said this his eyes bulged out and he asked me why, so I told him John wrote and added to his writings his gospel after he wrote those words. Then I told him just what John meant and wanted to know if John had anything to do with the compiling of the books which composed the Bible, or if the Bible was in existence in the shape we now have it in John's day. He saw the difficulty he was in, and changed the subject, telling us what was necessary to save a man. Belief without works was all that was required, but of course works were acceptable. I asked him if he thought a man could be saved if he was not willing to keep the counsel of God. He paused for a moment and then said it was necessary to keep the counsel of God. . . .

"We then mentioned baptism to him and said it was necessary to salvation as well as faith and repentance. 'No,' he said, . . . 'Where do you get such a doctrine as that?' I told him Christ said so. 'No! No!' he said, 'Not in *my* Bible! Not in *my* Bible!' and with these words he made off for *his* Bible. He handed it to me saying, 'Now show me where God says baptism is essential to my salvation.' I called his attention to what had been mentioned before that it was necessary for a man to keep the counsel of God to be saved and then without turning a leaf in the book opened *his* Bible to the 7th chapter of Luke and read the 29th verse to him. I began to read from the 24th verse in order to give him the thought. No longer did he say baptism was not the counsel of God. He saw he was trapped. Taking the Bible he read the passage over and over again, and after thinking awhile said, 'No, Christ does not say we cannot be saved unless we are baptized. Show me where he says it. Just show me. Stay with your position and I'll put you in a corner'. I turned to the 3rd chapter of John and read what the Savior said to Nicodemus. He had to take his Bible again and he read the verse over and over several times. I forced him to admit it meant baptism and he could not answer.

"He then began to get very warm, in fact angry, and danced up and down shouting in true Methodist style. I then read to him the words of I Peter 3:18-21. He paused and read it calmly as he had done before and confessed that he had not noticed it before. He then began to dance around again shouting, 'Christ or baptism. Which is it? Does Christ save us or does baptism?' It was so comical I had to smile a bit. We tried to reason with him but he was in too big a rage. I asked him if he would accept the words of Paul and he yelled 'No! I will not believe Paul!' 'And Peter?' I said. 'No! I won't believe Paul or Peter!' he said. 'It is either Christ that saves us or baptism. Which is it? If we are saved by baptism we have no need of Christ!' and he continued to dance up and down like a jumping jack.

"But we proved that the Bible he accused us of not believing in, *his* Bible as he called it, was the very book *he* did not believe in. There were many other things mentioned, too numerous to write, but never before was I assisted through the power of God more than at this time. He [Mr. Blood] set his own trap and was caught in it. Every corner he tried to put us in he was forced into himself. The spirit of the Lord was with us, we were there nearly two hours and mentioned many things: the apostasy, restoration, faith, baptism, etc., and on all these subjects he was silenced completely. Surely the Lord does choose the weak things to confound the wisdom of the wise. And it was due to his assistance that we were successful."

Joseph sought to engage the various ministers of religion in discussion. His feeling was that "they are teachers of the people and the people naturally follow them. I feel that they are in need of warning if anyone is, and they ought to have it. I want them to have it, too, where I can, for they should be left without excuse, and they cannot say the gospel was never presented to them." He even mailed a personal letter to about 200 ministers in Nottingham, Derby, and neighboring towns, together with a copy of a pamphlet explaining the Latter-day Saint beliefs, and invited them to send him literature on their beliefs:

"Dear Sir, In this enlightened age of free thought and religious liberty, when all men have a right to their respective views, I hope you will not be offended because I have taken the liberty of sending to you a pamphlet setting forth the fundamental principles of the faith of The Church of Jesus Christ of Latter-day Saints, the Church of which I am a representative.

"It is my desire that you peruse those principles carefully and compare them with the Holy Bible to see if they do not agree with that sacred record. 'To the law and to the testimony, if they speak not according to this word, it is because there is no light in them.'

"As a searcher after truth I desire that you kindly forward to me a pamphlet setting forth the fundamental principles of your faith, which, I promise you, I shall carefully read. My sole desire being that we might come to a 'unity of the faith.'

"If further information should be desired concerning the principles of The Church of Jesus Christ of Latter-day Saints, which are little understood by the Christian world in general, it may be had on application.

"Hoping you will oblige me in this desire, I am, Sir, Respectfully yours. . . ."

A few responded. Two of them well expressed the chaotic condition England found herself in regarding religion. The Reverend Perry Holbrook said, "The differences which separate us are so slight and the division among Christians cause such untold harm that I earnestly wish that good and true people would be content to hold their little notions in private. I believe that hundreds of people could conscientiously become members of the Church of England, if they would be content to *differ* from others without separating from them. Here instead of a hundred little causes struggling to maintain half empty buildings there would be one grand cause in a glorious work against iniquity, impurity and infidelity. . . ."

The Reverend S. Arthur Beery, also a minister in the Church of England, entertained similar feelings: ". . . I do quite agree that we should all teach the same thing. This being so it seems to me that it is much to be deplored that men should have severed themselves from the National church [Church of England] and so pandered to their own wishes that we find today several hundred different sects in England all divided rather by circumstantials than essentials, where a few centuries ago they were one. I certainly will read the pamphlet you so kindly sent, although I must confess that it seems to be published without authority."

England of course had never been "one" in religious belief, as the Reverend Mr. Beery suggested. From ages past it had been bathed in the blood of civil wars prompted by religious as well as political contentions, not only between Catholics and Protestants but among various factions of Protestants and of Catholics. King Henry VIII's beheading of two of his six wives was just one of the more dramatic manifestations of the unholy alliance of church and state in a land where people were oppressed and exploited equally by fat bishops and jaundiced kings. Nottingham had been made famous by the legendary Robin Hood who championed the cause of the little man by relieving the gorgeously arrayed clergy and royalty alike of some of their surplus wealth. Supposedly good Robin returned a portion of it to the overtaxed, over-burdened layman whose soul was somehow to be saved by enduring the wrongs heaped upon him daily by the corruptions in politics and religion. It was here at Nottingham, too, that one of the Catholic minded Stuart kings, Charles I, had unfurled his royal banner of defiance to Parliament, plunging England into bloody civil war as it took another tiny step in its slow and tortuous route toward responsible government.

Another of the ministers to whom Joseph wrote, George Hill, responded, ". . . It will perhaps excuse my delay [in replying], as well as explain the brevity of my answer, if I say at once that I have neither time nor taste for religious controversy. Some years ago I looked into the doctrines of the Mormons, and found them so utterly incredible that they cease to interest me. I have perused the pamphlets [you] sent to me, and find that my early judgment is well warranted. . . ."

But most of the ministers just ignored his letter. To Louie Joseph reported, "The ministers do not answer us now. I think they have had their heads together to see what they could do in order to put down this strange doctrine. I think they must have come to the conclusion that the best thing to do is to ignore us, to let our letters go unanswered. . . . These men do not want the truth. They are ministers by trade, because it is money in their pockets."

It was such behavior of religious leaders plus the daily indifference from the layman whose homes he tracted or whom he sought to engage in street meetings, that prompted Joseph to express several times in his journal and in his letters home that England had been warned sufficiently by the elders. One such comment was also prompted in part by a copy he received of a sermon by President George Q. Cannon in general conference in Utah. "He states that there are certain nations which have been warned almost enough. I certainly feel that England has been well warned. There are very few that we meet who have not heard of us and express themselves as knowing more of 'Mormonism' than we do, thus condemning themselves, being their own witnesses before our Father in heaven. We can get few to talk to us on the gospel with any intention of knowing the truth. I am of the firm opinion that this nation among others is almost gleaned. I went tracting this afternoon and delivered over 100 tracts with little success." The Church then used no referral system in its missionary program and relied pretty much on tracting. "We distribute over 10,000 tracts a month and visit about 4,000 houses, yet I don't believe one, or more than one, tract in every hundred is read," he told Louie.

Sometimes the British disdain for the Mormon elders was expressed more openly than by mere indifference. A butcher once threatened Joseph with a knife at the mere mention of the Church. And occasionally a street meeting was broken up by the audience pelting the elders with rocks, mud, manure, garbage, or anything else convenient at hand. Sometimes local ministers would try to keep them from speaking, but the policemen and some of the audience would usually intervene for them. All in all, Joseph felt that the missionaries were safer in England than they would be in some parts of the United States, even though "the names 'Latter-day Saints' and 'Mormon' are hisses and bywords among the people."

Joseph sometimes found that drunks were more inclined to listen to his message than ministers were. One day, for instance, "I went with Brother Pugmire to see a Methodist minister and had a long talk with him, upsetting some of his teachings. When we came away he told us never to call again for he had had enough of our doctrine." Yet, a month earlier he and another elder had traveled to a neighboring town where they had searched out a woman who was a member of the Church. "She is a faithful saint but her husband drinks and makes her life very miserable. . . . We saw Mr. Beardsmore, her husband, but he was so drunk he could hardly stand. But he seemed pleased that we had called. He says the gospel is true and the elders are the best men on earth and *some day* when he *quits* drinking he will be baptized. I talked to him awhile but felt it would do more good when he is sober. He receives the elders well and reads the [*Millennial*] *Star* every week."

Drunkenness and immorality were curses in England,

Joseph found. Rainy weather frequently kept him and the other elders from going out tracting, but so did holidays. The English had a wealth of holidays and there was even less use trying to talk religion to them then than on other days, partly due to their habit of being in their cups on a holiday: "April 13, 1900. The wind has been blowing fiercely all day and we had some rain this morning. Being Good Friday the people are all having a holiday so we did not go out tracting. . . ." "April 16, Monday. Today is Bank holiday so we have not been able to go tracting. The wind has been blowing fiercely. . . ." "April 17, Tuesday. We went tracting today but it resulted in no good as the people are just sobering up after their holiday." And so it went.

Having no better place for it, young Englishmen and women did their love making on the streets, especially on Sunday evenings, which Joseph found rather distressing. "Coming home from Arnold Sunday night, for a distance of about five miles the streets were so full of young people that I could hardly work my way through, and a good part of the time had to take [to] the road. You could not imagine what it is like hardly," he wrote Louie, "without seeing it for yourself."

Returning to his apartment about 10:30 one night after two weeks in England, Joseph said, "On our way home we saw more drunken men and women than I ever saw before in my life, and the women I believe out-numbered the men. I have seen more wickedness here in two weeks than I have seen at home in all my life." One of his missionary companions had a cousin in Nottingham who was a policeman and Joseph and the friend visited him. "He told us that the Mormons with their polygamy were saints in comparison with some of the people in Nottingham. He said that it was a common thing for men to exchange wives for a week at a time, etc." Being a polygamist's son Joseph must have been rather amused if not annoyed by this "favorable" comparison.

Many of the English were enthusiastic nature lovers. Among its other attractions Nottingham had a large park, presumably where Robin Hood and his brethren of Sherwood once trod. One warm July afternoon "Brother Lloyd and I went out on the 'Forest' to study. But our effort was a failure," Joseph confided to his journal. "The Spirit of God is not on that piece of ground, for it is a wicked spot. We saw things there in broad daylight that we could not imagine if we had not seen." Such was Victorian England.

While the English countryside was still dotted with castles and country estates, the Church with its few converts was in pretty humble circumstances. "Ever since I have been here and for a long time before," Joseph wrote to Louie in July, 1900, "the Nottingham saints have been meeting in a sort of suspension shanty over a stable about three rods back from the street—the last place on earth a person would look for a meeting room, and a place that would frighten away a timid investigator. They had a good place once, but it was torn down in order to make room for a railroad station, one of the best in England. We have had hard work to get a hall anywhere else, for everyone will not receive the 'Mormons.' They have paid about $1.75 a week for the old room that is not worth 10¢. But at last we have found another room and moved into it yesterday. It is an improvement on the other, but still is not the best on earth but as good as we can get, I suppose."

Perhaps because there were so few Englishmen who would even discuss religion with them, Joseph and some of his companions occasionally attended sessions of the "Brethren's Bible Class." To Louie he explained, "I may be called on at any time to address a congregation of Christians (?) who call themselves the 'Brethren.' I believe they know more about the Bible than any other of the sects we are among. They are the hardest sect we have met here. They have partly offered us the use of their hall if we would go and talk to them. But they want to question us as they feel led. If we get the chance we will go, for there may be some among them who are seeking for light and we may be able to do some good. If we will seek for the Spirit of Truth, we will be able to do some good. I hope we will get the chance to preach unto them, for it is not very often we get a chance to preach outside of our own meeting rooms unless it is on the street. If the way is opened up for us, then we will feel that the hand of the Lord is in it. We are his servants holding the holy priesthood, with a message to this nation, warning them before the gospel shall be taken away from them entirely, for I do believe that the day of the Gentiles is almost to an end."

He attended several of the Brethren's meetings. "But they muzzled us and did not permit us to speak," he noted after one such visit. "They . . . spent all the time on the subject 'saved by grace,' believing that all who call on the name of God shall be saved, no matter what their works may be, for salvation is a free gift to all, 'as free as the air we breathe,' their argument being that if we have to work then salvation is not free to us." It was this doctrine that seemed most prevalent in England and apparently was one cause of lack of interest in the Latter-day Saint message.

Among the many religions and pseudo-religions of the Nottingham area was a spiritualist cult. Joseph and some of the other elders attended several of its meetings, which were held in the same hall as the Mormons used for meeting: "Sunday evening Brother John Astle and I attended the spiritualists at their evening service. We both feel benefited by the visit as our testimonies in the gospel have been strengthened, and the workings of the Devil are made manifest. The evening was occupied by one of their leading lights of darkness who gave a lecture and compared spiritualism with Christianity."

Several days later Joseph and three other elders attended a rather spectacular session of the spiritualists, where the elders pitted the power of the priesthood against the power of Satan: "This evening Elders John Astle, Thomas R. Ward, Charles J. Dewey, and myself attended a meeting of the spiritualists in the Cabden Hall where we also meet on Sundays. The feature of the evening was character reading and spiritual descriptions by Mrs. Peters of Manchester, a clairvoyant. We went for the purpose of resisting the evil power and of strengthening our testimonies of the gospel. I have heard other elders testify that they have been strengthened in the faith and have seen the powers and cunning of Satan made manifest at such places, and I desired to be a witness for myself and for my personal benefit.

"After the meeting began and the woman prepared herself through prayer—I suppose to Satan—if I and my brethren can judge, there was a change came over her which was visibly manifest to us. I think the woman must certainly have been possessed. And if I ever saw the devil in my life I did in her. I think I shall remember the look on her face for some time.

"She began by giving several very general descriptions of different parties who were dead, that could apply to most anyone, and obtained affirmative replies from those in the congregation. When she first began giving her descriptions, she stated that there was a gate in front of her which blocked her way, or in other words a power opposing her. This statement was gratifying to us. After she had been giving descriptions of dead to different persons and had told a few fortunes, she suddenly changed and related as near as I can remember the following incident: She could see Nottingham, in fact traveled from one end of Nottingham to the other under the influence of which she was possessed, in vision. She said she had been in places where she had never been before and did not know the full meaning of it. She said she could see six men who had *come* to Nottingham and were not *of* the people of Nottingham, but they had come here for good and had brought a great deal of light with them, and would do a great deal of good here in Nottingham. After she had said this she said she could tell no more but those whom it was for would understand her remarks, and further it was somewhat of a mystery to her. After she had said this the vision left her and she began again to give character readings.

"Now, there are just six elders laboring here in

Nottingham: Elders S. W. Walker and Hyrum Bennion being the other two—they had remained home. We are the only *six* men in Nottingham who are *not* of the inhabitants and who *have* come among them for *good,* and who have brought *light* unto the inhabitants, and we certainly do intend to do *much good* if it is possible and if the Spirit of God assists. We all take it that no one else but we elders could fit in this description, and as she said the parties it was for would understand, we surely feel that we do. I feel that it is an admission of Satan that we are the servants of the Lord. Satan does at times tell the truth, as we learn from the scriptures. They [devils] testified of Christ wherever he went; they also knew Paul and Silas and others at different times, and testified of it.

"This was not the only thing that attracted our attention. She began to read the character of a young man who sat just in front of us, we being on the back row. She said he was a materialist and did not believe in spiritualism and asked him if it were not so. He answered in the affirmative. She then tried to prove to him her powers by describing a young lady to him. She said the young lady was a sister or a cousin to him and died while very young. She then called on him to affirm what she had said but he could not, for he knew of no such person. She then described to him a young man who was at the front in Africa [England was then waging war in South Africa] and gave his name as 'Charles.' But he knew no such person. The woman then suddenly left him and declared to the congregation that the four men who were sitting just back of the young man to whom she had been giving this description had a great deal of power and for that reason she had failed. It was the only time she had attempted to give a personal description to one who was not an avowed spiritualist, and she called the attention of the people to the fact that we *four* elders had foiled her in her purpose. It was another testimony from beneath that we were possessed with a great deal of power for *good.* Further, she testified that our power and influence in opposition had almost used her up, for she was exhausted. Of course we were there for the purpose of opposing her and the more power she called forth the harder we opposed in our secret prayers and faith with the result that we also, at times, felt as if strength was leaving us, and no doubt it was—the influence of which we are possessed. We feel that we accomplished our purpose and our testimonies have been strengthened.

"I do not care to go see them any more. I am satisfied. I again have seen the cunning of Satan revealed and we feel to rejoice in the truth of the gospel and the power of the priesthood. All the other elders declare that what I have written is correct as I read my statement to them."

Quite often in tracting the Mormon elders were asked if they believed in spiritualism. Such queries, plus Joseph's experience with the clairvoyant Mrs. Peters, brought to his mind a story his father once told him of two Mormon elders visiting a spiritualist, a medium, who asked if they would like to have him call back from the dead any particular person for them. Without identifying who he was the prankish missionaries requested that the medium call back Gadianton, perhaps the worst villain in the Book of Mormon. As the medium got into his seance calling for Gadianton suddenly there was a terrible disturbance in the room, the table and chairs were tipped over, things scattered helter-skelter, and the medium was thoroughly beaten up. When things finally quieted down and he recovered his senses, the shocked medium asked the missionaries, "Who in hell is Gadianton?"

One of the most effective uses that Joseph made of his priesthood while on his mission was in administering to the sick. He had been promised in his patriarchal blessing that he would enjoy the gift of healing, and this was seen manifest several times. Perhaps the most notable time was when he and another elder administered to little Georgie Lord, young son of John Lord, a convert. The boy was critically ill with lung congestion, his face having become discolored. Through the healing power of God he was restored to health and strength.

Louie had never been able to get Joseph to sing with her at the piano. Supposing that he would have to do some singing as a missionary she was anxious to learn how he was getting on with it. "You want to know how I am getting on with my singing," he replied. "Well, I have no voice in the first place, and what I have in its place is like a file. I would never be able to sing here if there was any sing in me. I am a singer after the order of Dr. James E. Talmage." But like many another missionary who thinks he cannot sing, Joseph eventually learned that you sing anyway. He and three other elders even organized a quartet known as "The Sagebrush Singers," to sing at street meetings. "After listening to us *sing*, people were glad to hear us *talk!*"

For recreation Joseph and the other elders occasionally played a game of football or attended football games between English teams. For two weeks in September 1900, Joseph, his brother Richards and seven other elders vacationed in London and Paris, attending the world's fair at Paris and touring historic sites in both cities. It was a delightful, restful change from the daily routine of missionary life. In Paris "we were happily surprised to see so many elders from Zion with whom we were acquainted at home." Among those who joined them in a tour of the fair was Thomas McKay, brother of David O. McKay. "It seems strange to be in a land where you cannot understand anyone or make them understand." He found the Paris fair interesting "but not as grand as the Chicago fair," which he had attended when 17 years old. The best part of his first day in Paris was being able to get some fresh fruit to eat. "I have eaten more fruit today than I have had all the while I was in England."

Joseph and 25 companions "hired a drag for the day and visited points of interest in Paris," including the Arch de Triumphe, the statue of Washington, statue of Joan of Arc, "the old church where the signal was given for the massacre of St. Bartholomew," the Notre Dame cathedral built in the twelfth century, the Tower of the Bastille, a cemetery containing the vaults of many historic Frenchmen, sites of the guillotines used during the French Revolution, and on other days they toured the Louvre, the great French building of art and antiquities; the tomb of Napoleon; down to the palace at Versailles, once occupied by French kings, Napoleon, Marie Antoinette and other notables.

In London the traveling elders visited the White Tower "where we saw all kinds of armour, some of which was worn by the different kings. We saw the blanket upon which General [James] Wolfe died at the Heights of Abraham in Canada. From there we passed out through the parade grounds to the Beauchamp Tower. This tower, which is not so large, is noted as the prison house of many persons of rank, some of whom were condemned to the block. After coming from the tower we stood on the spot, only a few feet away from the tower, where the scaffold once stood." He noted that on this very spot Queen Anne Boleyn, Catherine Howard, Lady Jane Grey, the Earl of Essex, "and many others were beheaded." They also visited "the Wakefield Tower where the crown jewels are kept. We saw the crowns, scepters, etc., of many of the kings and queens of England, including Queen Victoria's, the grandest of all." At Westminster Abbey they "saw the graves and tombs of many of the rulers and prominent men and women of England. . . . The coronation chairs are to be seen here also."

Discouraging as tracting and street meetings were, Joseph preferred them to the assignment he had the last year of his mission, that of being conference clerk. Stephen W. Walker, who had been Joseph's junior companion in the city of Derby, was appointed president of the Nottingham conference replacing George Ruff when Ruff's mission term was completed in June, 1900. Apparently at Walker's request, Joseph was called to return to Nottingham to replace Samuel A. Greenwood as clerk,

Elder Greenwood also having completed his term of service.

A time or two earlier Joseph had assisted Greenwood, a 19-year-old from southern Utah, with the job, and had substituted for him when he was sick. So he knew the demanding nature of the job: Writing letters for the conference president, receiving and distributing mail to the elders in the conference, making out monthly and yearly reports on the conference and mailing them to mission headquarters at Liverpool, receiving and recording tithing from church members in the Nottingham area and forwarding the money to Liverpool, distributing the weekly *Millennial Star*, the church newspaper in England, helping arrange for conference meeting places, buying supplies, assisting the conference president with a miscellany of chores, and substituting for him whenever he was gone to neighboring towns on visits. He also had a full share of kitchen duty. His time for tracting and teaching was now quite limited, and he chaffed at the constant routine of the clerical chores. To Louie he expressed his disappointment in not having more time for actual missionary endeavor: "President Ruff is going home next week and Brother Walker who was with me is going to take his place and he has decided that I am to spend my time from now on in Nottingham. . . ." And later, "I have had a stack of letters to answer for President W. besides sending money orders to different elders. I am thankful I do not have to stay here at this more than one year. That is just about 12 months more than I care for." And again later, "If I am here in the field two years then 18 months of that time will be 'killed' in the conference house."

It is reported that Conference President Stephen W. Walker, nine years older than Joseph Fielding, wrote home to say that Joseph Fielding was "very young, a little green, but he will leave his mark upon the world."

Joseph always arose early—whenever another missionary wanted to get up extra early he asked Joseph to awaken him. Joseph generally devoted the morning hours

Stephen W. Walker, Nottingham Conference president while Joseph Fielding was serving as clerk of the conference.

to writing letters, both personal and as conference clerk, then often spent the afternoons in visiting church members, studying, tracting, buying supplies for the conference house, or in other duties of the office. Frequent letters to and from Louie and his folks helped greatly to ease the trial of being so far from home for so long a time. Louie was very faithful in writing at least once and often twice a week, and Joseph wrote to her nearly as often. He exchanged weekly letters also with his father and mother. Several of his brothers and sisters also wrote occasionally, and once in a long while he received letters from other relatives or friends. His father-in-law once wrote to him, "I have always felt that you would fill a glorious mission and gain an experience that will fit you for the exalted station that you are destined to fill in the future."

The letters from home were so filled with sentiments of love and encouragement that they were a weekly boon to Joseph's morale. "My own precious Joseph," wrote Louie, "I do love you so much that I could not possibly tell you because it grows greater with each day that comes. I do trust you so entirely and have such perfect confidence in you that I am more happy in leaving you and in being left than I could possibly be if you were as giddy as some young men are. But I know you love duty far more than you do pleasure and so I have so much love and trust that I feel as though you are about as near being a perfect young man as could be."

Pressed flowers frequently were enclosed in Joseph's and Louie's letters to each other—and are still there today. The husband of a friend of Louie's was on a mission at the time, and she contrasted Joseph's warm and affectionate letters with the letters her friend received: "Such matter-of-fact, business-like letters as O— writes to her! It would break my heart if you wrote such cold little notes to me as Anne gets all the time. It is a thousand times worse than to have to wait a long time for a letter."

"Dearest," writes Louie another time, "I was made very happy this morning by receiving such a dear good letter. I felt repaid for waiting. . . . Thank you for the flowers you sent. You did not tell the names but the pansies I knew and Mama knew the others. . . . Be good to yourself, my darling, and remember I am here to love and pray for you and that I never forget you for one single moment. I *do* want to do as you say, 'be a brave good girl' and I try; but don't measure my desire by my success. I believe I have been and will be fairly brave. At least I have not exhibited the white feather before anybody. And I do make an *effort* to be good. There are a great many things to write about, but somehow I like best to write 'I love you.' I sometimes think I could write it over, a thousand times, and still wish to write it again. I am afraid if I did you would soon be ready to scold me but it is written in every word I write and in every stroke I make. . . . Bless you, my own precious husband, is my prayer always. Take good care of my property, for I hold you responsible for its safety. I am ever your Loving Wife, Louie."

Lonely as Louie was for Joseph she assured him that she was fully in agreement with his having accepted the mission call, and told him of a certain missionary in the Southern states "who got homesick and came home [early] to surprise his little frau. But I think he was the most surprised, for she would not let him touch her or come in the house (her mother's) so he stayed all night with a brother and started back the next morning and is now a very fine missionary. I admire her 'spunk' and I would want to do the same if I were in her place. She did just right."

Surely no husband ever had a more patient, loving, devoted wife waiting at home for him than did Joseph in Louie. As his mission term neared its close, she writes, on May 12, 1901: "My Beloved Husband, Tomorrow brings the two-year mark since you left home and begins the overtime which I hope will not be long. They cannot release you too soon to suit me, after the 1st of June. I am getting very anxious now. It takes a good deal to hold me now, I can tell you. I could easily start out and walk with a fair prospect of meeting you in N.Y. if energy were all that is necessary. But I am not going to try it, though I do feel as though I could. . . ." Anxious as she was to have him back home she urged him in her next letter to take advantage of some sight-seeing opportunities at the close of his mission, both in the British Isles and in America on his way home.

Joseph's letters were equally filled with love and devotion: ". . . I know that the work I have been called to do is the work of God or I would not stay here one minute, no, I would not have left home. But I know that our happiness is dependent upon my faithfulness while

I am here. I should be willing to do this much for the love of mankind when our Savior could suffer as he did for us. . . . Four days of my mission are now in the past. Every day will bring me nearer to you and I shall soon be home again. . . . Louie, you must cheer up, do not be downcast or feel bad. I am in the hands of our Heavenly Father and he will watch over me and protect me if I do his will. And he will be with you while I am away and watch over you and protect you in all things. I am well and shall try to do my duty while I am here. May God bless and protect my wife and keep her from all harm, and watch over all the dear ones at home, is the prayer of Your Loving Husband, Joseph."

In response to her mention of the young man who returned home early only to have his wife send him back again, Joseph wrote, "You need not fear that I shall come home as that young man you speak of—of whom I have heard before—and try to surprise you. I shall stay here until I am released if I can have the Spirit of God with me. I would rather stay here forever than come home without an honorable record and release, for I should never be happy and would only make you and our parents miserable. Neither could I look my friends in the eyes without a feeling of shame. I pray that I may have the spirit of the gospel and a love for my fellow man that I may be able to stay here until I am released honorably. If it were not for the many prayers that are offered up for me at home as well as my own I could not succeed."

The devotion he felt to duty and to improving his mind is expressed often, such as this comment in a November, 1899, letter to Louie from Derby: "My Beloved Wife, Another week has passed and I am that much nearer to you. . . . I am trying to learn something while I am here. Since I left Nottingham I have put my time in to study and I feel that I can hardly find a minute when I do not feel that I ought to be preparing my mind with useful knowledge. I feel that when I come home that more will be expected of me than I am ca-

115

pable of as it generally is with returned missionaries. They are generally supposed to have learned all that the Bible contains or else they have neglected their duties." Committing scripture to memory did not come easy for him for he adds, "But it must not be expected of me for I am rather dull of comprehension. I have tried all day to learn a passage of scripture and have not got it yet. But I am determined to learn it before I am through. It is the 9, 10, and 11 verses of the second chapter of 1st Cor. . . ."

There was also a close bond of love between Joseph and his father, who often expressed appreciation in his letters for Joseph's attitude toward the gospel generally and toward his mission. It is rather surprising that the elder Smith found time to write as frequently as he did to both Joseph and Richards. "I like your spirit, I have faith in your integrity, and I have pleasure and satisfaction in you," wrote his father. "I want you to cultivate wisdom and deliberate judgment and patience as well as the Holy Spirit and the love of God." Then he adds, *"The Salt Lake Tribune* and the hireling priests have stirred up a hot wave of persecution against the elders in the Southern States mission. They have mobbed and beaten a number of our elders and have burned and destroyed a number of our meeting houses. It is all in the democratic South." Sometimes he would send one son a carbon of the letter he had written to the other, especially when answering doctrinal questions that one or the other of them had asked, such as "do women ever become sons of perdition?" (the answer was no, and he tells why). Joseph so prized his father's answers that he copied them verbatim into his journal. His father also sent him money from time to time to help meet his financial needs. "I send you herewith receipt No. 1038 for five dollars, the like amount having been sent to Buddie [Richards]," he wrote on June 22, 1899. "And I hope you will receive it safely. Hyrum's [his oldest son's] expenses while he was in England averaged about ten dollars a month. While you and Buddie will no doubt be as economical as you can be, I do not want you to go hungry, naked, or without shoes, and I hope to be able to supply you what you may actually need over and above your own resources."

Joseph assured his father, "I shall be very careful of the means you send me. I do not spend anything unless I have a good reason for it. I take care not to spend anything for toffee, etc., as some of the elders do." To save on expenses he walked most everywhere he went, he darned his own socks, did most of his own washing. "I bought a colored shirt last week to wear around the house, for it saves my laundry bill, as well as my shirts," he told Louie. He kept ten dollars hidden in his purse in case of emergency, but had little money otherwise. He also told his father, "I am here to preach the gospel and I hope I will be able to do that well. . . . It is my desire to improve my mind and talents while I am here, that I may always be useful for something in life . . . I want to be right on all things and nothing gives me more pleasure than to learn something about the gospel. My desire is to become acquainted with it and gain wisdom."

The letters from home were generally optimistic and encouraging. But in the closing weeks of his mission in the spring of 1901 there were two sets of letters, from Louie and from his parents, that contained sad news: the first was of the death of President George Q. Cannon at Monterey, California, April 12—news that Joseph had earlier seen in the newspapers, and the second was of the death of his 18-year-old sister Alice, Sarah's daughter, on April 29. His journal entry for April 13 reads: "I received letters from Louie, my father and my mother. Each of them report that President George Q. Cannon is very sick in California, also that my sister Alice is very sick. Later the evening papers printed a telegram from America stating that President Cannon is dead." And for May 11: "I received letters from my father and my wife this evening containing the sad information of the death of my sister Alice. . . . It is a dreadful blow to us all. I did not realize the seriousness of her illness although

I knew she was sick. I fully expected to meet her again with the rest of the family within a few weeks, but the will of God be done. It is at such times that the hopes which the gospel present to us are most welcome. We shall all meet again on the other side to enjoy the pleasures and blessings of each other's presence, where family ties will no more be broken, but where we shall all live to receive the blessings, and realize the tender mercies of our Father in heaven. May I always walk in the path of truth, and honor the name I bear, that the meetings with my kindred may be to me indeed most sweet and everlasting, is my humble prayer. . . ."

At the time of Alice's death Joseph was himself in the hospital at Nottingham, one of the few times in his life he was ever hospitalized, and that was under protest. One of the elders had gotten smallpox, so the public health officer insisted on putting the other five elders at the conference house into the isolation ward of the local hospital, for two weeks, April 15-30. "We have made friends with the nurses and others who visited us during our imprisonment," Joseph recorded at the end of their confinement. "Many times we have had talks with them about the gospel, also left with them books to read. When we left the hospital, we sang a hymn or two which among other things impressed those who listened for we left them with tears in their eyes. I think we have made an impression at the hospital for good, especially with the nurses who confess that we are not the people they thought we were and they will now defend us at all times."

Through much of his mission Joseph was disturbed by a certain condition in the district which he recognized was not being properly handled. After reviewing the matter at some length in his journal, he makes this observation, which seems quite reflective of his attitude throughout his ministry: "It appears that some men—or most men—are afraid to do what they know to be right for fear of giving offense to their friends, or lose the respect of the people they have come to teach. . . . But the safest thing to do is to do *right*."

118

Two major historic events occurred while Joseph was on his mission: the world moved into the twentieth century, and Queen Alexandria Victoria of England died. She had been the reigning monarch of England for 64 years, since ascending the throne in 1837 at the age of 18. That was just shortly after the first Mormon missionaries, Heber C. Kimball and his associates, had been sent to England to introduce the gospel there. It was the year Joseph Smith and others fled from Kirtland, Ohio, to Far West, Missouri. Perhaps because England was the "mistress of the seas," with colonies in every part of the globe, Queen Victoria had become the world's number one celebrity. On her 81st and final birthday anniversary on May 24, 1900, Joseph noted in his journal at Derby, "Today the people have been celebrating the Queen's birthday. Brother McAllister and I went down to the market place to see the celebration."

The Queen died Tuesday, January 22, 1901. "We received the news tonight of the death of Queen Victoria which occurred at 6:30 this evening. The newsboys are shouting and running to and fro selling their papers. She has had a long and prosperous reign." To Louie he wrote, "The people feel somewhat solemn about it, for they know they have lost a true friend in her. Under her reign England has reached to the height of her glory, and I think had her Golden Age. Without doubt the people loved their ruler and could sing her praises from their hearts, but after a long reign they have at last received a change. They now sing to the king, Edward VII, but not with the vigor nor with the same ring that they did before, for the life of the Prince of Wales does not command the respect that his mother did." Eleven days later, Saturday, February 2, Joseph notes in his journal: "Today the funeral of the Queen took place in London. Nottingham like other cities has been all stir. It has been raining hard all day."

The Queen had been a widow for nearly 40 years, her husband and consort, Prince Albert, having died in 1861, the year the United States became embroiled in civil war. The Queen probably never did know of a rather spectacular event she missed: In one of his sermons in the late 1830's, Sidney Rigdon, then the Prophet Joseph's first counselor in the church presidency, had assured the brethren that come the day of the great Battle of Armageddon, blood would run as high as a horse's girth in the streets of London, and he would step forth in the power of the priesthood, march into the castle and lead Queen Victoria out by the nose!

News of one of the worst disasters in Utah's history had reached Joseph on May 3, 1900: "We saw by today's papers that day before yesterday a terrible explosion had occurred in the Pleasant Valley Mines at Scofield, Utah, causing great destruction and the loss of life of nearly all the employees who were in the mine at that time. The worst destruction that ever took place at home," he noted in his journal. Many of the men killed and injured by that explosion were converts to the Church from the British Isles. Reflective of the national prejudices that continued among church members and other American immigrants, a prejudice that even today causes civil strife in the British Isles, was the observation given in a book prepared on the Scofield mine disaster, that in this dire emergency "even the Welsh helped out!"

A few days prior to Joseph's mission release in June of 1901 the British mission presidency was changed, with Presidents Platte D. Lyman and Henry W. Naisbitt being released and Elder Francis M. Lyman of the Council of the Twelve being appointed. Joseph accompanied Stephen W. Walker and Charles C. Rich Pugmire to a special meeting at Bradford, in the Leeds conference area, May 25, at which the outgoing and incoming presidents met with elders from several of the conferences, including Joseph's brother Richards and William Armstrong, who had left Salt Lake City with them and was now president of the Grimsby conference.

While at Bradford Joseph received a letter from his father requesting him to visit the village of Toppesfield in Essex County in southern England "and see if I can find any genealogy. So I shall go there soon. President Francis M. Lyman informed me that I would be released to sail for home on June 20th." Joseph brought the Nottingham conference records up-to-date on June 1 and turned them over to J. S. Dixon, who was succeeding him as conference clerk. He left the next morning for London, then onto Toppesfield where he was successful in gathering many Smith names from the records of the old parish church there, through the courtesy of the local vicar, Reverend H. B. Barnes.

As Joseph prepared to return home, he received a letter from Louie informing him, "Your father is thinking of coming to meet you if he can leave. President Snow has made up his mind to go east within a short time so your father does not know whether or not he can come to meet you. Your mother wants to go with him; so does Aunt Sarah. So I don't know how they will manage it. Perhaps Papa and Mama will come out a little way to meet you. I shall not come to meet you but will be just as glad to see you as though I did come."

Joseph gave his farewell address in Sunday services at Nottingham June 16, wrote a final letter from England to Louie on June 18, enclosing flowers from Toppesfield —which are still in the letter today, left Nottingham Wednesday morning, June 19, and met his brother at Liverpool later in the day. They sailed from Liverpool Thursday afternoon, June 20, aboard the steamer *Commonwealth* and arrived in Boston Friday, June 28, where they met their father, Richards' mother, Sarah, and two of their sisters, Minerva and Ina. Perhaps Sarah had been favored over Julina for the trip because of having recently lost her daughter Alice. Joseph had expressed the hope in a letter to Louie that if anyone came east to meet them that she would be among the party, but she chose not to make the trip. Bishop Charles Nibley, a close personal friend of President Smith, and later to become the presiding bishop of the Church, was also in the group from Utah.

After five days of sightseeing in the Boston area, the party entrained for Buffalo, New York, where they visited the Pan American Exposition, again visited the nearby Niagara Falls, then headed west aboard the Nickel Plate railroad, on July 5, and traveled via Chicago, Kansas City, Pueblo, Colorado, and finally arrived in Salt Lake City on Tuesday, July 9, "where I found my wife, mother and all in good spirits and health. I was indeed glad to be home once more after an absence of two and more years. For a few days after my return I visited in Ogden."

"O Ye Mountains High . . ."

On Becoming a Historian
and a Defender of the Faith

There was a feeling of autumn in the air as Joseph walked briskly from the tabernacle to his home. It had been an interesting session of October general conference. Joseph's father had been advanced from second to first counselor to President Lorenzo Snow, after serving for half a year as his only counselor, since the death of George Q. Cannon the previous April, 1901. President Snow's son-in-law, Rudger Clawson, a member of the Council of Twelve, had been sustained as second counselor, succeeding President Smith. The vacancy in the Council of Twelve, stemming from President Clawson's advancement, had not been filled. Naturally there was anticipation as to who might be appointed.

Next day word came that President Lorenzo Snow was critically ill. Three days later, on October 10, he was dead, at the age of 87, and Joseph Fielding Smith Sr. was to become the sixth president of the Church, at the age of 63. Brigham Young Jr. and John Willard Young had both been ordained apostles February 4, 1864, nearly two and a half years before Joseph F. Smith. But there had been no vacancy in the Council of Twelve at the time of any of the three ordinations, and when a vacancy next occurred, on October 8, 1867, when Amasa M. Lyman was dropped, the members of the Council of Twelve voted to give membership to Joseph F. Smith in preference to either of the Young brothers. John W. Young served for a time as first counselor to his father, and he was the youngest man ever ordained an apostle in this dispensation, at age 19. But he never was admitted into the Council of Twelve and eventually drifted from the Church. Brigham Jr. was admitted to membership in the Council October 9, 1868. President Lorenzo Snow decided on the policy that seniority would be determined by date of acceptance into the Council rather than by date of ordination as an apostle. Thus Joseph F. Smith rather than Brigham Young Jr. now became president of the Church, with Brigham becoming president of the Council of Twelve, until his death in 1903.

Interestingly, both Presidents Wilford Woodruff and Lorenzo Snow had prophesied that Joseph F. Smith would sometime become president of the Church. Thirty-seven years earlier in the Hawaiian Islands when President Snow, then a member of the Council of Twelve, nearly lost his life by drowning, he declared that the Lord made known to him "that this young man, Joseph F. Smith . . . would some day be the Prophet of God on the earth." President Woodruff was once relating to a group of children some incidents in the life of the Prophet Joseph Smith. "He turned to Elder Joseph F. Smith and asked him to arise to his feet. Elder Smith complied. 'Look at him, children,' Wilford Woodruff said, 'for he resembles the Prophet Joseph more than any man living. He will become the President of The Church of Jesus Christ of Latter-day Saints. I want everyone of you to remember what I have told you this morning.'" After President Woodruff's death, President Snow told Joseph F. Smith that the spirit of God whispered to him that he, Joseph, would succeed him, Lorenzo, as president of the Church.

Inasmuch as President Snow had already designated Rudger Clawson to be a counselor in the presidency and the recent conference had voted to sustain him, there was supposition now that he would be retained as such, although he had not yet been ordained to the position. And knowing of the close personal friendship that existed between President Smith and Bishop Charles W. Nibley, many anticipated that Nibley also would be chosen as a counselor. But both suppositions were mistaken. President Smith chose as his first counselor 80-year-old John R. Winder, a former ward bishop whose name was—and still is—practically unknown in the Church. As his second counselor he chose Anthon H. Lund, 57, a member of the Council of Twelve, church historian, and a convert from Denmark. He chose his eldest son, Hyrum Mack Smith, Edna's boy, to become a member of the Council of twelve, filling the vacancy created by the advancement of President Lund. Elder Clawson was retained in his position in the Council of Twelve. The new presidency and apostle were ratified at a solemn assembly of the Church in the tabernacle on November 10, 1901. Joseph was one of the proudest persons in the audience, to be able to raise his hand in a sustaining vote for both his father and eldest brother Hyrum. He was also particularly fond of President Lund who had greatly befriended him.

When Joseph had reached home from his mission in July, one of his first concerns was to get a job. While casting about for employment he called to see his former boss in the wholesale grocery department at ZCMI and was immediately offered work there in his old position. "Not much!" he said, remembering the long hours and meager pay. "I'll look around for awhile first." The very thought of returning to his old job made his shoulders ache. Besides, the wage was inadequate for rearing a family, as he hoped to do. Joseph's older brother-in-law, Alonzo Pratt Kesler, was able to get for him five weeks' work in the Salt Lake County Clerk's Office, where he was paid at the rate of $260 per month, three times the salary he had received at ZCMI.

Joseph was next offered a permanent government position, as an inspector of pool halls, bawdy houses and other places that sold beer and liquor, and to collect excise taxes, his territory to include Utah, Idaho and Wyoming.

The job paid quite a handsome salary and was respectable enough in nature even though it would bring him into contact with some unsavory characters. The man who previously held the position had been dismissed for having succumbed to temptation along the road. The good salary would certainly help Joseph to get a house built. Joseph mulled the offer in his mind a few days. Tentatively deciding against it, he conferred with his father about it before making a firm decision. His father advised him to decline the offer. "Remember this, son," he said, "the best company is none too good for you." So Joseph declined the job, and a few days later he received an offer he liked much better: Anthon H. Lund offered him a staff position in the Church Historian's Office. With his fondness for the Church and for history, it was a job that seemed tailor-made for him. Gladly he accepted it, starting work there October 1, 1901, just a few days prior to his father's becoming church president and Lund a counselor. Joseph's choice of jobs was one of the most important decisions of his life.

Joseph Fielding found Anthon H. Lund a pleasant person to work for, and showed his loyalty to him years later in a rather forceful way: a certain man came to his house to launch a complaint against Lund. "I would not listen to any criticism of my beloved President Lund," President Smith later recalled. When the visitor persisted, he was asked to leave the house. When he refused to do so, Joseph Fielding removed him from the house and yard, in a maneuver best described as by-the-seat-of-the-pants diplomacy. The week after Lund was appointed to the church presidency, October 17, 1901, he invited Joseph to become a member of a weekly prayer circle which the brethren conducted each Wednesday afternoon in the Salt Lake Temple.

Heaven knows there were plenty of problems for them to pray about, for *The Salt Lake Tribune* and other anti-Mormon newspapers, magazines and book publishers throughout the United States kept up a running attack on the Church. Although the practice of plural marriage had been officially suspended by the Church in 1890, it was far too enticing and lucrative a subject for the press and politicians to let quietly die. Curse the Mormons for it, but don't let it die! Mormon polygamy helped to sell books and helped to build circulation of newspapers and magazines. To denounce the Mormons helped politicians get elected to office and win brownie points with their constituents.

Being on the staff of the Church Historian's Office, where an effort was made to compile everything pro and con written about the Church, Joseph Fielding became acutely aware of the flood of derogatory material that was deluging the country. Now as president of the Church his father was singled out for particular attack, especially in the fact that he had continued living in plural marriage after the Manifesto.

Antagonisms sometimes make strange bed-fellows, for with some people the easiest way to love your enemies is to hate your friends. Such was the case at this time with several of the men who became most vindictive in their denunciation of the Mormons and especially of Joseph F. Smith. These men included one of Utah's first two United States senators, Frank J. Cannon, elected in 1896 when Utah achieved statehood, and another early United States senator from Utah, Thomas Kearns, elected in 1901.

Cannon was a capable and ambitious person who took a particular delight in politics, and had helped to organize the Republican Party in Utah. While Joseph Fielding was on his mission to England, Frank Cannon was in England briefly on a business trip, and upon learning of a favorable impression Joseph Fielding had made on certain prominent individuals in England, he had written a gracious letter to President Joseph F. Smith commending his son. Cannon was a son of President George Q. Cannon. But even though his parents were polygamists Frank was much opposed to the doctrine and to those who continued living it. After his father's death in 1901 he grew ever more hateful toward President Joseph F. Smith. He published a series of nine articles in *Everybody's* magazine and later published much the same material in a book, *Under The Prophet In Utah,* depicting President Smith as "a religious fanatic of bitter mind" and a "cruel despot."

Thomas Kearns as a young man had become a millionaire miner in Utah, with his Silver King mine at Park City. With the backing of President Lorenzo Snow, Kearns, a Catholic, was elected to the United States Senate in 1901 for a four-year term. He also bought *The Salt Lake Tribune* in 1901, after it had opposed his candidacy. President Snow, who had appointed Reed Smoot to be an apostle in 1900, dissuaded him from seeking the United States senatorship in 1901, when he gave his support to Kearns. But President Joseph F. Smith, who succeeded President Snow as head of the Church in October, 1901, about the time Kearns bought the *Tribune,* took a different view of the Church's role in politics. He endorsed Smoot's candidacy for the other Senate seat from Utah in 1903, and Smoot was elected. Although they were both Republicans, Smoot and Kearns, Utah's two United States senators, did not get along well. Kearns had been opposed to Smoot's candidacy because he was an apostle of the Church. Because of the anti-Mormon feelings, Smoot's seat was contested and the issue was not finally decided until 1907 when the Senate voted in Smoot's favor, overriding the negative decision of its committee on elections. President Smith declined to endorse Senator Kearns' hopes for re-election in 1905. George Sutherland, a non-Mormon with a Mormon background, was elected to the office. Tom Kearns in his farewell address to the Senate bitterly denounced the Mormon Church for its alleged continued participation in politics, and its alleged continued practice of plural marriage. He labeled the Church a monarchy, and called upon the Senate to take further stringent measures against it.

So polished and harsh a speech was it that knowledgeable persons agreed it had been written for him by

Ex-Senator Cannon, who was much more gifted in speaking and writing than was Kearns. And it was no surprise when Kearns employed Cannon as his chief editorial writer on *The Salt Lake Tribune*, to wage war against the Church. From 1904 until they finally sickened of their own efforts in 1911, Kearns and Cannon and their associates sunk the *Tribune* to new lows of irresponsibility in their anti-Mormon editorial crusade.

"*The Salt Lake Tribune* in those days wrote editorials and pictured my father as one of the basest and most miserable creatures that ever walked the face of the earth," recalled President Joseph Fielding. "And that instilled into the hearts of the sons a feeling of revenge and the time came when the boys, when they were old enough, decided that they would go down to the *Tribune* office and give the editor, who was an apostate, a thrashing of his life." But their father learned of their plan and forbid them to do it. So Joseph contented himself with making an editorial reply, publishing it in the two newspapers in Ogden, the *Standard* and the *Examiner*. "I wrote an article today for publication in defense of my father," he noted on March 18, 1905. "For a long time past a very bitter anti-Mormon feeling has existed against the President of the Church, and the 'Mormon' people. Frank J. Cannon is the most bitter anti-Mormon of the entire number and as an editor of *The Tribune* made many vicious assaults on the presidency and the Church."

Cannon, Kearns and company also revived the old anti-Mormon Liberal party, now giving it the name of the American party, to help wage their fight against the Church. While they were unsuccessful in getting their candidates into state or national offices, they did gain control of Salt Lake City government for several years, electing their candidates for mayor in three successive elections, 1905, 1907, and 1909. Interestingly, there seemed to be quite a cross-over vote, some Mormons supporting the American party despite its anti-Mormon stand, and some Gentiles or non-Mormons supporting the Democrat or Republican candidates. When Kearns finally quit his anti-Mormon crusade in the *Tribune* in 1911 he gave as one reason the fact that many Gentile merchants, while paying lip service to his endeavor, declined to really support him in it.

While never really interested in politics as such, Joseph Fielding during this period became involved to the extent of attending the local Republican rallies to help as he could toward getting into office men who were not hostile toward the Church. Even when the church leaders gave their endorsement to non-Mormon candidates, such as President Snow had done with Tom Kearns in 1900-01, there were howls of protest from a variety of sources, but chiefly from the defeated candidates. The most sustained wail, however, came in the wake of Apostle Smoot's election to the Senate in January, 1903. In his private journal Elder Smith noted, under March 5, "Honorable Reed Smoot took his seat as United States Senator from Utah today. The ministers of this city have tried to stir up an opposition that he may be denied his seat, many false reports have been circulated; but all to no effect."

Others, including apostate Mormons, joined the ministers in a formal protest to Congress against Smoot's being seated because he was an apostle and thus represented a mixing of church and state. He was also incorrectly charged with being a polygamist and thus a violator of the law. Smoot's father, Abraham O. Smoot, Provo's first mayor, was a polygamist, but Reed Smoot was not, and this charge was later withdrawn. In fact, at a time when the members of the Church presidency and Council of the Twelve and other general authorities were quite divided in their attitude toward continued living of polygamy, Smoot was one of those who strongly favored its being discontinued.

For four years, from January, 1903, through February, 1907, a heated war of words was waged in the press, from the pulpit and in the halls of Congress over whether Reed Smoot was to be allowed to continue serving as a United States senator. President Snow in 1900 had dissuaded Smoot from seeking the position because of the controversy that would ensue. President Joseph F. Smith at times must have wondered whether he made the wise decision in letting him accept the office in 1903. In 1898, Brigham H. Roberts, member of the Council of Seventy and a polygamist, had been elected to the House of Representatives and was then denied his seat, even though most of his political support had been from non-Mormons. But Smoot not being a polygamist, there were no legal grounds on which he could be denied. Even so, the Senate's committee on privileges and elections which had conducted the lengthy hearings, from March, 1904, through June, 1906, submitted a majority report recommending that he not be allowed to continue serving in the Senate. The vote was eight to five. A minority report recommended to the contrary, and in February, 1907, four years after he had been elected to the position, Smoot won a majority vote of the Senate as a whole allowing him to continue. Perhaps significantly, the five senators signing the minority report favorable to Smoot each represented a state in which the Mormons had figured prominently, including the state of Vermont, whose earlier congressmen had been so hostile toward the Mormons. The five were: Joseph B. Foraker of Ohio; Albert J. Beveridge, Indiana; William P. Dillingham, Vermont; A. J. Hopkins, Illinois, and P. C. Knox, Pennsylvania.

As President Joseph F. Smith predicted to Bishop Charles Nibley and other intimates, Smoot's membership in the Senate, if once achieved, could eventually have a good influence in behalf of the Church. Smoot served in the Senate for 30 years, became one of its most influential members, and a friend and confidante of Presidents Theodore Roosevelt, William Howard Taft, Warren G. Harding, Calvin Coolidge, and Herbert Hoover. He became chairman of the powerful Appropriations Committee. The presence of a Mormon apostle in the Senate, while vexatious to some, did indeed help break down the long standing anti-Mormon prejudices.

During the four-year controversy over Smoot's eligi-
bility, Joseph Fielding, as a clerk in the Historian's Office,
spent considerable time searching out material for sub-
mission to the Senate to substantiate the fact that Mormons were loyal citizens of the United States, material
to refute the charges being made that the Church sought
the overthrow of the government, that its leaders were
guilty of treason, etc.

President Theodore Roosevelt visited Salt Lake City
on May 29, 1903, to get some further feeling about the
Mormons, and decided to give Smoot his full support.
But so determined were the Church's enemies to oust
Smoot, that even the backing of the popular Roosevelt
had less influence than might have been expected in such
a case. The following February the Senate committee
on privileges and elections subpoenaed President Joseph
F. Smith and some other Church leaders to go to Washington and testify under oath as to the charges leveled
against them regarding their continued practice of plural
marriage, their allegiance to the United States, and other
points, both pertinent and impertinent. Among those accompanying President Smith to the witch hunt was his
son Hyrum, member of the Council of the Twelve. For
the first several days in March, 1904, the Latter-day
Saints prophet was grilled by the senatorial investigators.
Under questioning he candidly admitted that he and
others had continued living in plural marriage following
President Woodruff's issuance of the Manifesto. But he
denied having married additional wives or authorizing
others to do so contrary to the laws of the land since the
Manifesto, and he staunchly affirmed his and the Church's
loyalty to the United States despite the abuse they had
suffered in a land of supposed religious liberty.

It was probably just as well that Joseph Fielding
did not accompany his father to the hearings. Even at a
distance of 2,000 miles, at home in Salt Lake City, he
was incensed at the grilling to which his father was subjected. "The 'siege' in Washington continues with my
father on the stand," he noted in his journal entry of

March 4, 1904. "He has been forced to answer all kinds of questions which have been asked by moral lepers who are unworthy to unloosen his shoes, and some of these vile creatures are, too, members of the committee of privileges and elections." Years later in writing a biography of his father he cited particularly the prejudiced action of the chairman of the committee, Julius C. Burrows, senator from Michigan. "Mr. Burrows was a [nephew] of a former member [Sylvester Smith] of the Church who traveled with the Prophet Joseph Smith and his company in what was known as Zion's Camp to Missouri in 1834; but who was a trouble maker and finally was excommunicated from the Church. Mr. Burrows seemingly inherited all the hatred engendered into the heart of his [uncle], and manifested throughout the investigation, which took many months, a bitterness and spirit of unfairness very unbecoming in such a presiding officer." Senator Fred T. Dubois of Idaho was another of the committee who was particularly abusive. "Mr. Dubois was naturally mean and despicable and an arch-enemy of the Church who had bitterly antagonized its members in Idaho for many years," observed President Smith in the biography of his father. For several years Dubois had served as a federal deputy marshal in Idaho, determined to stamp out the practice of plural marriage. Senator Jonathan P. Dolliver, one of the eight submitting the majority report recommending Smoot be ousted from the Senate, did so solely for political expediency. As soon as he was safely re-elected himself, he reversed his stand and voted with the Senate majority to reject the committee's majority report and sustain Smoot. Burrows and Dubois were later defeated in their bids for re-election to the Senate. President Smith notes that Dubois then sought for a federal appointment and Burrows for federal favors for some clients, and Senator Smoot, the man they had so severely abused, was the one to whom they each had to appeal. Magnanimously Smoot granted each of them the favors asked.

During this same period the Reorganized Church of

Jesus Christ of Latter Day Saints was making rather strenuous efforts to discredit the "Utah" church and to proselyte its members. Joseph Smith, son of the Prophet Joseph Smith, was president of the Reorganites, and his counselors were his son (the Prophet's grandson) Frederick M. Smith and Richard C. Evans. Several doctrinal differences existed between the two churches, including the right to succession in the church presidency, priesthood authority, plural marriage, blood atonement, and rebaptism. The Reorganites claimed that the Prophet's son was the rightful heir to the church presidency, rather that Brigham Young or any other. They also claimed that the Prophet Joseph neither taught nor lived plural marriage, but that this "abominable doctrine" was introduced by Brigham Young; likewise blood atonement and rebaptism. When The Church of Jesus Christ of Latter-day Saints suspended the practice of plural marriage in 1890 the Reorganites considered it a victory for them, and stepped up their missionary efforts in Utah, hoping to win other "concessions" from the Utah church.

At best it was a sad situation, that after Joseph and Hyrum Smith had been so close and loyal to each other, that now their sons, President Joseph Smith of the Reorganized Latter-day Saints Church and President Joseph F. Smith of The Church of Jesus Christ of Latter-day Saints, should be engaged in a public controversy over which church was right and which was wrong; and that their grandsons should also be caught up in this war of words. None regretted it more than President Joseph F. Smith and his son Joseph Fielding. Joseph F. Smith, before he became president, had visited in the Midwest a time or two with his cousin, Joseph Smith. On the first visit Joseph Smith, son of the Prophet, had been friendly, but on a visit to him a few years later Joseph F. found him antagonistic. Apparently, this negative feeling persisted to the end of his life. Years earlier upon visiting with Brigham Young and others in Salt Lake City he had concluded that he should reunite with The Church of Jesus Christ of Latter-day Saints. But apparently either his mother or some of her associates dissuaded him from this wise decision.

Although Joseph Fielding saw his father's cousin, Joseph Smith, son of the Prophet, a number of times, he apparently had little contact with him and did not enter the controversy personally against him. But he did do battle with Joseph Smith's two counselors, Frederick Smith and Richard Evans, and also with W. H. Kelley, president of the Reorganized Latter Day Saints Council of Twelve, and with Amos Milton Chase and others who served as missionaries to the Utah-based Mormons.

The *Daily Star* of Toronto, Ontario, Canada, in its issue of January 28, 1905, published an interview with Mr. Evans in which appeared statements that Joseph Fielding considered to be a "wilful misrepresentation of the doctrines of the Latter-day Saints and the unwarranted abuse of the authorities of the Church." Joseph Fielding sent a letter to the editor refuting Evans' statements, and further correspondence between the two men followed, some of it also being published in *Zion's Ensign*, a Reorganized Latter Day Saints publication. This dialogue resulted in publication of one of Joseph Fielding's first booklets, *Blood Atonement and the Origin of Plural Marriage*, containing the correspondence between the two men and affidavits from several widows of Joseph and Hyrum Smith to irrefutably document the fact that plural marriage had been introduced into the Church by Joseph Smith rather than by Brigham Young.

Accompanied by his uncle John Smith, the church patriarch, Joseph on May 22, 1905, visited Peter Lott "and obtained the family Bible of Cornelius P. Lott which contains the Lott family record including the sealing of C. P. Lott and his wife for eternity, also the marriage of Melissa Lott to the Prophet Joseph Smith." On June 29, 1905, Joseph Fielding "had a talk with Aunt Lucy Walker Smith at the Beehive House in the afternoon when she told me many of her experiences in Nauvoo and of her marriage to the Prophet Joseph Smith and that she also knew personally and positively that the

Partridge sisters and Sarah and Maria Lawrence were also the Prophet's wives."

On September 24, 1905, Joseph and his mother called on Catherine Phillips Smith, a widow of his grandfather, the Patriarch Hyrum Smith. Mrs. Smith lived in East Jordan. She was old and sick. "We found her in a very weak condition but her mind was perfectly clear. She told us that a short time before her sickness four members of the Reorganized Church had called at her home with the object in view of having her deny her testimony as given in her affidavit in which she testifies that she was married to the Patriarch Hyrum Smith. They remained at her home a good part of the day and did their worst to get her to contradict her statement, which they could not do. I shall quote her own words: Said she, 'They tried to get me to tell a lie and deny that I was married to the Patriarch Hyrum Smith, but I would not do it. I never have lied and will not now. My affidavit is true. They asked me if my mother knew of my marriage, and I told them that the Patriarch first asked my mother if she was willing for him to marry her daughter, and she said he could ask the daughter and she could do as she pleased. I told them that the Prophet Joseph sealed me to the Patriarch Hyrum Smith as his wife for time and all eternity; and they tried to get me to deny it, and I would not do it, for it is true. I told them the truth. They annoyed me very much, and I finally told them to leave my house, and never enter it again.' " Aunt Catherine died two days after Joseph Fielding and his mother visited her.

Frederick Smith visited in Salt Lake City a number of times and Joseph and Louie exchanged dinner dates with him and his wife and also took them on a tour of the city, up City Creek Canyon, out to Saltair, and otherwise hosted them. It was on invitation of President Joseph F. Smith that Frederick first came, to attend a Smith family reunion on the occasion of the 104th birth anniversary of Hyrum. There was also a pleasant exchange of letters between Joseph Fielding and Frederick, and relationships seemed warm and cordial. But underneath the smooth surface remained the old animosities, with Frederick and his father and other Reorganites feeling a deep resentment toward the Latter-day Saint leaders. Added to their other grievances was a new one in 1905 when the Church announced plans to build a monument to the Prophet Joseph Smith in Sharon, Vermont, on the occasion of his centennial birth anniversary. The Prophet's son and grandson seemed to feel that the Utah church had no right to do that.

The duplicity in Frederick's behavior was astounding. "Frederick M. Smith and wife and little daughter spent the evening at my place," wrote Joseph Fielding in his journal for June 30, 1905, "had supper and enjoyed themselves—so they said, and appeared very friendly. That same day he wrote a bigoted, contemptible open letter to the people of Royalton and Sharon, Vermont and the people of the United States, in which he protested against our people building a monument to the memory of his grandfather the Prophet Joseph Smith which is going to be done by our people, the Latter-day Saints. He accused the leaders of the Church of all manner of wickedness, called them law breakers and declared that they and the people were not worthy the fellowship of honorable people. Yet he would come to my house and eat at my table, accept the kindnesses of my father and the hospitality of the leaders of the Church, and thereby show himself a hypocrite. He left his open letter with the daily papers when on his way to my home in the evening."

Next morning Frederick called on Joseph at his office, "to have a heart to heart talk with me, and to see how I felt about his article in the morning papers. I told him frankly what I thought. A discussion followed in which the subject of the introduction of plural marriage was discussed. I showed him from the Reorganized writings that *his church* taught that the Prophet Joseph Smith in-introduced that doctrine. He admitted to me that the *sealing* of husbands and wives for *eternity* was practiced in Nauvoo in his grandfather's day and declared that if his grandfather introduced plural marriage—which he practically admitted that he did—that it only lessened him in his (Frederick's) estimation. He became very excited and had to retract some statements that he made in his argument."

In the gall of bitterness, Frank Cannon as chief editorial writer for *The Salt Lake Tribune* at this time was heaping calumny upon the Church generally and upon President Joseph F. Smith particularly. President Joseph Smith of the Reorganized Latter Day Saints and his son and counselor Frederick attended the general conference of the Church in the Salt Lake Tabernacle in October, 1905, thinking perhaps they would be there to see the collapse of the Church. "Frederick M. Smith and his father Joseph were present and attended the sessions on the first day and were sadly disappointed at the unanimity of feeling, as they had been led to expect a division in the Church," wrote Joseph Fielding in his journal. "*The Salt Lake Tribune*, which is bitterly attacking the President of the Church and the Mormon people generally, led them to believe that the Latter-day Saints were hopelessly divided. But the people were never more united, judging from the spirit at the conference. . . ."

Three months later Frank Cannon was collaborating with Frederick Smith in an attack upon the Church leaders. "I wrote a reply to a vicious attack on the authorities of the Church which appeared in the *Saints Herald* [the RLDS newspaper] signed by Frederick M. Smith and written by him and Frank J. Cannon," Joseph noted in January, 1906. In 1844 the Prophet Joseph, the Patriarch Hyrum, the Apostles John Taylor and Willard Richards had stood together in Carthage Jail bravely facing the bullets of assassins. The Smiths had given their lives and John Taylor had been severely wounded. Yet here now was the grandson of the Prophet and the grand-nephew of President Taylor jointly fomenting hatred toward the grandson of Hyrum and the gospel cause for which the earlier generation had offered their lives! Strange indeed are the quirks of history.

Reorganite ministers and missionaries in Utah became extremely outspoken and abusive in their attacks on the Latter-day Saint leaders, so much so that President Lewis Shurtliff of Weber Stake invited his son-in-law to come to Ogden and lecture on the subject of the Reorganized Church and the question of succession in the presidency. Joseph Fielding later published this talk and other materials he had gathered as a booklet in 1907, *Origin of the "Reorganized" Church: The Question of Succession.* A second edition was published in 1909 with additional information on differences in the doctrines of the two churches.

Happily, the behavior of another whose family had splintered off from the Church was much more positive: John Rigdon, son of Sidney Rigdon, decided to return to the Church. Sidney, it will be remembered, had sought to establish his own church in Pittsburgh, Pennsylvania, after his abortive effort to take the leadership of the Latter-day Saint Church following the death of Joseph and Hyrum Smith in 1844. Sidney died at Friendship, New York, in 1876, the year Joseph Fielding was born. His old age had been spent in loneliness, bitterness and disillusionment. John Rigdon and others of the family naturally had partaken of his negative feelings toward the Church. At Joseph Fielding's request, a representative of the Church had called on John Rigdon in the East and had made friendly overtures to him. After some careful soul searching John Rigdon decided his father had been mistaken. He visited in Salt Lake City at April conference in 1905. "John W. Rigdon, son of Sidney Rigdon, came in the Historian's Office and left with me a package of letters written by his father," noted Joseph Fielding on April 5, 1905. "He desired that they be filed away in the office. He also presented to the President of the Church for safe keeping a cane that was made out of the oak box in which the Prophet's body was carried from Carthage to Nauvoo after the martyrdom June 27, 1844. The cane bears the following inscription: 'Presented by Brigham Young to Sidney Rigdon 1844.' It is one of a number that were made by President Young." Two months later, June 4, 1905, Joseph attended a Sunday meeting in Ogden at which Rigdon "spoke of early Church scenes."

While serving as a clerk in the Historian's Office Joseph decided to compile the history of his line of the Smith family. His father sent him and Licurgus A. Wilson, who had been working with him on genealogy, back to Essex County, Massachusetts, to seek names and data. Here in the heart of America's infamous witch hunt country they spent most of the month of July, 1902, visiting the old Robert Smith farm at Boxford, Asael Smith's farm near Topsfield, and "searching all old records of wills, deeds, court trials, etc." in the courthouse at Salem. They found that President George A. Smith, counselor to Brigham Young, had erected a monument in 1873 to their Smith ancestors in Topsfield cemetery. George Francis Dow, secretary of the Essex County Historical Society, was most cooperative in their efforts, turning over many records to them, and later invited Joseph Fielding to write a sketch of the Smiths for the society. The booklet, *Asahel [sic] Smith of Topsfield, Massachusetts, with some Account of the Smith Family*, became the first of Joseph Fielding's many publications. It was read to the society at Topsfield by Mr. Dow. In 1905, Joseph also wrote pamphlets or universal salvation and salvation for the dead.

Through the kindness of his father and President Anthon H. Lund, Joseph Fielding had opportunity to take several other trips of interest during this first decade of the 1900's. One was to the historic church sites in Missouri in August, 1904, in company with his father-in-law. The two men visited Independence, Gallatin, Adam-ondi-Ahman, Far West and other sites of interest, as well as an exposition fair at St. Louis. At Adam-ondi-Ahman, where the Prophet and others had discovered an ancient altar, they found that "the portion of the ancient altar which was visible when our people first settled there has been destroyed by parties who were seeking for gold which was erroneously said to have been buried there by the Mormon people. . . . The altar was built on the highest portion of a bluff or mound on the north bank of Grand River in a sharp bend of the same. To the south and west is the small but beautiful valley of Adam-ondi-Ahman through which Grand River flows. The country is rolling prairie land covered with farms, but very sparsely settled." It was with a feeling of reverence that Joseph and his father-in-law looked upon this site where the Ancient of Days was said to have assembled his people.

Far West also had a strong emotional appeal for Joseph for it was here that his father was born, and his grandfather taken captive along with the Prophet Joseph. Of Far West he noted in his journal, "It is one of the most beautiful spots for the location of a city in the world. The temple lot stands on the highest rise, and the corner stones of the temple which were laid by the elders in 1838 are still resting in the position in which they were placed. The public square—now a field—was in the centre of the town and included the temple lot. It was on this square that the Saints were forced at the bayonet point to sign away their property to defray the expenses of the mob which drove them from the state. My father was born there November 13, 1838, just 11 days after his father was carried off a prisoner by the mob. Today the evidence of a settlement has all disappeared and the land has been converted into farms and pastures. . . ."

At Gallatin, Joseph and President James G. Duffin of the Central States Mission "called on an old man by the name of [Joseph] McGee and had a talk with him" concerning the history of the Missouri country and particularly the conflict between Mormons and anti-Mormons in the early days of the Church. Mr. McGee was 17 years old when the Mormons were driven from Far West in 1838. He had a keen recollection of those days of violence and bloodshed. He also remembered the Prophet Joseph. "I saw Joseph Smith throw [John] Brassfield, the champion wrestler of the county, the first two falls out of a match of three [best two in three]," McGee told them. "He was a powerful man. Brassfield you know was one of the guards in charge of the Smiths when they escaped from Missouri and the people always blamed him and the other guards for their escape. William Morgan was the sheriff and the people were so enraged that they rode him on an iron bar so violently that he died shortly after. The Missourians were mostly from the southern states, principally Kentucky and Tennessee. They were hospitable and would feed a stranger and lodge him, yet they were a rough, uneducated class, very quarrelsome and delighted in fighting even among themselves."

The Prophet Joseph had predicted that the Missourians would reap the whirlwind of their misbehavior, and Mr. McGee had seen the fulfillment of that prophecy. No state was more divided in its loyalties between North and South during the Civil War. McGee had served as a major in the Union Army until the loss of his sight in 1864. "During the war the Major served in the army operating along the border counties, principally in Jackson and other counties where such awful depredations and pillaging were so prevalent. . . . He said that there were more Union men than Confederates in Daviess County, but that the whole section of country in and around Missouri was terribly divided, neighbors fighting neighbors, sons against fathers, in the opposing armies. Especially in Jackson County was the suffering great." It was in this area also that William Quantrill and his band of cutthroats operated, exploiting and terrorizing people regardless of their allegiance to North or South. And here it was that Jesse and Frank James and their gang, some of them previously associated with Quantrill, operated, through the very counties that the Mormons and anti-Mormons had disputed.

Joseph's major travels had all been eastward until September of 1905 when his father invited him to accompany him on a train trip to northern Mexico for the dedication of the Church's academy in Juarez. They also visited church colonies at Dublan and elsewhere, then came home via California, where Joseph got his first glimpse of the Pacific Ocean. A highlight of the trip was a visit to Catalina Island.

Joseph Fielding enjoyed another pleasant journey in December of 1905 when he accompanied his father, his father-in-law, his older brother Hyrum, and 26 others to Sharon, Vermont, for the dedication of the Joseph Smith Monument, on the Prophet's one hundredth birth anniversary, December 23, 1905. "Early Saturday morning, December 23rd, we were all conveyed in carriages from South Royalton to the birthplace of the Prophet Joseph at Sharon to attend the dedication. I cannot express my feelings as I drew in sight of the magnificent monument and home that had been erected at that place, but I felt that I was on sacred ground, a place dear to me, one which I had desired to see. The dedicatory services were conducted by President Joseph F. Smith and were most impressive. About 400 persons were in attendance. Elder Junius F. Wells related the difficulties overcome in rearing the monument and related the history of its erection. . . ." It was Wells who had proposed the idea of the monument, and was commissioned by the church presidency to head the project—despite the opposition felt to it by the Reorganites.

Before returning home the dozen Smiths in the monument party visited Smith family sites in Essex County, Massachusetts, while the others visited in Boston. The group also visited Palmyra, Manchester, and the Hill Cumorah, which Joseph Fielding refers to in his journal as the site of the last great battle between the Nephites and Lamanites. "A grand view of the valley in which the death struggle took place between the Nephites and Lamanites can be seen from the top of the hill." On their return journey they also visited the Kirtland Temple and cemetery, and made a side trip from Chicago to Kenosha and Racine, Wisconsin, as guests of the Bain Wagon Company. They reached Salt Lake City on New Year's Day, 1906, feeling so enthusiastic about the trip that they decided to form a society of those who had made it and hold an annual reunion. By the following May 16, Joseph Fielding had ready for the bindery a booklet he had prepared on the monument proceedings.

Joseph Fielding made yet another visit to the historic church sites and Smith family sites in May of 1907, when his father asked him and his brother David to go to Boston to greet their brothers George and Willard as the latter two returned from their missions to Scandinavia. The four Smith brothers visited Sharon, Royalton, South Royalton and Tunbridge, Vermont, the latter being the birthplace of their grandfather, Hyrum. They visited Rochester, Palmyra and Manchester, New York, the Hill Cumorah, Buffalo, Niagara Falls, Kirtland, Ohio and other spots of interest.

President Heber J. Grant and party on Hill Cumorah on the occasion of the one hundredth anniversary of the visitation of the Angel Moroni to the Prophet Joseph Smith. From left to right, Elder James E. Talmage, Elder Joseph Fielding Smith, President Grant, and Elder Rudger Clawson. Date— Sept. 22, 1923.

In the Church General Conference in April, 1906, Joseph was advanced from a clerk in the Historian's Office to the position of an assistant historian, succeeding Orson F. Whitney, who was sustained as a member of the Council of Twelve. Other assistant historians were: B. H. Roberts, Andrew Jenson and Amos Musser. George F. Richards and David O. McKay were appointed to the Council of Twelve at this same conference, along with Whitney. The three vacancies had been created by the death of Apostle Marriner W. Merrill of Richmond, Utah, and the requested resignations of Apostles John W. Taylor, son of President John Taylor, and Matthias F. Cowley. Elders Taylor and Cowley were casualties of the anti-Mormon crusade being waged by ex-Senators Thomas Kearns, Frank J. Cannon, Senators Julius C. Burrows and

President Heber J. Grant and party in the Sacred Grove, Sept. 22, 1923. From left to right, President John H. Taylor, Elder Joseph Fielding Smith, Elder Rudger Clawson, President Grant, Augusta Winters Grant, Elder James E. Talmage, and President B. H. Roberts.

Fred Dubois and others in connection with the Reed Smoot hearings in Congress. Taylor and Cowley were two of the general authorities who felt strongly that plural marriage should be continued and they had personally married additional wives as well as performing plural marriages for others after the Manifesto. When they declined to appear before the Senate committee investigating Smoot, and as the anti-Mormon pressure over the issue continued to mount, President Smith reluctantly asked for their resignations. Their exercise of the priesthood was suspended. Years later in his old age Elder Cowley was again allowed the use of the priesthood. Elder Taylor was later excommunicated for taking still more wives, then in 1965, nearly half a century after his death, he was vicariously reinstated to Church membership and priesthood, with President Joseph Fielding Smith of the Council of Twelve officiating in the ceremony. Elder Merrill's resignation would also have been requested had he not died just when he did, for he too had continued performing plural marriages, according to his grandson, Dr. Milton R. Merrill, a biographer of Senator Reed Smoot.

In June, 1906, two months after the three non-polygamist apostles were sustained, the senatorial committee concluded its hearings on the Smoot matter. From then until February 20, 1907, when the Senate majority voted for Smoot to retain his seat, Cannon, Kearns, and other anti-Mormons intensified their attack to a feverish pitch, hoping to manipulate public sentiment to the point that the Senate would expel Smoot. In the midst of this barrage of words, President Smith deemed it wisdom to take an extended tour of the European missions. With Joseph's assistance, he departed on July 22, in company with his friend Bishop Charles W. Nibley, and a wife and daughters of Nibley.

"I was in council with a number of brethren considering local conditions," Joseph noted on September 17, 1906, "and the feelings of bitterness existing in the hearts of anti-Mormons toward my father, and the wicked, malicious fight that is being made on him. *The Salt Lake Tribune* publishes daily articles of the worst kind filled with bitterness and threats against the President of the Church, and to some extent those who call themselves brethren partake of the same spirit and fight the work of God, mostly in secret, but occasionally in political and other gatherings." A week later he "went to the county attorney's office with other members of the family and members of the First Presidency and apostles quorum to be examined by the attorney in regard to a charge made by C. Mostyn Owen—one of the meanest and vilest creatures on earth—against my father." Two months later the apostate Owens was successful in his efforts to have President Smith fined for continuing to live in plural marriage. Joseph Fielding notes that he, Joseph, "went with my father to the 3rd district court where he was fined $300.00 for living with and caring for his wives, on complaint of C. M. Owen, a devil incarnate."

In December, as the vote on Smoot neared, Senators Burrows and Dubois "made speeches in the United States Senate in the Smoot case and bitterly attacked the Church." In an effort to counteract the influence of these speeches, the Cannon editorials in the *Tribune* and other hostile comments, the church presidency in January, 1907, appointed a committee "to prepare data for a defense of the Church against assaults made upon it by its enemies. The members of the committee," noted Joseph Fielding, "were: Orson F. Whitney, David O. McKay, B. H. Roberts, Richard W. Young, Nephi L. Morris, James E. Talmage, Franklin D. Richards, Legrande Young, and myself." This likely was the first instance of David O. McKay and Joseph Fielding Smith serving together on an assignment, or being closely associated. For several days the group met to consider material for use in trying to improve the Church's public image. At the following April conference this was used for an "Address to the World," by the church presidency, refuting the lies being fomented against the Mormons, and proclaiming once again the true nature and purposes of the Church.

Seldom in his journal does Joseph Fielding make any personal comment, pro or con, regarding men appointed to positions in the Church, beyond the fact of their appointment, but when Anthony W. Ivins, president of the Juarez Stake, was sustained as an apostle at the October, 1907, conference, replacing George Teasdale who had died, Elder Smith comments, "This was a most excellent choice." Ivins later became a counselor to his cousin, Heber J. Grant, in the church presidency.

In December, 1907, Charles W. Nibley was appointed as the presiding bishop of the Church, Bishop William Preston having become mentally incapacitated. Bishop Nibley chose Orrin P. Miller and Joseph's younger brother, David A. Smith, as his counselors.

The above picture shows a group of general authorities with their wives standing in front of the old Deseret News Building on the corner of South Temple and Main Street, now the location of Hotel Utah. Four of the general authorities in the picture have served as president of the Church, Joseph F. Smith, Heber J. Grant, George Albert Smith, and Joseph Fielding Smith.

In addition to his duties in the Church Historian's Office, Joseph Fielding assisted his father with correspondence, serving unofficially as a secretary to him from time to time. He also filled a number of church positions, usually as many as five concurrently: he was what is now called a home teacher, (then known as a block teacher), a home missionary, a branch Sunday School superintendent, a president of the 24th Quorum of Seventies, a member of the Salt Lake Stake high council, a Sunday School teacher, a Mutual teacher, a member of the general board of the Young Men's Mutual Improvement Association, a director and secretary of the church-sponsored Utah Genealogical Society, a member of the Church's Religion Class general board, and treasurer of the Mormon Tabernacle Choir.

Four of Joseph's brothers had left for missions in April, 1905: Alvin and Chase to Great Britain and George and Willard to Scandinavia. George had been serving as treasurer of the Tabernacle Choir. Already carrying a heavy load of church assignments, Joseph was asked to replace George as choir treasurer. Although he never did sing in the choir, Joseph for the next two years as treasurer attended rehearsals and performances of the choir. Thus it was that years before he ever met and married Jessie Evans, and years before she ever joined the choir and achieved notoriety as a soloist, Joseph Fielding Smith himself was an officer in the famed Mormon Tabernacle Choir!

The YMMIA appointment, made May 27, 1903, and continuing until his call to the Council of the Twelve in 1910, required considerable travel, by train and by horse and buggy, to the various stakes of the Church. Generally he and one of the representatives of the YWMIA would travel together and be the principal speakers at the MIA sessions in the particular stakes to which they were assigned. So, long before becoming a general authority Joseph Fielding was well indoctrinated in the practice of stake visits. With his multiplicity of assignments, he also became well indoctrinated in meetings. Reading through his daily journals prompts one to wonder whether any other person in the history of the world ever attended quite so many meetings. Each Wednesday afternoon and evening, for instance, he had three meetings to attend: Religion Class general board meeting at 4:00 P.M., MIA general board meeting at 5:00 P.M., and stake high council meeting at 7:30 P.M.

The church-wide Religion Class board assignment, beginning in January, 1909, also entailed considerable travel to the various stakes. It was the hope of the brethren that through this Religion Class effort the saints could be brought to a greater understanding and appreciation of the gospel. As someone once challenged a testimony bearer, "You know the gospel is true, but do you know the gospel?" Through the Religion Class program more men and women would *know the gospel* and be reminded that we are here to *work* out our salvation, not *wait* out our salvation.

It was in this first decade of the 1900's that Joseph Fielding became deeply involved in development of the Church's genealogical program which today is quite universally acclaimed as the best in the world. He was one of the organizers of the church-sponsored Utah Genealogical and Historical Society, became its first secretary and the first editor of the *Utah Genealogical and Historical Magazine*, the first edition of which was published in January, 1910—a week late because Joseph had to do most of the work on it right in his house while in quarantine, caring for his second daughter Julina who was afflicted with scarlet fever. The magazine, which he not only edited but personally mailed out, was "to be published in the interest of temple work and to instruct the saints in the collection of their genealogy."

In the fall of 1909 Joseph in company with Bishop Joseph Christenson of the Society made an extensive tour of libraries in Chicago, Washington, D. C., New York, Boston and other cities, carefully observing how they handled their filing systems, indexing, shelving, and all other aspects of their operations which might be pertinent to development of a full fledged genealogy library in Salt Lake City. Several years earlier he had visited the Newberry Library in Chicago, and now again marveled at the extensive collection it had in genealogy, by contrast with the meager holdings at that time in the Salt Lake genealogy library. Today, thanks in large part to the pioneering efforts of Joseph Fielding Smith, the Church's library is much larger than the Newberry in genealogical materials.

With increasing frequency Joseph was called on to give talks in various wards of the Church on the importance of genealogy and temple work. His booklet on *Salvation Universal* attracted considerable attention also, and helped to stimulate interest in genealogy and temple work, which the Prophet Joseph Smith had declared was the most important assignment of the Latter-day Saints. This vicarious work for the dead which the Church had been authorized to perform came to occupy an ever greater role in Joseph Fielding's life. Seemingly his extensive involvement with it was one of the factors which helped to qualify him for his call to the Council of Twelve early in 1910.

Joseph personally witnessed an example of how vicarious work for the dead could be a comforting, uniting influence in a family: one of the most puzzling characters in church history is Amasa M. Lyman. The Prophet Joseph thought so well of him that when he decided to drop Sidney Rigdon as his first counselor in the church presidency, he ordained Amasa Lyman to succeed him. But the saints refused to drop Rigdon and so Amasa was never put into the church presidency. He was appointed to the Council of the Twelve Apostles instead. Years later Brigham Young received a disturbing report that while serving as president of the European missions Elder Lyman at Dundee, Scotland, had preached a sermon denying the atonement of Christ! He called Lyman in and questioned him closely. Lyman is reported to have admitted doing so, claiming that he taught nothing but what he had heard from the Prophet Joseph! Brigham Young sternly warned him to never preach such doctrine again. He was deprived of his apostleship in 1867. Sometime later he preached this false doctrine again, and so Brigham Young excommunicated him, in 1870, and Lyman died outside the Church, in 1877. One informant attributes his strange preachment to the fact or alleged fact that he had been tampering with spiritualism and was getting his inspiration on the wrong wave length. Whatever the reason, it was quite unbecoming a professed apostle of the Lord, to say the least.

Three years after Amasa's death his son Francis Marion Lyman became a member of the Council of Twelve. In 1903, upon the death of Brigham Young Jr., Francis M.—he generally went by Marion—became president of the Council of Twelve. It was tough to think of his old dad being in Purgatory instead of Paradise. How could they get the door open for him? Under the date of January 12, 1909, Joseph Fielding records the answer in his journal: "At 4:00 p.m. I went to the temple with my father, where President Francis M. Lyman was baptized by Elder John Henry Smith, for and in behalf of his father, and was confirmed, etc. by Joseph F. Smith. Presidents John R. Winder and Anthon H. Lund, Elder George Albert Smith and Patriarch Albert W. Davis were also present." It was comforting to have power to bind on earth and in heaven and to loose on earth and in heaven.

Joseph's habit of assisting his father with his correspondence led to further close association with him, beyond what any of the president's other sons enjoyed, unless it was his oldest son Hyrum, an apostle. With increasing frequency Joseph accompanied his father on various assignments and journeys, and occasionally substituted for him. Apparently as a member of the MIA General Board Joseph in August, 1908, had been a speaker at the Box Elder Stake Conference in Brigham City, and while there was a house guest of Stake President Oleen H. Stohl. Nine months later, "I went to Brigham City at the request of my father to dedicate the Second

Ward meeting house in Brigham City. They were very desirous of having *him* offer the dedicatory prayer, but as he was suffering from a severe cold he sent me in his stead. I was met at the station by President Oleen H. Stohl and Bishop Thomas H. Blackburn." Joseph dedicated the Second Ward Church house all right, and also inspected improvements that had been made in the Brigham Fourth Ward chapel. What he did not mention in his journal—but apparently shared with his family later—was the fact that when he stepped off the train at the Brigham City depot, President Stohl and Bishop Blackburn were deeply disappointed. They viewed him with long faces. "I could bawl," the stake president said. "We were expecting the president of the Church and we get a boy instead!"

Chapter 7

"The Lord gave and the Lord hath taken away"

On Becoming a Father, and a Widower

Up and down the lot they walked, first this way and then that, stepping off distances, setting one rock here and another there, for markers. "The stairs should be here," said Joseph. "And the dining room will start here," said Louie. "And the kitchen over here." "And let's have a pantry here, filled with lots of pies," said Joseph. Affectionately he squeezed Louie's hand, and they stole a quick kiss in broad daylight. It was a warm summer evening in 1901, just a short time after his return home from the mission to England.

Papa and Mama Smith had again made available to them the northwest corner room in Julina's house, and Louie had it all redecorated by the time Joseph had reached home. After Joseph F. became president of the Church in November, 1901, he and Julina and their unmarried children moved into the Beehive House, the official residence of the church president. Joseph and Louie then had additional rooms in the house at 333 West First North. Still, it was not like having a home of their own. Each time they passed the vacant lot that Papa and Mama had given them as a wedding gift they talked of the day when they would build their dream home. Happily they envisioned just how the house would look, where each room would be. It would be a large house, built of brick, three stories high—counting the basement, of course—with lots of bedrooms for lots of children they were going to have some day. It would be a beautiful house, with a big green lawn and plenty of tall trees around it.

At 25 years of age Joseph and Louie had the best years of life ahead of them. They were flat broke at the minute, that's true. But they were rich in faith in the future. Having never gone on a first honeymoon they also did not go on a second one, following Joseph's return from England. It was sufficient just to be together. Sufficient? It was wonderful! The two years and more of being apart had just enhanced the joy of being together. The long days and nights of loneliness were forgotten now in the happiness of having each other within arm's reach.

New Year's day, 1902, the first New Year's day they had been together in the twentieth century, they spent at Louie's folks in Ogden. This would be a great year for them. Joseph was enjoying his job as a clerk in the Historian's Office, where he had been employed now for exactly three months. He was earning a respectable if modest wage, and by careful management they were putting a little money into savings each month which, together with the worth of their lot, would one day make a down payment on the cost of building a house. This year they would build a house. This year, hopefully, they would start on their family.

Louie became pregnant within the month, and unfortunately had a most miserable time of it, being sick much of the time, especially through February, March, April and May. Her burden was emotionally lightened by the prospects of their getting their house built. They decided to start in the spring when the weather permitted. By April they had a house plan drawn up and Joseph submitted it to a builder named Matthew Noall. There was an old foundation of a house on their lot, at 165 North Second West, which apparently had been occupied by a Fielding relative. In the evenings as his time permitted Joseph cleared this foundation away and otherwise prepared the lot for a building. He measured and marked off the space, hired George Nebeker for $10 to dig a hole for a cellar, and another $20 to work on the cellar. He had rock and sand trucked in, and on June 17, the day after Louie's 26th birthday anniversary, he obtained a building permit, and their house was soon on its way up. Poor Louie, meantime, had gone to Ogden to stay with her mother for several weeks, and on June 18 Joseph received a phone call with the worrisome news that she had taken worse. Joseph spent the Fourth of July holiday with her in Ogden prior to leaving on a genealogy search trip to Essex County, Massachusetts.

Such was Louie's difficulty through her pregnancy that at times it seemed she would lose her baby. But on Thursday, September 18, 1902, at 5:15 in the morning at their home at 333 West First North, in Salt Lake City, "Louie was delivered of a fine 9 lb. baby girl. She has suffered extremely during the night. We both feel very grateful to our Heavenly Father, for without His blessing we never would have been so prosperous." On Friday, September 26, "Our baby was blessed this morning by its grandfather L. W. Shurtliff and given the name of Josephine." Louie had continued "very sick and has suffered very much pain from the time of her confinement," and they feared for her life. But as the days and weeks rolled by she gradually improved, and little Josephine was doing well. Despite the difficult time Louie had, parenthood was a joyous experience for the young couple. When five months old baby Josephine became quite ill, but through the healing power of God she was made well.

With meetings nearly every night of the week and practically all day Sunday, plus working six days a week at his job in the Historian's Office, Joseph did not get to spend as much time at home as he would like to have done. Come summertime he did take an occasional day off to take Louie and the baby out to Saltair or for a drive up one of the nearby canyons. Louie and baby Josephine spent quite a few days each year with her parents in Ogden, sometimes for a few weeks at a time. These trips to

Ogden were really about the extent of Louie's travels. That she never accompanied Joseph on any of his various trips probably reflects the custom and attitude of the time, that the woman stayed at home. It may be too that she simply did not care for travel. And seldom did she accompany him to meetings, the theater, sports events and other activities that occupied some of his time.

It took a year for the construction of their house, and a handsome house it was, large and stately, built of brick, with a large front porch, facing to the east. On the ground floor were a parlor, sitting room, dining room, kitchen, pantry, bedroom, bath and hallways. Upstairs, to be finished later, would be several bedrooms and a study for Joseph. He was anxious to get the main floor of the house done in time for Louie's 27th birthday anniversary, and on June 16, 1903, he noted in his journal. "Today is Louie's birthday. I moved the cook stove into the new house this evening, David and Wesley [his brothers] helping me. The carpet men from the Co-op Furniture Company also laid a carpet." Early next morning and the following evening, and for three days thereafter, he continued with the chore of moving, taking time out, however, to go "with Brother Jonathan Openshaw to visit [some] slothful Seventies."

There can be no question but what Louie was a good cook and took loving care of Joseph. When he was working at ZCMI in the early days of their marriage, he weighed 150 pounds. By December 22, 1903, his weight had increased to 176. He enjoyed generally good health, but had considerable difficulty with his teeth. He was plagued with toothaches. He tried to persuade a number of different dentists to pull several of his teeth, but they declined to do so. Instead they severed the nerves to try to relieve the discomfort. One tooth gave him so much distress, however, he finally did persuade a dentist to extract it. Years later he got them all extracted in favor of dentures and declared it was one of the smartest things he ever did. His father while still in his 40's had had his teeth extracted also.

In his assignment in the Church Historian's Office Joseph was required to do considerable intensive reading, including proofreading on upcoming manuscripts such as the seven-volume *Documentary History of the Church.* For months he and President Anthon H. Lund and B. H. Roberts and occasionally Orson F. Whitney read proof on these volumes, which had been edited by Elder Roberts. He also served on manuscript committees, such as one on *The Prophet Joseph Smith as a Scientist,* by John A. Widtsoe, who would later become a general authority, and he did considerable indexing on various volumes. He also pored carefully through thousands of pages of early church historical documents, such as personal diaries, and the early records of the Relief Society. His own writing efforts and genealogical research were also taxing on the eyes, and by April, 1904, he found it necessary to have them tested for glasses. Most of his adult life he had to wear glasses.

Joseph Fielding Smith, as chairman of the publications committee, checks a manuscript with associates. From left to right, Elders Stephen L Richards, Joseph F. Merrill, Joseph Fielding Smith, John A. Widtsoe.

Despite the strain on his eyes, the opportunity of carefully going through these early church documents was a fascinating and rewarding one, helping to thoroughly orient him in church history and doctrine. "Today," he notes on July 11, 1904, "I found certain promises and statements concerning the restoration of the Melchizedek Priesthood in the patriarchal blessing pronounced by the Prophet Joseph Smith on the head of Oliver Cowdery in 1833. The blessing is recorded in [Great] Grandfather Joseph Smith's Patriarchal Blessing Book and refers to the prophecy of Joseph, son of Jacob. Why it has never been used before now I do not know."

Besides sitting on an occasional case as a member of the stake high council, from the time of his appointment in March, 1904, he as a citizen was also summoned to jury duty on some civil cases in the courts of Judge Samuel W. Stewart and Judge Thomas D. Lewis in June of 1904. These cases required several days of his time.

In the early summer of 1905 Louie again became pregnant. Fortunately she had an easier gestation this time, although she was not entirely free from trouble. Their second child and daughter was born on Monday, February 5, 1906, at 9 A.M., with Joseph's mother, Julina, serving as midwife, assisted by his sister Julina. A week later his father "blessed my baby and gave her the name of Julina after my mother." Josephine was now about three and a half years old, and was delighted to have a baby sister. Joseph would have preferred a boy, so as to have one of each, but the more important thing was that the baby was safely born and mother and child were doing well.

It was at the following April conference that Joseph was advanced from clerk to an assistant church historian, which meant not only greater responsibilities but a modest salary increase. He and Louie decided to have the top floor of their house finished. Workmen began the project on May 10, and for a historian that was an auspicious day to commence, for that was Golden Spike day, 37 years since the transcontinental railroad was completed at

Promontory. It was also just three weeks after the devastating San Francisco earthquake and fire, which had destroyed a fourth of the city and killed many.

Early in 1907 an epidemic of the dreaded spinal meningitis swept through Utah, "and baffles the skill of the physicians who are powerless to cope with it." Joseph and Louie in common with other parents kept an anxious watch over their children for any symptoms of it. The disease struck close. "My cousin Albert J. Davis lost a daughter a few days ago with the dreadful malady," he noted on March 24. But fortunately it passed by the Smiths.

At October conference time, 1907, Joseph "gave $50 for stock in Zion's Publishing Company which was organized by our people at Independence for the purpose of publishing books, tracts, etc." To Joseph, with his interest in writing, editing, compiling, and publishing, this was a most satisfying investment.

Another satisfying investment was one of time spent in the temple. (Louie had served as a temple worker for a time in 1901.) On November 1, 1907, "With Louie, I spent the greater part of the day in the Salt Lake Temple, one of the happiest days of our lives and the most profitable to us." Their happy days together were fast coming to a close. Joseph's sister Leonora "Nonie" Nelson died the following December 23, a few days after giving birth to a stillborn child. "Christmas day was spent by the family in sorrow." They buried her the day after Christmas.

Louie was again pregnant, and the sorrowful experience of the Nelsons seemed to cast a heavy shadow upon hers and Joseph's future. Joseph spent New Year's day "at home with my wife and babies." It would be Joseph's and Louie's last New Year's day together. On January 21, Joseph and his brother David A. "went to the city cemetery where we examined locations for [a] burying ground for our family, the object being to buy property for that purpose that would be of use for at least a century where all our dead could be buried together." Next day their father went back with them to help make a choice. "We will have David petition the city council for a reduction on one site which is now $4,000 per lot. The piece consists of 14 lots, one of which belongs to Joseph Nelson and it is there that my sister Leonora is buried."

By the fore part of February Louie was clearly having serious problems in her pregnancy. She was suffering from pernicious vomiting. The doctors seemed helpless to remedy the malady. Both Joseph and Louie were now feeling anxiety for her health. Joseph's mother Julina, who had enjoyed such remarkable success as a professional midwife, was consulted, but was unable to give relief. Louie was administered to, but still the problem persisted. "My wife has not been well for several days," Joseph noted on February 12, "and I had her prayed for by the brethren in the [temple prayer] circle." And on March 6, "Louie has not improved during the past week and her condition is quite serious."

Joseph later noted, "During the remainder of the month of March I spent my time at home and at the Historian's Office, principally at home where I felt that I was needed. I felt also, that I was justified in neglecting all other duties and in devoting my time and attention so far as possible to my sick wife and our babies." Seeking reassurance, he turned to the scriptures. Somewhere was there not a statement to the effect that although a woman shall suffer in child bearing, nevertheless she may be preserved? Joseph reread the passage, from the Book of Moses, but found not the comforting line he sought. It read only: "Unto the woman, I, the Lord God, said: I will greatly multiply thy sorrow and thy conception. In sorrow thou shalt bring forth children, and thy desire shall be to thy husband, and he shall rule over thee."

In helpless anxiety Joseph watched Louie becoming daily worse. For Louie it was a terrifying experience. She wanted so desperately to continue living, to successfully carry her baby full term, to be well enough to care for her two little baby girls, to stay with them and Joseph. She was only 31 years old, too young to die. There was so much to live for. So much. . . .

Death, and with it relief from suffering, came on March 30, at 4:45 A.M. In the depth of grief and anguish Joseph, seeking the balm of expression, confided to his journal, "During this month which has been one of constant anxiety and worry for me, I have passed through trials and experiences of the deepest and most painful kind. And through it all I have depended on the Lord for strength and comfort. After suffering most excruciating pain for three or four weeks and after an illness covering a period of nearly two months my beloved wife was released from her suffering Monday, March 30, 1908, and departed from me and our precious babies, for a better world, where we patiently and in sorrow await a meeting which shall be most glorious."

To Louie Joseph paid this heartfelt tribute, "She died firm in the faith and true to every principle of the gospel which she lived in righteousness. A purer, nobler, truer companion and mother there is not to be found in the whole earth. Her entire life was devoted to the gospel and the love of her fellows. She was constantly engaged in doing good. She loved her husband and babies dearer than her life and for them she laid it down. Every action on her part for them was one of love and unselfish devotion. She sacrificed self and her own comfort for those she loved and her example is one to be emulated by her children and all her loved ones. She received the blessings of the house of the Lord and lived the law of the Celestial Kingdom where she shall sit down never again to depart therefrom, and be crowned with immortality and eternal life, among those who have entered into the Church of the Firstborn, who shall receive a fullness of all things according to the promise of our Eternal Father."

In the depth of sorrow Joseph then cries out to the Lord, "O my Father in heaven, help me, I pray Thee, to so live that I shall be worthy to meet her in eternal glory, to be united again with her, never again to be separated, throughout the countless ages of eternity. Help me to be humble, to trust in Thee. Give me wisdom and knowledge of heavenly things that I may have power to resist all evil and remain steadfast to Thy *truth*. O Lord, help me, grant unto me eternal life in thy Kingdom. Guide my footsteps in righteousness, give unto me Thy Whole Spirit. Help me to rear my precious babies that they shall remain pure and spotless throughout their lives, and when we have finished our course, take us unto thy Celestial Kingdom, we pray thee. In the name of our Redeemer, let it be, Amen."

After writing into his journal an obituary of Louie, reviewing her life's activities, Joseph added this plaintive note, "With a sick heart I acknowledge the Lord and trust in Him for His help and comfort, for in Him only can I trust securely."

Funeral services for Louie were held on Thursday, April 2, in their home ward, the Salt Lake Seventeenth Ward. Forlornly Joseph and his two little daughters, five-year-old Josephine and two-year-old Julina, sat together numbly listening to the speakers extol Louie's virtues. Little Julina could not comprehend what had become of her mother, and it was hard for Joseph to try to explain to her. At Joseph's request the speakers for the service were Bishop John Watson of the Ogden Fifth Ward—Louie's former ward, and three apostles, David O. McKay, George Albert Smith and George Albert's father John Henry Smith.

With the funeral past, the cortege wound its way sorrowfully to the city cemetery, where Joseph, his brother David and their father had so recently arranged for a family burial plot. ". . . for dust thou art, and unto dust shalt thou return. . . . The Lord gave, and the Lord hath taken away. Blessed be the name of the Lord."

Chapter 8

"Is it good for man to be alone?"

From Sorrow to Happiness

Hour after hour Joseph sat rocking his baby Julina, through the gloom of the evening and well into the night, before the little two-year-old girl finally cried herself to sleep. Fretfully she slept, suddenly waking up crying out for her mother. "I want my mama!" she sobbed. Sometimes her tears would start five-year-old Josephine to crying also. Day after day and night after night it was the same. Little Julina could not be comforted. To the burden of grief that Joseph already bore in his loneliness for Louie was added the anguish of daily experiencing the sorrow of his little daughters, and being unable to console them in their loss.

Finally, reluctantly, Joseph decided to accept his parents' invitation for him and his children to move into the Beehive House where his mother and sisters could more readily help care for Josephine and Julina. They did not wish to leave their home, for it was here that they had their most vivid memories of their wife and mother. To take his little ones from here would perhaps make things even worse. Yet there seemed to be no good alternative. He could not continue to be both father and mother to them, and with Louie gone their once happy house now seemed as dark and gloomy as a tomb.

Despite the loving attention of his mother and sisters at the Beehive House, the two little girls continued to sorrow; especially Julina. She just could not adjust to the loss of her mother. It rent Joseph's heart to hear her cry. When Louie died he was so heart-broken he thought he would never marry again. But one day his father, after listening to little Julina's cries, said, "Joseph, you have got to find a mother for those little girls!" His father-in-law also urged him to remarry.

Joseph sought guidance through prayer in choosing a girl he should ask to marry him, someone who would be a good mother to his babies, someone who would take a loving interest in them and be able to win their affection. He wanted someone also who, like Louie, shared his love of the gospel. Like his father before him, he found such a girl right in the Church Historian's Office where he worked. She was 18-year-old Ethel Georgina Reynolds,

Daughters of Louie and Joseph Fielding Smith, Josephine and Julina, as they appeared two months after their mother's death in the year 1908.

daughter of George C. Reynolds, a member of the Council of Seventy. Ethel was beautiful, gracious, friendly, and talented. She was a good conversationalist, she played the piano well, she had been ward organist at the age of 11, and she loved the gospel.

On June 16, Louie's birthday, two and a half months after her death, Joseph, with his sister Ina, had taken Josephine and Julina to Ogden and spent the day with Louie's folks. A week later they made a second visit. To be close to her parents seemed to ease the sting just a little. Josephine was allowed to spend the Fourth of July there, and the next day Joseph and baby Julina went up for her, staying overnight before returning to Salt Lake.

Over that Fourth of July weekend Joseph made his decision. He would carefully court Ethel Reynolds. If her response was favorable and if she and his two little girls took well to each other, he would propose to her. If not, then he must look elsewhere. On Monday morning, July 6, not without trepidation, he watched for an opportunity to speak privately to Ethel and asked her if she would go with him and his two little daughters that evening for a ride out to Wandamere, a park on 27th South and Fifth East. Ethel, all smiles, said yes, she would be glad to go with them. Joseph breathed a sigh of relief.

But that evening as he, with Josephine and Julina on the streetcar seat beside him, called at the George Reynolds home he again found his heart pounding like a school boy's on his first date. The vivacious Ethel soon put him at ease and, of more importance, he saw with great satisfaction that within a matter of minutes after they had again boarded the streetcar for Wandamere, Ethel had managed to get Julina to sit on her lap, and had engaged both her and Josephine in happy conversation. The four of them had fun in the park together that evening, eating hot dogs, drinking soda pop, walking along the flower strewn trails, watching the fun seekers go down the chute-the-chutes into the water, and riding on the miniature railway and taking a rowboat ride together on the lake, and watching the big white swan swimming gracefully through the

water. As they rode homeward that evening, Joseph, looking from the radiantly beautiful Ethel to his two sleepy
but happy little girls, knew that he was on the right track.
He hoped Ethel would think so too.

Although he was daily with her in the office, Joseph
waited 10 days before asking Ethel for a date again, and
this time he apparently left the babies at home. In his
journal he notes only, on July 16, "Was at the office all
day. Spent the evening with Miss Ethel G. Reynolds." The
following Sunday, July 19, was his birthday. He would be
32 years old, 14 years older than Ethel.

Joseph had been asked to speak in the Murray Second Ward Sacrament Service Sunday evening. It being his
birthday why should he not have the treat of Ethel's companionship? He asked her to go with him. Yes, certainly,
she would be delighted to go with him. In church, Joseph
spoke to the question, "Have we departed from the doctrines taught by the Prophet Joseph Smith?" It was in answer to a talk given there a short time before by an elder
of the Reorganized Latter Day Saints Church. Sitting in
the congregation Ethel Reynolds found the sermon an interesting one, and felt a growing pride in the fact that this
handsome, fluent man at the pulpit had shown a personal
interest in her. That evening after the meeting as they sat
together in the Reynolds' parlor Ethel presented to
Joseph as a birthday gift a two-volume copy of Ralph
Waldo Emerson's Essays, "which I value very highly," he
noted in his journal.

Through the rest of the summer of 1908 Joseph Fielding Smith was a frequent visitor at the George Reynolds'
house. He and Ethel became well acquainted with each
other's family. Joseph admired George Reynolds' abilities
as a writer. He had produced several volumes of church
literature. But mostly he admired his daughter. The more
he knew her the better he liked her. And the feeling was
mutual. On August 20, "Ethel G. Reynolds went through
the temple for her endowments today, at my request."
Clearly it was a commitment to marriage. Still, it was not
easy to make the emotional adjustment. Deep feelings

President Joseph F. Smith riding in his early-model car near his home in the Beehive House, corner of South Temple and State Street. Members of his family enjoyed the ride.

for Louie sometimes seemed to intrude upon his course of action. Two days after he and Ethel attended the temple together they visited Louie's grave, taking Josephine and Julina with them. It was a solemn moment.

Joseph's father sensed the inner struggle he was having and sought to assure him that his course was the right one. In his journal for August 27 Joseph appreciatively made this entry, "Today my father presented to me a gold watch with his best wishes and good will." To further show his confidence in Joseph he sent him that weekend to Brigham City as a substitute speaker for himself at the Box Elder Stake conference.

Mutual Improvement Association conferences took him on a number of out-of-town trips during the following weeks. But most of the time he was in Salt Lake City and much of the time with Ethel. It was convenient of course to be working in the same offices. Ethel as well as Joseph liked church history, and somehow it was always more interesting to hear his version of historical events. Just now the most interesting of all church history was that which was in the making in the Church Historian's Office, involving a son of the church president and a daughter of a president of the Seventies.

Teasingly Joseph told Ethel he could not marry anyone so young, he would have to wait until she was at least 19 years old. That was a safe tease because her birthday was on October 23. They spent the evening together, and set their wedding date for Monday, November 2.

Come November 2, Ethel looked especially beautiful in her bridal gown. And Joseph was happier than he had supposed he ever could be again in this life. Although Louie's death had been an extremely sorrowful experience for him, Joseph had found that, as the scriptures taught, all things work to the good of those who love and serve the Lord. He had never doubted the correctness or the goodness of plural marriage, for he had seen the love and happiness in his father's family. He knew for a certainty that his father loved each of his wives with a fullness of love, even as a good father or mother loves each child with a fullness of love. But now of his own experience he knew that it was possible for a man to fully love more than one woman, for the love that he felt for Louie was in no sense diminished by the love he felt for Ethel. Nor did his love for Louie diminish his love for Ethel. He came to realize more keenly than he ever had before the wonderful, magical quality of love, that it is not something to be portioned out, something that must be divided up, like a cake, or a handful of money. But rather that it is a divine substance that grows ever greater with the giving, that the more you share it, the more you have.

Years later he would write to Ethel, ". . . O how thankful I am that you were sent to me in the hour of trial and my need! I do feel a little tender just now, as I read your precious, gloriously so, letter and think of your abundant goodness and love and thoughtfulness for me. . . . You do not know how often I have thanked the Lord that I made no mistake when I needed a companion. You were sent to me. You just had to come for I know you belonged to me. . . .

"When I was a youth, I was only 21, I loved a girl and she loved me, and we were married. We were happy all the time and two little girls came to our home, and two babies were never born that were more welcome. I loved them deeply for they are mine. . . . Louie and I were happy. We were blessed with each other's companionship for ten years, and then she was taken away and I was left broken hearted and lonely with my two little girls. In the midst of my sorrow—and it was greater than many may think—I knew it was my duty to find other companionship. I was so instructed by my father and by President Shurtliff and I knew it was right. I prayed about it and desired to be led aright, and a little girl, in years scarcely more than a child, but in understanding a woman, was sent to me. I learned to love her and she came to me a great comfort and blessing. . . . Today she is so much a part of my life (and I have not forgotten the love nor overcome the longing for that other companion) that I could not live without her. O my Father help me to be grateful for her. How my heart fills with joy when I think that she is mine forever. We have been happy and that happiness shall grow and become greater and deeper in the eternity to come, where joy is made complete. Thank the Lord for the gospel, . . . for the knowledge that the family organization shall continue complete forever if we are faithful. Yes we shall dwell together all of us in unity, joy, in that land where all tears shall be wiped away and wickedness and sorrow shall have no place. Yes, there shall be no life for me without you, but life will then have a deeper meaning. . . ."

There in the majestic Salt Lake Temple on that Monday morning of November 2, 1908, Joseph entered into a fullness of celestial marriage. Holding hands with Ethel across the altar, looking into her beautiful face, hearing his father's voice as he performed the sealing ceremony, knowing that Louie with her understanding of the gospel would approve of this moment, Joseph felt that he had never been closer to heaven. "This forenoon, in the Salt Lake Temple at 11:30, Miss Ethel G. Reynolds was sealed to me for time and all eternity, by my father."

Four pictures of Joseph Fielding Smith's second wife, Ethel Georgina Reynolds, mother of nine of his children.

Ethel with small daughter, Naomi, July 1911.

Ethel's sister, Bertha Russell, scheduled a shower for the new Mrs. Joseph Fielding Smith. Mrs. Russell lived on the avenues in Salt Lake. Josephine was now in first grade, and Ethel arranged with Joseph's sister Emily to leave little Julina with her at the Beehive House while she attended the shower. But when Ethel got off the streetcar and stopped at the Beehive House to leave Julina there, the little girl threw her arms around her new mother and clung to her. "I want to stay with you," she cried. Emily, who had been very kind to Julina, tried to persuade her to stay, just while her mother was to a party. But Julina would not be entreated. "It's all right," said Ethel, pleased that the child had grown so fond of her. "Julina will go to the party with me." And she did.

Joseph offered to take his bride on a wedding trip. But she would not hear of it. She wished to begin immediately making a home for Joseph, Josephine and Julina. So it was that on the day of their wedding the big brick house at 165 North Second West was reopened. The lights went on again. Life came back into the house. Its tomb-like silence gave way to the happy laughter of children. What for several months had just been a house was once again a home as the magic of a woman's touch breathed life into it. Gratefully, Joseph knelt in thanks to a loving Father in Heaven.

The Newest Apostle

For an hour or more the Church Presidency and Council of Twelve Apostles, meeting in the Salt Lake Temple in April, 1910, had discussed various men as possibilities to fill the vacancy in the council occasioned by the death of President John R. Winder on March 27, and the subsequent advancement of Apostle John Henry Smith to the presidency. But to every name suggested there was some exception taken. It seemed impossible to reach any unanimity of feeling in the matter. Finally President Joseph F. Smith retired to a room by himself and knelt in prayer for guidance. When he returned he somewhat hesitantly asked the 13 other brethren whether they would be willing to consider his son Joseph Fielding Smith Jr. for the position. He was reluctant to suggest it, he said, because his son Hyrum was already a member of the council and his son David was a counselor in the Presiding Bishopric. Church members, he feared, would be disgruntled to have another of his sons appointed as a general authority. Nevertheless he felt inspired to offer Joseph's name for their consideration. The other men seemed immediately receptive to the suggestion and sustained President Smith in it.

Apparently President Smith confided the choice of Joseph to his mother prior to the conference announcement. Joseph's sister Edith S. Patrick says, "I remember mother telling us that in 1910 father came home from his temple council meeting and seemed very worried. When asked what was troubling him, he said that Joseph had been chosen as one of the Twelve. He said the brethren had unanimously selected him and he said now he, as the president, would be severely criticized, having his son made an apostle. Mother told him not to worry one minute as to what people might say. She knew the Lord had chosen him and said she knew he would be a credit to his calling."

"I never expected to be called into the Council of the Twelve," Joseph Fielding remarked years later, "because my brother Hyrum had been called into that council before . . . and so, having a brother in the council I never expected anything of that kind would come to me." It was the custom at that time *not* to notify the chosen person in advance but rather to let him hear of his appointment when his name was read in conference for a sustaining vote. Thus it was that when Joseph Fielding left for conference on April 6, 1910, he had no knowledge of having been selected. Not even his father, mother or brother had told him.

"As I was going to the tabernacle to attend meeting . . . Ben E. Rich, who was the president of the mission in the Southern States [and whose former sister-in-law, Alice Kimball, was a wife of President Smith] met me as I crossed the street. He put his arm on my shoulders. . . . He said to me as we went to cross the street to the tabernacle, 'Are you going to take your place up on the stand as one of the Council of the Twelve today?' I said, 'Brother Rich, I have a brother in that council. There is no reason for you or anybody to think that I would be called into that council. I am not looking for it or anything of that kind.' "

As he entered the tabernacle a doorkeeper also bantered with him. "Well Joseph, who is the new apostle to be?"

"I don't know," replied Joseph. "But it won't be you and it won't be me!"

As an assistant historian Joseph had a reserved seat on the bottom row on the stand. As he sat taking notes he, like everyone else in the room, except the few who knew, was wondering who the new apostle would be. Heber J. Grant, number two man in the council, was called on by President Smith to read the names of the authorities for a sustaining vote: Joseph F. Smith as president; Anthon H. Lund, first counselor; John Henry Smith, second counselor; Francis M. Lyman, president of the Council of Twelve, and as members, Heber J. Grant, Rudger Clawson, Reed Smoot, Hyrum M. Smith, George Albert Smith, Charles W. Penrose, George F. Richards, Orson F. Whitney, David O. McKay, Anthony W. Ivins, and—. As Elder Grant read down through the list of the apostles, just before he reached the new name, the impression swept across Joseph's mind that the name to be read might be his. Yet when he actually heard his name read, "I was so startled and dumbfounded I could hardly speak."

With dozens of well wishers waiting after conference to shake his hand and congratulate him upon his appointment, Joseph was late getting back to his home. He hoped Ethel and the children had not yet heard the good news, for he wished to be the one to tell them—and tell them in his own way: "I guess we'll have to sell the cow," he said. "I haven't time to take care of it any more!"

Joseph was 33 years old at the time of his call to the Twelve. As President Smith had anticipated, there was some dissatisfaction with his having appointed a second son to the council. To some it seemed a heavy case of nepotism. Yet those who felt disgruntled about it would likely find no fault in more than one son of a king becoming a prince. Predictably Frank J. Cannon and *The Salt Lake Tribune* viewed the appointment with disdain. They had long referred to the Church as the "church of relations" rather than the "church of revelations." In an editorial entitled " THE CHURCH OF THE SMITHS," Cannon and the *Tribune* declared:

Joseph F. is losing no time unnecessarily in his well defined purpose and process of Smithizing the Mormon church. In other words, the present monarch is doing all in his power to make of the entire institution a belonging of the Smith family, as a heritage to them forever.

On Wednesday afternoon, President Joseph F. Smith selected Apostle John Henry Smith as counselor to fill the vacancy created on account of the death of the late John R. Winder. This necessitated the filling of a vacancy in the apostolate, of which John Henry was a member. In order to fill up the quorum Joseph F. kindly loaned the distinguished services of his son, Joseph F. Smith, Jr. So we see that the Smiths are increasing in numbers in the hierarchy, there now being seven of the royal gentry in the governing body. Joseph F., John [the patriarch to the church], John Henry, George A., Hyrum M., Joseph F. Jr., and David A. form the brilliant galaxy of Smiths that now adorns the controlling body. One may turn to the right or to the left, move to the front or back up, and one will bump into an official Smith. Gaze where one may in the hierarchy and the sight takes in a front or rear elevation of a Smith. There isn't a single Mormon pie but there is a Smith finger in it. The saints pay allegiance to Smiths, they contribute money to Smiths, the Smiths spend that money and they are Smiths who tell tithe payers to mind their own business if asked what they do with the funds. It is a system of nepotism seldom witnessed in history— everywhere the omnipresent, robbing, non-accounting, lawbreaking Smiths, until the Mormon people actually begin to look and feel Smithy.

Joseph F. has waited a long time for this day, when he and his would come into what he thinks is his and theirs by taking the Mormon church into the Smith household and ownership.

Years later Heber J. Grant, who by then was president of the Church and who was present in the council meeting in the temple the day Joseph was chosen in 1910, assured a group of the correctness of the decision: It was at a Smith family reunion. President Grant pointed to Joseph Fielding and said, "That man was called by direct revelation of God. I am a witness to that fact."

If indeed "the proof of the pudding is in the eating," perhaps the best evidence of the wisdom of Joseph's appointment to the council lies in his performance as a general authority for nearly three-quarters of a century. The humility with which he accepted the calling, and the prevailing feeling in the Church that he was a good choice, are reflected in his journal entries at this time: "The reading of my own name as an apostle to fill the vacancy caused by the removal of Elder John Henry Smith from the Quorum of the Twelve and his promotion to the First Presidency, came to me, as to the entire assembly, as a most sudden and to me unexpected shock, and left me in complete bewilderment from which I have not in days recovered. I feel extremely weak and pray to my heavenly Father for strength and guidance in my great responsibility that I shall not falter nor fail to perform all that is required of me. Oh, my Father help me, guide me in thy truth and fit and qualify me, for I am weak, that I may indeed be thy servant and have thy Holy Spirit to guide me and direct my feet in the path of wisdom as one of the special witnesses of thy Beloved Son, who died that I might live and be numbered among His chosen people through faithfulness to his gospel and obedience to his laws. Give me strength and courage and buoy me up that I may be worthy to bear thy name and labor in thy Kingdom and in the knowledge and testimony of the truth, for I know the gospel is true and through obedience thereto is salvation through the name of Jesus Christ whose servant I am called to be. . . .

"At the close of the afternoon session of conference and the adjournment for six months, I received the following note from Sister Susa Young Gates, who has always been a true friend to me and for years has hoped and prayed for me that I might some day be an apostle. 'My Beloved Joseph F. Jr. Let me ease the fulness of my joy by telling how grateful I am to God for this beautiful thing. Don't you see now that God is pleased with your earnest, modest labors—and most especially has He not thus indicated His own approval of the grand cause which you have so eloquently espoused? I have felt this coming for some time. I am so happy. Your Aunt Susa.' "

From Apostle-Senator Reed Smoot in Washington, D.C. came the telegram, "God bless you in your apostleship. Be true and loyal to your leader." And Joseph notes, "This I shall try always to do. I have also received a number of letters, telegrams, etc., from friends who rejoice at my great blessing, which feeling I believe to be quite universal although there are those who are not pleased. Elder Ben E. Rich, President of the Eastern States Mission [he had earlier been president of the Southern States Mission] who has always been a friend to me, and one year ago predicted that I should be called to this great responsibility, was one of the first to give me the hand of fellowship and his blessing, faith and constant prayers. May the Lord bless him.

"This morning [April 7] I met in the Temple with the First Presidency and was ordained an apostle, to be an especial witness for the Redeemer of the world, my father being mouth and the following brethren, who were present, assisting, each laying his hands upon my head: Presidents Anthon H. Lund, John Henry Smith of the first presidency who were just previously set apart to their calling, President Francis Marion Lyman, and the following brethren of the Twelve: Heber J. Grant, Rudger Clawson, Hyrum M. Smith, George F. Richards, Orson F. Whitney, David O. McKay and Anthony W. Ivins, and Patriarch John Smith.

"Elders Reed Smoot, George Albert Smith and Charles W. Penrose were absent, the first in Washington, the second in St. George where he is sorely afflicted and Brother Penrose in England, from which mission (Europe) he was this day released to be succeeded by Elder Rudger Clawson.

"President Francis M. Lyman instructed me in the duties of my calling and told me that I had been called by revelation from the Lord. He said he had watched me for a number of years and while on the trip to Vermont [at time of the dedication of the Joseph Smith Memorial Monument in December, 1905], both going and coming and while there, he had watched me and felt at that time in his heart that I should some day be an apostle, which prediction has been made by several others, all of which predictions I received lightly and without thought of their fulfillment."

*April 26, 1910, a few days
after appointment to the Council.*

July 19, 1914, age 38.

July 19, 1918, age 42.

July 19, 1920, age 44.

*Four pictures of Joseph Fielding Smith during younger years as a member of
the Council of the Twelve.*

Three years later, in a second patriarchal blessing, this one from Patriarch Joseph D. Smith at Scipio, Millard County, Joseph Fielding was told, ". . . you were called and ordained before you came in the flesh, as an apostle of the Lord Jesus Christ to represent his work in the earth."

When ordained an apostle Joseph was given the specific charge to preach repentance. This he would do, and his doing so plus his own strict adherence to gospel standards, would prompt some to regard him as a rather cold, unfeeling individual, an authoritarian rather than a humanist. But casual impressions can be completely wrong. From his bed of affliction in St. George, in April, 1910, Apostle George Albert Smith, a third cousin to Joseph and later to become president of the Church, sent his congratulations: ". . . We have always loved you and we admire very much the disposition you manifest to be kind and generous to all." Those who knew Joseph Fielding Smith best through the years found as George Albert Smith that it was indeed his disposition "to be kind and generous to all."

Chapter 10

"And the voice of warning shall be unto all people . . ."

As a Member of the Council of the Twelve

It had been a long hard day of traveling for Joseph Fielding and his senior companion, Francis Marion Lyman, president of the Council of the Twelve. They had started out by train but had then switched to horse and wagon after reaching rail's end as they moved along to their stake assignment in a remote area of southern Utah. A representative of the stake had met them at the railroad depot and was driving them to their destination. The three men sat side by side on the wagon seat. It was a rocky road and the wagon was frequently jolted as the wheels ran over the rocks. Elder Lyman was a giant of a man with a tender bottom, and with each heavy jolt of the wagon he would complain to the driver, admonishing him to use more care. After an hour or so of such rough riding they hit a really large boulder, and the wagon bounced so hard that it nearly threw them from the seat. Lyman turned and glared at the driver. After a moment of silence the driver said, "Well, I hit it, didn't I?" His reply so amused Joseph Fielding that he remembered it 50 years later.

"Let me tell you another story about President Lyman," he offered. "I used to travel quite a bit with him, going to stake conferences. One day we were held by a flood and could not get to our journey's end, so we had to stop along the way. The only hotel—I guess you would want to call it a hotel—that was available was nearly filled; there was only one room left. President Lyman said he would take it. I did not know what was going to become of me. But he took the room and they put a cot in the hall for me. And what do you think he said to me? I guess I should not tell this. He said, 'I never sleep with anyone but my own wife!' So I had a cot put out in the hallway and I slept out there all night."

In Joseph Fielding's early days in the Council of the Twelve, it was rather unusual to stay in a hotel at all, whether in a room or in the hallway. Usually the brethren on their visits stayed with the stake president or some other LDS family in the community where the conference was being held. Through years of visiting they learned which of the brethren had wives who were good cooks, and which were not so good. President Lyman, who had been making the rounds for years, was especially fond of rich, thick cream, and in a certain community had stayed with a family where he was always served plenty of cream —on his mush, on pies, on fruit, on anything he desired to put it on. As he and Joseph Fielding came to this community on a stake visit, he said nothing to Joseph about the cream business, but to Joseph's surprise he said, "You go along and stay with the stake president. I'm going to stay with Brother so and so"—the man whose wife had always served him plenty of cream.

Joseph Fielding was well treated in the stake president's home, even being served cream for breakfast. Later in the morning when he joined President Lyman at the tabernacle Lyman looked very disgruntled. The first thing he asked Joseph was, "Did you get any cream for breakfast?" Joseph assured him he had. "Well then," he said, "after meeting I want you to pack up your things and trade me places, for I didn't get any!"

Once Elder Smith took a newly appointed general authority with him on a stake assignment. They stayed at the home of a stake president in a little farming community. The stake president had a large family. Evidently his wife had briefed their youngsters on table manners prior to the arrival of the visitors, and had placed restrictions on the number of servings they could have of various items. Hot rolls were served, and during the course of the meal the woman asked Brother Smith's companion whether he would care for another roll. "I really shouldn't," said the visitor, "I've had three already." "Three?" exclaimed one little child in surprise. "You've had seven! I counted them."

Elder Smith did not often take his wife with him on stake visits, but occasionally he did. One time they were kindly invited to have breakfast with a family of limited means. They were served oatmeal with cream. There were five small children in the family. The children ate in the kitchen, while the Smiths and their hosts ate in the dining room. After breakfast, as the Smiths were about to leave, Ethel stepped into the kitchen to say goodbye. She noticed that the children had only skim milk for their oatmeal. Ethel realized that the cream had been taken for her and her husband. She had five one dollar bills in her purse, and she placed one under each child's plate.

At President McKay's funeral service in 1970 President Smith recalled, "In the early days of his ministry the brethren used to go out on assignments two by two. Often President McKay and I went together. We would travel as far as we could by train and then the local brethren would meet us with a white top or a wagon. Sometimes we continued on horses or mules or by ox team. Many times we slept out under the stars or in such houses or cabins as were available."

Some hosts were abler than others. "You know, as I said, we used to travel by any conveyance we could get, even in my day, and I have traveled almost every way that you could think of, to get to stake conferences. I don't think that I was ever on the back of a mule. I may have been. But sometimes we would go on horseback to get to our destination. Now, out to one of these distant parts one time we held our meeting. A brother was very anxious that I should go home with him because he lived near to the railroad and I would only have a few miles to go to get a train. So would I please come and go home with him. So I went with him. When I got there I found that the only place that he had where I could sleep was a shanty where he kept his pieces of bacon and other pieces of meat. There was a cot in there and the meat was hanging from the ceiling. They had a large dog, and I spent the night with the dog in this little shanty, and the dog and I had a very comfortable night together. Well, in those days we had all kinds of experiences. . . . Now our brethren are not satisfied unless they can get into an airplane. They are getting so the train is not good enough any more."

As an apostle, Joseph Fielding never had to endure persecution such as his father and other earlier apostles had. Nor was he ever in danger of Indian attacks or other perils of pioneer life such as they had been. The government's persecution of the Mormons was pretty much a thing of the past also, although there continued in the world for many years a heavy prejudice against the Mormons. But as an apostle he did considerable traveling and like any traveler he was sometimes subjected to hazards.

One especially close call he had was on a trip to New Mexico via southern Colorado. This was the same trip in which he had the overnight stay with the dog in the shanty. To Ethel he wrote, "Mama Dear, I am at Salida, Colorado, waiting for the train. I have just sent you a telegram so you will know my plan is changed, not because I will it but of necessity. I have had some new experiences and am glad they are over, or I hope they are. I am going to write them and then take the letter with me and you can read it instead of my telling it. I have time to fill in anyway. I arrived in Denver Thursday without anything of interest happening. That evening I started for Alamosa, where I expected to arrive Friday morning and then continue my journey. Everything went well until we reached LaVeta, when our train stopped between two and three o'clock in the morning, then we remained there. I awoke and realized something was wrong and did not sleep after three a.m. I heard two porters talking and gathered that we would be detained for forty minutes more. This gave me encouragement for I knew I could reach my destination if we got away that soon. However, we remained and I got up at six o'clock and learned that a landslide and wrecked train were ahead of us. I was told we could not get away before noon. I knew that meant we would probably stay there all day or longer. The time for our departure kept changing and it was after ten p.m. when we began to move.

"In the meantime I sent a telegram to President Elmer F. Taylor at Kirtland, New Mexico, that I would not arrive until Saturday night. . . ." Finally after another sleepless night and day of travel Elder Smith reached Kirtland, New Mexico. "It was late before I got to bed, for we held a meeting after my arrival. Sunday I was kept very busy and after the night meeting returned to Farmington [New Mexico] where I was to take the train at 4:20 a.m. on the journey home. I was invited by a Brother _____ to stay at his place until the train was due to leave and accepted the invitation. I perhaps would not have done so had I known the circumstances. He with his wife and four children were living in two small rooms in a shanty. He very kindly gave me a bed in one room where I remained from midnight until 4 a.m., sharing the room with one of the children, the family dog, and his supplies, while he and his wife and the other children occupied the other room. For reasons which I need not explain I was glad to get out and take the train at 4 a.m. I started on the return journey, reached Durango [Colorado], changed trains—these trains are narrow gauge—and got along very well until about 90 miles from Alamosa. I was dreaming of the continued journey to Denver, and then home on schedule time, and a pleasant meeting with you all, when there came a sudden crash and I was thrown almost out of my seat, as were all others. This was followed by another jar and then we stopped. One man said, 'What was that?' I said, 'That means trouble; we are going to stay here for some time.' I went out and discovered that the engine of our train was toppled on its side, the reason being that the rails, ties, and all had slid on the loose mud under them. Fortunately no one was hurt. If the accident had happened about five seconds sooner or about fifteen feet, we all would have been hurled down the mountain side about 200 feet, and seriously hurt if not killed. If it had happened fifty feet farther on, the same thing would have happened. Where the engine fell was the only place where the earth was banked up high enough to catch it and arrest the fall. Fortunately all the cars stayed on the track. . . . I pray there will be no more mishaps. I have gone three nights without sleep. My eyes hurt and my head aches. But I will soon be home. With love, Papa."

To Elder Smith the long, lonely, tedious hours of travel were perhaps the least desirable aspect of being an apostle. Nearly every month for several days he was gone from family and loved ones. Fortunately there were ways to help pass the time, such as preparing notes for the upcoming conference talks, writing letters home, reading, and, for Joseph Fielding, writing poems. Through the years he composed several poems, and four of these were eventually set to music and published as LDS hymns. The four are: "The Best Is Not Too Good For Me," with music by Tracy Y. Cannon; "Come, Come, My Brother, Awake! Awake!" with music by Evan Stephens; "Does the Journey Seem Long?" with music by George D. Pyper, and "We Are Watchmen on the Tower of Zion," with music by Alexander Schreiner.

The Tower of Zion song was sung by the Mormon Tabernacle Choir at the laying of the cornerstone of the Oakland Temple May 25, 1963, with Jessie Evans Smith as soloist. Other hymns of his have also been sung by the choir. The hymn, "The Best Is Not Too Good For Me," was prompted in part at least by the advice his father gave him when as a young man he consulted his father about taking a government job, mentioned earlier. "Remember son," said his father, "the best company is none too good for you." The poem states:

By faith I walk on earth's broad plain,
With hope forever in my breast;

If valiant to the end, I'll gain
A glorious mansion with the blest.

O Father, lead me by the hand,
Protect me from the wicked here,
And give me power that I may stand
Entrenched in truth, to me made clear.

The best is not too good for me
That heaven holds within its hand,
O may I falter not but see
Thy kingdom come o'er all the land

His tender concern for his wife Ethel and his young-sters, and also his devotion to duty, are beautifully reflected in his composition of the poem, "Does the Jour-ney Seem Long?" Ethel was several months pregnant at the time, and perhaps feeling rather tired and discouraged. Joseph Fielding had to leave home once again, this time on a stake assignment to Holbrook, Arizona. Traveling by train via southern California—then the fastest route—he penned a letter to his family during a train stopover at San Bernardino, on April 18, 1924. The poem was included as part of the letter:

"My Beloved Mama and Kiddies: I arrived here this morning one hour late, but still have two hours to wait for the Santa Fe train out of Los Angeles to take me to Hol-brook, where I hope to arrive tomorrow morning about 6:30. I am trying to help the time along as much as possi-ble, but fear I do not succeed any too well. . . . I am pray-ing for you, and hoping you will try to take things as easy as you can, and make yourself as comfortable as possible while I am away, and I assure you I will be back just as soon as I am able to get away. . . . We have so far to go to get here by going through California. If we could fill in the Grand Canyon of Arizona, then we could come here by way of St. George or Kanab, and save time—provided we had trains running that way. But what is the use specu-lating or dreaming? I find myself against the reality and I am here, will have to stay until my duties are done, and then you may be sure I will waste no time in returning. . . .

"Mama, I am thinking of you and wish I could be

with you constantly for the next few weeks, to help take care of you. I will help you all I can as it is, and hope you will be able to *feel* my influence. Tell the children to be kind to you and to each other. I hope they will do all they can to make your burdens light. I hope they will not be cross and out of patience with each other nor quarrel over dishes. If they only *knew* and could realize what it all meant I know they would not do those things. Bless you all. May the Lord be kind to you. I know He will. I was thinking of home and of you and lots of things on the way down, and tried to amuse myself and pass the time along yesterday as I spent the day on the train and wrote what follows, as I was thinking. I mean it so don't make fun of me, will you?

> Does the journey seem long,
> The path rugged and steep?
> Are there briars and thorns on the way?
> Do sharp stones cut your feet
> As you struggle to rise
> To the heights through the heat of the day?
>
> Is your heart faint and sad,
> Your soul weary within,
> As you toil 'neath your burden of care?
> Does the load heavy seem
> You are forced now to lift?
> Is there *no one* your burden to share?
>
> Are you weighed down with grief,
> Is there pain in your breast,
> As you wearily journey along?
> Are you looking behind to the valley below?
> Do you wish you were back in the throng?
>
> Let your heart not be faint,
> Now the journey's begun;
> See! There is *one* who beckons to you.
> Look upward in gladness,
> And take hold of his hand,
> He will lead you to heights that are new.
>
> He will care for you tenderly
> All the day through;
> Will share in your burden and pain.
> He will pray for you fervently,

Pray now for you
And joy you will shortly obtain.

Good bless you, with love, Papa."

A month later after their baby was born—they named him Douglas—Joseph Fielding wrote to Ethel again, not from the distance of a stake trip but from his office in Salt Lake City, further expressing his feelings toward her and the poem he had written: "Mama Dear, I owe you a letter. . . . Since I came home I have been thinking of sending you that delayed letter, even if I am at home. Tonight I will be away, and will miss you greatly and our tiny baby boy. How I hate to go and leave you. The letters you sent me when I was in Arizona were so sweet that they brought tears to my eyes when I read them and I uttered a prayer for you, my Mama dear, and was happy in the thought that you belonged to me. That which I wrote to you in rime, I wrote because I knew how miserable you were feeling at the time in your discomfort and that you were fretting over my absence. I too was feeling very uncomfortable in knowing I would be away so long at a time when you needed me at home, and when I left it was hard to keep back the tears. I do love you, Mama, dear, and want you to be happy. Now your discomfort is over and we have been blessed with one of the sweetest baby boys that any one ever had. And how precious he is to us all.

"When I sent you that letter with the poetry, I told you not to show it, and if you didn't like it to burn it, and you answered me by saying that I had misjudged you in thinking such a thing, and you expressed the hope that I would try to write something again. You don't know how much good it did me to have you answer me in that way. I have written a great deal on doctrinal lines, and my writings have been published from time to time over my name. I have a confession to make to you now. I have written 'poems,' *a few* before, and some of them have been published, but not with *my name attached*, and no one knows it, except the editor of the paper, and I don't know if he even knows that they were mine. Some I have written, while on the train alone, to pass away the time, and they have been only for my own amusement, and afterwards I have destroyed them. I have done this because I have not claimed any ability in that line, and did what I did for my own amusement. . . ."

He told her in the letter that he had been attracted by a poem entitled "Compensation," by Charleton Everett Knox and published in the *Deseret News* a few months prior. The Knox poem had inspired a further poetic effort of his own, and to Ethel he wrote, and included in the letter, a poem he entitled, "I'll Be Waiting for You."

Yes, I'll wait at the end of the lane,
  When the toil of the journey is through,
Though clouds over head fill my heart now with dread,
  I'll be waiting, waiting, for you.

When the day's work has come to an end,
  And the duties and cares are all past,
I'll be watching for you, dear heart kind and true,
  With love that forever shall last.

When the journey of life shall be o'er,
  And the gates of death I shall pass through,
O mine you will be in eternity;
  Dear heart, I'll be waiting for you.

"Josephine calls this 'mush,' maybe it is. But remember I went away feeling rather blue and under the circumstances was in a state of mind to do such a mushy thing. Please forgive me.

"Mama, I want you to be happy and will do all I can to make you so. . . . Take good care of my poor little boys, the tiny one and the runaway. The others can help take care of themselves. I am proud of them, and all my little flock. The Lord bless them and you and me. . . . With love and a prayer, I remain, forever, your companion. Papa."

As a member of the Council of Twelve, Joseph Fielding in common with the other apostles had the standing assignment of helping to direct the missionary activities of the Church. Each month he spent several hours in helping to set apart and instruct newly appointed missionaries. A few times he made tours of some of the missions. And in the opening days of World War II he directed the evacuation of the missionaries from Europe. Unlike some of the authorities, he did not serve as a mission president. Rather he had several specific assignments which required that he maintain his headquarters in Salt Lake City. These assignments, during his years as a member of the Council of Twelve, included: several years as an assistant church historian, followed by 49 years as church historian and recorder; secretary, editor, vice president, and then for 30 years president of the Genealogical Society; a member of the presidency of the Salt Lake Temple, first as assistant or counselor to Anthon H. Lund, later as a counselor to George F. Richards, and from 1945 to 1949, president of the temple. He also filled specific assignments in both the Sunday School and Mutual Improvement Association.

A few months prior to becoming an apostle he had taken another tour to the East, partly to visit libraries with a genealogical department. In a letter to Ethel from Chicago in October, 1909, Joseph expresses amazement at the genealogical holdings of the Newberry Library there, in contrast to the Church's meager holdings: ". . . This afternoon we spent at the Newberry Library in the Genealogical department where we learned some things and one of them was that we are carrying on a very important work; one which is bound to grow and be great, but very *insignificant* just now in its proportions. We could take the [LDS] Genealogical Library together with the whole Historian's Office and lose it in the one floor of the *Newberry* Library that is used for genealogical work, and the librarian told us their library was not nearly as large *as it ought to be.* They have over *236,982* volumes in their library, while we have about *1400.* Don't you think we are rather small? They have *everything* that we have and over 235,000 volumes more. . . . They have an index that covers volume after volume, taking the whole side of the wall of a room perhaps 60 feet long. In it you can find any name in the library from A to Z and back again. I can see one thing, which is, that we have a great deal to do."

It is to Joseph Fielding Smith's credit that the LDS

Church Historian Joseph Fielding Smith with his assistant historians, Andrew Jenson and A. William Lund.

Room 304, used as the Church Historian's Office for 53 years by Joseph Fielding Smith.

Genealogical Library today dwarfs the Newberry Library in holdings, and is in fact the largest genealogical library in the world. The phenomenal growth it has enjoyed in a few decades reflects the enthusiasm and energy of this man who was determined that the Lord's program should be second to none.

In considering church history it is easy to get in the habit of thinking of all Mormon Smiths as being related to the Prophet Joseph or Hyrum Smith. Such of course is not the case. And at least one Smith not of Joseph Fielding's line entered significantly into his life, in 1913: Joseph Fielding, together with Joseph W. McMurrin of the Council of the Seventy, was visiting the Millard Stake conference. The Millard Stake patriarch was another Joseph Smith, this one Joseph D. Smith, a native of England and the first person to be ordained a patriarch in the Manti Temple. Although Joseph Fielding had received a patriarchal blessing at age 19 from his uncle John Smith, he received while visiting Millard Stake a second patriarchal blessing, on May 11, 1913, from this Joseph D. Smith. In his journal he offers no explanation but merely mentions in connection with his conference trip that "while in Scipio I received a blessing from Patriarch Joseph D. Smith." In his old age he did not recall any reason particularly for receiving it, but the wording suggests that perhaps he was seeking further guidance as to what the Lord required of him. And the blessing does enumerate several important aspects of his ministry:

A Patriarchal blessing given by Patriarch Joseph D. Smith of Fillmore, at Scipio, Millard County, Utah, May 11, 1913, upon the head of Joseph Fielding Smith Jr., son of Joseph F. and Julina Lambson Smith, born July 19, 1876, in Salt Lake City.

Brother Smith, in the name of the Lord Jesus Christ and by the power of the priesthood conferred upon me to bless, I seal upon you a patriarchal blessing, as it is the desire of your heart to know what the Lord requires of you. You have been greatly blessed in your birthright, and you were called and ordained before you came in the flesh, as an apostle of the Lord Jesus Christ, to represent his work in the earth. You are of Israel, and are entitled to every blessing that the gospel imparts through obedience to its laws. You have never known the time when you did not believe and feel within your very bones that Joseph Smith was a Prophet of God and that his mission was divine. You have been blessed with ability to comprehend, to analyze, and defend the principles of truth above many of your fellows, and the time will come when the accumulative evidence that you have gathered will stand as a wall of defense against those who are seeking and will seek to destroy the evidence of the divinity of the mission of the Prophet Joseph; and in this defense you will never be confounded, and the light of the Spirit will shed its rays upon your heart as gently as the dews that fall from heaven, and it will unfold to your understanding many truths concerning this work that have not yet been revealed. And you will indeed stand in the midst of this people a prophet and a revelator to them, for the Lord has blessed you and ordained you to this calling, and it will come upon you as naturally as the night shall follow the day. There is a great work for you to do. Your humble spirit, if you continue, will open up to your mind truths that you have never before thought of, and you will hestitate to make them known. There will always be safety in doing this to your father while he lives, and to those who may succeed him, before you present them in public. You will always be in possession of the spirit of revelation regarding your individual affairs and much will be given to you that will be of profit to the Church at large. Your counsels will be considered conservative and wise, for the Lord has anointed you with that oil of gladness above many of your fellows. Your family will grow up and bless your name, and your influence with your sons and daughters, in connection with your wife, will hold your children in the gospel path and not one shall be lost. I bless you with wisdom to use the knowledge that God will give you in the furtherance of his work in the earth, and in the preserving of your body until you have completed all you have been sent to do.

I seal these blessings upon you with all of your former blessings, in the name of Jesus Christ, Amen.

That Joseph Fielding highly regarded this second patriarchal blessing is evidenced by the fact that in the back of his journal for the year 1937—24 years later— he copied that portion of it which appears from the 11th to the 20th line as it is reprinted above. For years, including through the 1937 period, he felt somewhat embattled in trying to keep the Church from drifting away from fundamental doctrine. This blessing no doubt was a comfort to him in that effort.

President Anthon H. Lund, counselor to President

Joseph F. Smith, continued to show a special interest in Joseph Fielding. In addition to being a member of the church presidency Elder Lund was also church historian and recorder and president of the Salt Lake Temple. After his call to the Council of the Twelve Joseph Fielding continued serving as an assistant historian and in 1919 was called to be first assistant to President Lund in the Salt Lake Temple. In February 1916, Joseph Fielding and Patriarch Hyrum G. Smith had been set apart by the church presidency "to officiate in the Salt Lake Temple and other temples, in all ordinance work." He comments, "We will commence our labors as soon as possible and devote our spare time to that labor according to our appointment." In the days following he spent considerable time in the Salt Lake Temple. In October, 1934, he did the temple ordinance work for Oliver Cowdery, who is a sixth cousin to him, and he was instrumental in having the ordinances performed for Oliver's family and ancestors.

Despite his earlier unsatisfactory relationships with Joseph Smith, son of the Prophet, and Frederick Smith, son and counselor to his father in the Reorganized Church presidency, Joseph Fielding did not lose interest in them. In 1914, from November 19 to December 9, he had the pleasure of taking a missionary tour with his father and mother, his sister Emily, George Albert Smith, President and Mrs. Charles W. Penrose and Bishop and Mrs. Charles W. Nibley, through the southern and western states. Their first major stop was in Independence, Missouri, for the dedication of an LDS chapel there. While at Independence they had an opportunity to visit once again with the Prophet's son and some of his family. "We found him very feeble, blind and deaf, and apparently a disappointed man, whose life indeed has been a failure," he noted in his journal. And to his wife Ethel he wrote:

"Between meetings yesterday all the members of our party excepting President Penrose and wife called on Joseph Smith, my father's cousin, and his family, and were received very cordially, especially George Albert. You know he [the Prophet's son] remembers some things that I have done, and my father too has been quite emphatic in defense of the truth and outspoken at times, which has not pleased the Reorganites. However we were very kindly received by him and more especially so by his wife, who is a very fine appearing woman of strong character who impressed me very well. She has three sons—little fellows—who look far more promising than do the older boys in my judgment. I have some hopes for them in the future. Joseph Smith of the Reorganized Church is very feeble, quite deaf and also blind. It was really a sad sight to look at him as he now appears and to reflect upon his condition and to realize that his life has been more than wasted, for he has been found all his days since 1860 fighting the truth which his father so faithfully labored to establish in the earth. I am convinced that he feels himself in his declining years that his life has been wasted. If he were young and could start over again with the knowledge he now has, I am sure he would never take the course that has led him [to] where he is today.

"Fred[erick], his oldest son, is in Massachusetts going to school trying to obtain a degree in sociology that he may be prepared, so he has said, to assist his people in colonizing—a thing that our people have been doing since the exodus more successfully than anyone else, without college degrees. It is the practical work and the help of the Spirit of the Lord that reaches results—and we have reached them. George Albert said Fred had taken the wrong course; he ought to have joined us and learned colonizing in the right way. We are told here that Fred has not taken a very active part in church work for some time, and many of his people have complained of his activity in other directions and inactivity in the church. I would have been pleased to have [again] met his wife, for she is a very excellent woman—far superior to Fred. I have met them both and know them pretty well. I believe we could convert her if it were not for her husband.

"Well, I hope some day to see some of the Prophet's family in the Church and it is quite possible, for the younger boys look more promising to me. Brother [Samuel

O.] Bennion [mission president there] says he expects to convert their mother when their father's influence is no longer felt. I hope he is right. I think the Spirit of the Lord will prevail with some of them at some time in the future, but just when and how, I do not know. I gave Israel, the second son, an invitation to come out and see us whenever he felt so inclined. He emphatically informed me that he held no position in their church and was in nowise connected with or engaged in the ministry. We invited him to our meeting and had him sit on the stand, which I think embarrassed him somewhat, but did him no harm. . . ."

Although not participating in politics as such Elder Smith continued his interest in political and civic affairs. Like his father, he favored the Republican party, was a conservative, and was a champion of the prohibition efforts made in Utah from time to time. Frequently he was disappointed in the outcome of elections, especially local ones in Salt Lake City. A revealing and typical comment was prompted by the elections in November, 1915: "Election day. W. Mont Ferry was elected mayor of Salt Lake City, by the help of many 'Mormon' votes. He has been in the past a hateful anti-Mormon, anti-Prohibitionist and unworthy individual. He has shown bitterness for the Mormon people, and in my judgment the Latter-day Saints show a wonderful lack of good sense in elections." And a year later: "Election day. I voted the Republican ticket which was overwhelmingly defeated in Utah and which lost in the nation." That is the year Woodrow Wilson was reelected president.

His other Church assignments did not leave Joseph Fielding much time to participate in its business affairs. But in January, 1916, he was elected a director in the church-owned Zion's Savings Bank and Trust Company, and continued to hold the position through the years, and in time became its longest serving board member. He also became a director of its Beneficial Life Insurance Company.

Joseph Fielding played his first game of golf in 1916. Through the years he had assisted his father with correspondence and other matters, and the older his father became the more he looked to Joseph Fielding for such assistance. President Smith and Joseph Fielding's mother Julina had observed their golden wedding anniversary on May 5, 1916. But the previous year President Smith's wife Sarah Ellen Richards, and also a daughter Zina, had died. The sorrow of their deaths and the infirmities of old age had taken their toll and his health was not good. Joseph Fielding had planned to leave on a stake visit to Canada in August, 1916, but his father requested him to cancel the trip and stay near him. Later in the month his father and mother decided to spend a few days in southern California, hoping it would be helpful to his health. A week later Joseph Fielding received word that his father wanted him to join them at Santa Monica and also bring his father's wife Edna. For a week he assisted his father with correspondence and in between times played golf with him and with his brother Wesley. "I spent the forenoon with my father writing letters," he noted on August 26, "after which he, Wesley and I went out and played golf. The first time I ever saw the game. My father seemed to enjoy it and is playing for the exercise he gets in the open air."

His father in his late 70's continued in poor health, and Joseph Fielding spent an ever greater amount of time helping him. Francis M. Lyman, president of the Council of the Twelve, also fell into poor health and died in November, 1916. He was succeeded as council president by Heber J. Grant, a cousin of Joseph F. Smith. Stephen L Richards was appointed to fill the vacancy in the quorum. He was a grandson of Willard Richards and thus a nephew of President Joseph F. Smith, whose deceased wife Sarah Ellen was a daughter of Willard Richards.

The year 1918 was one of the most difficult in the life of Joseph Fielding Smith, for in that year both his beloved father President Joseph F. Smith and his oldest brother Apostle Hyrum Mack Smith died, one at age 80 and the other at 45. Hyrum's wife also died, and so did Joseph Fielding's brother-in-law Alonzo P. Kesler, Donette's husband. That was the year of the terrible flu epidemic, which swept over much of the world, killing millions, including thousands in Utah. But the flu was not the cause of death of any of these four relatives of Joseph Fielding. Hyrum died on January 23 of complications from a ruptured appendix, including peritonitis. An appendectomy was performed and it appeared for a time that he was recovering, but within three days he died. Joseph Fielding, who at his father's request had gone with George Albert Smith and administered to Hyrum a few hours earlier, commented, "I thought he would surely recover, for I have felt that he had a mission to perform and surely would be spared. . . . We did all that we could for him and tried to exercise faith, but it appeared that all that we and all Israel could do in faith and prayers could not avail. . . . The whole family is cast under a cloud of sorrow and gloom, and yet, with it all, our hearts are filled with joy because of the faithful, honorable, and worthy life of our brother. My father, himself stricken in years, bears up wonderfully under the sorrow, for that blow which comes to him is a severe one indeed." Hyrum's widow gave birth to a son September 17, and died seven days later, leaving five children orphans. Kesler died of accident injuries.

The death of his oldest son had a telling effect on President Smith. His health continued to decline. "When the sad news was revealed to President Smith he was heart-broken," reports Joseph Fielding. "In the midst of his fears, he had prayed and pleaded with the Lord, but his soul was filled with foreboding anxiety. In his grief he cried, 'My soul is rent asunder. My heart is broken, and flutters for life! O my sweet son, my joy, my hope! O I love him still. I will love him for ever more! . . .'"

Joseph Fielding spent many days with his father during that final year of his life, taking dictation, tending to numerous chores for him, and taking him out for rides in the car. During the last six months of his life, much of the time confined to his room because of illness, President Smith "dwelt in the presence of the Spirit of the Lord," as Joseph Fielding states it in his biography. "I have not lived alone these five months," he declared at the October general conference six weeks before his death. "I have dwelt in the spirit of prayer, of supplication, of faith, and of determination; and I have had my communications with the Spirit of the Lord continuously."

The most remarkable of the manifestations he enjoyed is known as "The Vision of the Redemption of the Dead." This vision he received on October 3, 1918, the day before general conference convened. Two weeks later Joseph Fielding wrote the vision as his father dictated it to him, and another two weeks later read it to his father's two counselors and the Council of the Twelve for their acceptance. It received their unanimous endorsement, and was subsequently published in *The Improvement Era.*

President Smith related that he had been "pondering over the scriptures and reflecting upon the great atoning sacrifice that was made by the Son of God for the redemption of the world, and the great and wonderful love made manifest by the Father and the Son in the coming of the Redeemer into the world, that through his atonement and by obedience to the principles of the gospel mankind might be saved." He read the third and fourth chapters of the first epistle of Peter, touching upon the redemption by Christ and his preaching "unto the spirits in prison." He reported that as he "pondered over these things which are written, the eyes of my understanding were opened, and the Spirit of the Lord rested upon me, and I saw the hosts of the dead, both small and great. And there were gathered together in one place an innumerable company of the spirits of the just, who had been faithful in the testimony of Jesus while they lived in mortality, and who had offered sacrifice in the similitude of the great sacrifice of the Son of God, and had suffered tribulation in their Redeemer's name. . . .

"Among the great and mighty ones who were assembled in this vast congregation of the righteous were Father Adam, the Ancient of Days and father of all, and our glorious Mother Eve, with many of her faithful daughters who had lived through the ages and worshipped the true and living God. Abel, the first martyr, was there, and his brother Seth, one of the mighty ones, who was in the express image of his father Adam. Noah, who gave warning of the flood; Shem [whom the Prophet Joseph identified as Melchizedek], the great High Priest; Abraham, the father of the faithful; Isaac, Jacob, and Moses, the great law-giver of Israel; Isaiah, who declared by prophecy that the Redeemer was anointed to bind up the broken hearted, to proclaim liberty to the captives, and the opening of the prison to them that were bound, were also there."

Other individuals he saw in the vision included Ezekiel, Daniel, Elias, Malachi, several of the Nephite prophets, "the Prophet Joseph Smith, and my father, Hyrum Smith, Brigham Young, John Taylor, Wilford Woodruff, and other choice spirits who were reserved to come forth in the fullness of times to take part in laying the foundations of the great latter-day work, including the building of the temples and the performance of ordinances therein for the redemption of the dead. . . . I observed that they were also among the noble and great ones who were chosen in the beginning to be rulers in the Church of God. Even before they were born, they, with many others, received their first lessons in the world of spirits, and were prepared to come forth in the due time of the Lord to labor in his vineyard for the salvation of the souls of men."

In vision President Smith saw the Savior appear to the righteous spirits who had been awaiting the resurrection, and he saw the great joy that prevailed there. "But his ministry among those who were dead was limited to the brief time intervening between the crucifixion and his resurrection; and I wondered at the words of Peter wherein he said that the Son of God preached unto the spirits in prison. . . . And as I wondered, my eyes were opened, and my understanding quickened, and I perceived that the Lord went not in person among the wicked and the disobedient who had rejected the truth, to teach them; but behold, from among the righteous he organized his forces and appointed messengers, clothed with power and authority, and commissioned them to go forth and carry the light of the gospel to them that were in darkness, even to all the spirits of men. And thus was the gospel preached to the dead. . . . And so it was made known among the dead, both small and great, the unrighteous as well as the faithful, that redemption had been wrought through the sacrifice of the Son of God upon the cross. Thus was it made known that our Redeemer spent his time during his sojourn in the world of spirits, instructing and preparing the faithful spirits of the prophets who had testified of him in the flesh, that they might carry the message of redemption unto all the dead unto whom he could not go personally because of their rebellion and transgression, that they through the ministration of his servants might also hear his words."

Here then was a major revelation to Latter-day Saints, an important addition to the body of church literature, received by Joseph Fielding Smith Sr., sixth president of the Church and nephew of Joseph Smith Jr., first president of the Church, and dictated to and recorded by Joseph Fielding Smith Jr., then one of the apostles and prophets and later tenth president of the Church.

By early November President Smith was critically ill. On November 10, a Sunday, "My father's children gathered today at the Beehive House where we held meeting and administered the sacrament. A number of the boys spoke and our father also said a few words to us while he sat propped up in bed. Today is the 17th anniversary of the day when he was chosen and sustained by the people as president of the Church."

Next morning, notes Joseph Fielding, "We were awakened about one a.m. by the blowing of whistles which we understood to mean the unconditional surrender of Germany to the Allied Nations. The reports in the paper state that the terms were signed early this morning in France. The German Kaiser, who was forced to abdicate, has fled into Holland. Anarchy reigns in many cities in Germany. My father prophecied many months ago that peace would come to the nations after those who were responsible for the war were humiliated in the dust. All day long our city has been in an uproar and the streets filled with rejoicing people who have been wild with joy." Thus ended World War I.

Two days later, on November 13, "My father reached his 80th birthday." Four days later, November 17, "The counselors in the Presidency, the Council of the Twelve, and the Patriarch met in the Temple at noon and prayed for President Joseph F. Smith who has gradually been failing since the general conference. Today he is suffering extremely from plurisy and is very weak."

On Monday, November 18: "My father is in a critical condition. With others of the family I was at his bedside a good part of the day. All night long David A., Alvin and I together with my mother, Aunt Edna and Aunt Mary watched at his bedside. He suffered considerable pain and begged Presidents Grant and Lund who called in the evening to pray that he might be released. He rested easier towards morning but grew weaker and about 10 minutes before five peacefully passed away. All Israel and many not of our faith mourn this day, Tuesday, November 19th."

Joseph Fielding further noted in his journal that "Several times during the past two weeks he has called me to his bedside or to his room where he was sitting, and has given me instructions pertaining to his personal affairs. . . . He gave me his power of attorney several days ago and by that power I was able to transact some of his business. . . ." Joseph Fielding and several other sons were appointed executors of his estate.

President Smith's counselors and the Council of the Twelve spent their weekly meeting on Thursday, November 21, "in testimony and eulogy." "No [indoor] public funeral could be held as the city and state were under quarantine because of an epidemic of influenza which was sweeping over all the earth," recorded Joseph Fielding in a biography of his father. "All public assemblies, theatres and entertainments including the holding of meetings and funeral services in buildings, had been suspended by order of the law. As the solemn cortege quietly passed from the Beehive House to the city cemetery, [on Friday, November 22] thousands of people thronged the streets with bowed heads. Many of these had in the past expressed bitterness and enmity towards President Smith, but now they stood and mourned. As the remains passed the Cathedral of the Madeleine, the bells in the tower tolled solemnly and the Catholic priests paid silent respect to the distinguished dead. . . ." Speakers at the graveside services were Bishop Charles W. Nibley, President Heber J. Grant and President Anthon H. Lund, who conducted the services. President Charles W. Penrose offered the dedicatory prayer and benediction.

On Saturday, November 23, the day following the funeral service, "The apostles met in the temple at 9 a.m. and there completed a reorganization of the presidency, with Heber J. Grant as president of the Church and trustee for the body of religious worshippers known as The Church of Jesus Christ of Latter-day Saints, with Anthon H. Lund and Charles W. Penrose as counselors. Anthon H. Lund was also set apart as president of the Council of the Twelve with Rudger Clawson as the acting president," noted Joseph Fielding in his journal. The following week the presidency and Council of the Twelve reorganized the Sunday School and Mutual Improvement Association. "David O. McKay was chosen as superintendent of the Sunday Schools and he chose Stephen L Richards and George D. Pyper as his assistants. Anthony W. Ivins was chosen as superintendent of the MIA and he selected B. H. Roberts and Richard R. Lyman as his assistants. President Anthon H. Lund was chosen and sustained as president of the Salt Lake Temple, and Junius F. Wells was appointed to labor in the Historian's Office." The two men selected to head the two auxiliaries, McKay and Ivins, were later chosen by President Grant to be counselors in the presidency.

Melvin J. Ballard was selected in January, 1919, to fill the vacancy in the Council of the Twelve occasioned by the death of President Smith and the advancement of

Heber J. Grant to the presidency. It was next day that Anthon H. Lund, first counselor to President Grant and also president of the Salt Lake Temple, announced the selection of Joseph Fielding as his first assistant in the temple presidency, and Albert J. Davis, Joseph's cousin, as his second assistant.

When President Lund died two years later, 1921, his jobs were divided. Charles W. Penrose succeeded him as first counselor in the church presidency, with Anthony W. Ivins becoming second counselor in Penrose's place; Apostle George F. Richards succeeded him as temple president—and retained Joseph Fielding as a counselor until 1935, and Joseph Fielding succeeded him as church historian and recorder. Time-wise this latter was his number one job for the next half century. The Historian's Office employs quite a number of people, and Joseph Fielding soon acquired a reputation among them as a very considerate and understanding boss, one who expected the best effort from each employee, but was not demanding. He would remind them that they were working for the Lord, not for him, and that their best effort was none too good for the Lord's work. He also had the reputation of being an extremely hard worker himself, working long hours and seldom taking any vacation time. He bought a manual on typewriting and learned how to type well. He called his the scriptural system: "Seek and ye shall find." Through the years he typed many of his own letters and manuscripts. As an assistant historian he chose A. William Lund, a son of President Anthon H. Lund to whom he had so long served as an assistant. Shortly before his death in 1971 A. William Lund, after a lifetime of working closely with him, commented to the authors, "President Joseph Fielding Smith is the finest man I've ever known."

Another longtime associate, Rubie McKinlay Egbert, his secretary, insists that she never heard him say an unkind word to or about anyone. She like his other associates found he always showed concern about their personal welfare and happiness. "He has wanted the employees to be happy," commented another of his assistants, Edyth

Romney. "He did not watch or question to see if we were doing our work as it should be done. . . . His trust in us has inspired us to want to do well."

Joseph Fielding Smith in a familiar pose answering questions on his typewriter.

Rubie Egbert, for 52 years secretary to Joseph Fielding Smith.

Mrs. Romney also noted that "If a person received a misunderstanding or was unhappy following an interview with President Smith, and he knew about it, he recalled his visitor and gave him another opportunity to explain his condition, and sometimes the person emerged from the president's office with a smile replacing tears." She tells of a young returned missionary coming to the Historian's Office one day looking for work. President Smith told him there were no openings available, and the young man turned away disappointed and discouraged. "When President Smith was informed by his secretary that the missionary was not physically able to compete in positions in industry because of an injury, President Smith said to call him back, and he was given a chance to work."

It was a comfort to Joseph Fielding to have his mother Julina continue living for 17 years following the death of his father. She was a frequent visitor in his home, and he in hers. Unfortunately she suffered a bad fall late in 1935, and died on January 10, 1936, at the age of 86. "She never recovered from a fall in which she fractured two ribs a few weeks ago," noted Joseph in his journal. At the funeral service two days later President Heber J. Grant and Elder Reed Smoot of the Council of Twelve were the speakers.

It was upon the recommendation of Elder James E. Talmage that Joseph Fielding was invited into membership in the prestigious Victoria Institute or Philosophical Society of Great Britain, an association of outstanding scholars of the world. Membership in the society is made by election and the number of members who reside in the United States is small. And as a member of the Council of the Twelve Joseph Fielding also served as a member of the board of trustees of Brigham Young University since 1912, and of the Church Board of Education since 1917. In more recent years he served as chairman of the executive committee of the BYU board and was instrumental in the growth and development of that school to one of the best in the world.

Along with his multiplicity of church duties and home responsibilities, Elder Smith somehow found time to continue his writing and compiling of books and articles. His assignment as church historian of course was conducive to these efforts, including his book, *Essentials in Church History*, first published in 1922 and revised and published in later editions through the years; his compilation of the *Teachings of the Prophet Joseph Smith*, first published in 1938, and a biography of his father, *Life of Joseph F. Smith*, published also in 1938, on the occasion of the centennial of his father's birth. It will be recalled that before he became a member of the Council of the Twelve he had authored several booklets on history and doctrine, at least one of which, his *Blood Atonement and the Origin of Plural Marriage*, is still being republished. Two of his earliest books on doctrine are *The Way to Perfection* published in 1931, and *The Progress of Man* published in 1936. His later books have been largely a compilation of his sermons, magazine articles, and personal correspondence. They are as follows: *Principles of the Restored Gospel*, 1942; *The Signs of the Times*, also in 1942; *The Restoration of All Things*, 1944; *Church History and Modern Revelation*, in two volumes, 1953; *Man, His Origin and Destiny*, 1954; *Doctrines of Salvation*, in three volumes, 1954-56; *Answers to Gospel Questions*, in five volumes, 1954-66; *Elijah the Prophet and His Mission* and *Salvation Universal*, 1957; *Take Heed to Yourselves!*, 1966, and *Seek Ye Earnestly*, 1970. The three volumes of *Doctrines of Salvation* were compiled and edited by his son-in-law, Bruce R. McConkie. The five volumes of *Answers to Gospel Questions, Take Heed to Yourselves!*, and *Seek Ye Earnestly* were compiled and edited by his son, Joseph Fielding Smith, Jr.

Perhaps no other person ever had greater opportunity for service in the Church than did Joseph Fielding Smith. As a missionary, teacher, Sunday School superintendent, high councilman, general board member, historian, recorder, temple president, genealogy president, university board chairman, business director, trustee-in-trust, prophet, seer and revelator, and president of the Church, he performed countless important functions. Yet, it seems very likely that his greatest and most lasting influence in the Church is as an author. Sermons, stake conference visits, ordinations, instructions, recordings, appointments, executive decisions and all the other activities involved in the various offices he held are essential to the functioning and progress of the Church, of course. But there is something permanent, lasting and influential about the printed word that transcends the influence of any of these other activities. President Smith obviously recognized this when at an advanced age he was asked what his advice to young people would be and his reply was, if they have any talent for it, that they write.

No matter what else he was engaged in, whether clerking in the Historian's Office, serving as an apostle or what, he always watched for opportunity to write, to get facts and ideas down in print. "In the beginning was the Word." In a letter to his missionary son Lewis in 1938 he observed that while he used to get his exercise in playing handball, swimming and other sports, he now got his exercise typing manuscripts for books and manuals. Such is the lot of the writer.

Let a person hear a sermon or lecture or lesson, and no matter how good it is or how impressed he may be with it at the moment, a day or two later he is hard pressed to remember even what the subject of it was. Not so with words in print, and particularly a book. A book is there today, tomorrow and forever. It can be kept, handled, read, referred to as often as a person has need. It is lasting. If it is of value to begin with, then it is of lasting value, an influence for good through the years. Jobs, positions come and go, no matter how well or poorly filled, and who occupied them yesterday is forgotten by tomorrow. But the book, the Word, continues on. Although Joseph Fielding is no longer upon the earth, yet his name, his influence, appears on bookshelves in homes throughout the Church, teaching truth, exhorting to right.

Joseph Fielding Smith was a controversial author, in that he hewed right to the line of gospel principles as he understood them. He refused to compromise, refused to popularize, refused to accommodate deviant views. Some readers found such an approach objectionable. Others took a particular delight in it. "I have just finished the wonderful book, *The Way to Perfection*," wrote an attorney to him in 1932. "I can assure you Brother Smith, speaking from 52 years experience in preaching the gospel at home and abroad, that I have never received so much information as I have from your book. . . ." Charles A. Callis, a fellow member of the Council of the Twelve, wrote to him from the mission field, "You have a well informed mind and I read everything you write, that comes into my hands, with deep satisfaction and spiritual profit. When you preach and write you cause people to think." Dr. John A.

Widtsoe, a fellow apostle serving in the mission field, declared, "You have done an exceedingly fine piece of work in *The Way to Perfection.*" In response to another letter of commendation of his *Way to Perfection,* this one by Samuel O. Bennion, a mission head and later a general authority, Joseph Fielding gives a candid view of his feelings on how Church doctrine should be taught: "In this day of 'vain philosophy' and bowing down to, and the worshipping of, science, so-called," he wrote in 1931, "there are many members of the Church who are hungry for the gospel and apparently do not find it. It has become unpopular to preach the unadulterated gospel in the stakes of Zion. We have so many men who are *educated* and they can see nothing only through the eyes of the teaching of the world. [They seem to think] Simple faith and belief in the gospel must be interpreted in the terms which philosophy teaches. It is in the mission fields where the truth is taught. Seldom does a speaker here at home refer to principles of the gospel, or the teachings of our Lord, or one of the prophets ancient or modern, but they can tell you what such men as Dr. Fosdick, or Dr. Cadman, or Mr. VanDyke has to say or what this professor or that has said, but the people are hungering for the *truth.* And how to correct this condition I do not know. I am doing what I can, but under some handicap. Recently a very learned discourse was published setting forth the theories of men and trying to harmonize the gospel truth with these theories, and such things we have to contend against. . . ."

That Joseph Fielding continued to feel such concern is evidenced from his sermons and writings, including a journal entry of December 28, 1938, the year he published *Teachings of the Prophet Joseph Smith* and the *Life of Joseph F. Smith.* Now, 100 years after his father's birth and 20 years after his death, he observed in his journal, "I attended sessions of meetings for the institute teachers, held in the assembly room on the fourth floor of the Church Office Building. I cannot say that I was very greatly edified. Too much philosophy of a wordly nature does not seem to mix well with the fundamentals of the gospel. In my opinion many of our teachers employed in the church school system have absorbed too much of the paganism of the world, and have accepted too readily the views of uninspired educators without regard for the revealed word of the Lord. What to do about it I do not know. It is a problem for the Presidency to consider. It is a very apparent fact that we have traveled far and wide in the past 20 years [since his father's death]. What the future will bring I do not know. But if we drift as far afield from fundamental things in the next 20 years, what will be left of the foundation laid by the Prophet Joseph Smith? It is easy for one who observes to see how the apostasy came about in the Primitive Church of Jesus Christ. Are we not traveling the same road? The more I see of educated men—I mean those who are trained in the doctrines and philosophies now taught in the world, the less regard I have for them. Modern theories which are so popular today just do not harmonize with the gospel as revealed to the prophets, and it would be amusing if it were not a tragedy to see how some of our educated brethren attempt to harmonize the theories of men with the revealed word of the Lord. Thank the Lord, there is still some faith left and some members who still cherish the word of the Lord and accept the prophets. Surely the world is ripening rapidly for the destruction, and Satan has power and dominion over his own. If any are saved surely the Lord must soon come and have power over his Saints and reign in their midst, and execute 'judgment upon Idumea, or the world.'"

Among the general authorities as well as throughout the Church generally Joseph Fielding achieved a reputation as an outstanding authority on church doctrine and history. From President Heber J. Grant he once received a letter acknowledging his supremacy in this important area. Just two days following the institute teachers' meetings which displeased him, he received a visit from President Grant: "President Heber J. Grant, his wife Augusta, my brother Willard and his wife Florence called at our home this evening," he noted in his journal of December 30, "and paid us a short and pleasant visit. At the request of President Grant, Jessie and I sang a duet for them, which seemed to please them even if my part was not very good. Jessie also sang a solo which was good. We appreciated very much their visit." Then the next day, an errand took him to the President's office. "While I was in the President's office I was handed a letter by President Grant and had some conversation with him concerning myself. He manifested a very friendly spirit. When I opened the letter and read it I was deeply touched."

Written on December 31, 1938, the letter also expresses President Grant's concern over Joseph Fielding's working so hard all the time. In part the letter reads, "My dear Joseph: I was delighted last night to listen to you and your good wife sing. I am thankful to think that you are going to take a little bit of time to sing and to visit with your loved ones, instead of working, working, working. I am sure that the singing will prolong your life.

"I don't want to flatter you, Joseph, but I want you to know that I consider you the best posted man on the scriptures of the General Authorities of the Church that we have. I want you to prolong your life, I want you to make a business of trying to take care of yourself. . . . Your father worked altogether too hard. . . . He took a greater interest in the welfare of other people than almost any man who ever lived. He was my ideal of all the brethren from my childhood up to the day of his death. . . . May you be enabled to work less and accomplish more, is the prayer of my heart." There is no evidence that Joseph Fielding worked less, but certainly he accomplished more. And his life was indeed prolonged, for another 33 years and more, enabling him to one day become president of the Council of the Twelve and then president of the Church.

On Rearing a Family

It was a warm summer day, and particularly pleasant in the mountains. Joseph Fielding, Ethel, and several of their youngsters were pleasure climbing at Brighton, with a picnic lunch in hand. The blue sky overhead, with fluffy white clouds here and there, a gentle breeze whispering through the pine trees, the fragrant scent and colorful sight of wild flowers on grass-covered slopes, the birds singing, and the fresh invigorating mountain air all combined to make it a delightful experience.

"We climbed Sunset Peak which looked into the Salt Lake Valley below," recalled Julina many years later. "I will never forget this tremendous sight, with the lake like a silver ribbon far to the west. While there Father told us the story of the coming of the pioneers down Emigration Canyon, the mouth of which we could see from this point high above the valley. He pointed out the mouths of several canyons which we could see. As he told the story of the pioneers, I could actually see the horse carrying the two men as they scouted the valley in advance of the rest of the people. I remember that they were told by Brigham Young to bear to the north, which they forgot and headed south since some reeds in the Sandy-Draper area looked inviting. In the process one of the men lost his coat which was a terrible thing in those days."

Despite his extremely busy life and travel schedule as

an apostle, Joseph Fielding never forgot his father's admonition, which he in turn gave to others, that the most important responsibility in the gospel was responsible parenthood. To this day his children remember with delight the precious hours that they spent with their father, including stories of his travels that he told them at the breakfast or dinner table, picnics in the nearby canyons, trips to Saltair with a homemade lunch and a freezer of ice cream—Ethel made the most delicious ice cream, and it was a weekly treat through the heat of the summer. There were nights under the stars when he would teach them of astronomy, tieing it into the gospel and the glory of God and his infinite creative powers.

Stories of church history were favorites with the children. "I remember the day, evening that is, after supper dishes on a certain June 21," recalls Julina, "when I was about 12 years old, when he sat out on the back steps of that great big porch that went across the back of the house on Second West, and told me why it was necessary for the Prophet and Hyrum to give their lives, to seal their testimonies with their blood. It had seemed such a waste that two such men had been killed so needlessly." Good teacher that he was, Joseph Fielding had utilized the anniversary month of the martyrdom to tell the children of the Prophet's and Patriarch's death.

As a wife, mother and companion, Ethel Reynolds proved all that Joseph Fielding had hoped for, and more. Louie's two daughters, Josephine and Julina, adored her, as she did them. Ethel became pregnant shortly after marriage, and her first child, a daughter, was born the following summer, on August 9, 1909. They named her Emily, after Joseph's first wife, Louie Emily "Emyla" Smith, and also after his sister Emily. Joseph of course had hoped that his and Ethel's first child might be a boy. As the years went by he almost despaired of ever having a son. Fifteen months after Emily's birth another daughter was born, on November 16, 1910, and they named her Naomi. Fortunately Ethel's pregnancies were free from the complications that Louie had suffered. A third daughter was born

215

to her 16 months after Naomi's birth, this one on March 26, 1912, and they named her Lois, perhaps because of its similarity to Louie. The five little girls were dearly loved. Joseph Fielding had a pet name for each of them. Josephine he called "Dodo," the same nickname his father had given to Joseph's oldest sister, who had died when only three years old. Julina was called "Ninie." Emily was "Emilykins." Naomi was "Monie." And baby Lois with a loving father and mother and four older sisters to spoil her did not really need a name at all.

But Ethel knew that Joseph despite his love for the girls greatly desired to have a son, and in fact she did too. Surely the next one would be a boy. Think positive, think a boy, make boy-kind of baby clothes, he advised her. And sure enough it worked; the next one was a boy. Their first son checked in on December 18, 1913. It was Christmas morning one week early. A more welcome son never arrived. Joseph Fielding Smith was the happiest man in the Council of the Twelve. It did not require the use of the Urim and Thummim, nor even a family council, to decide that the name would be Joseph Fielding Smith III. Five daughters and now a son. Life was beautiful.

Six children might have been deemed an adequate sized family by some. But not so with the Smiths. It was in fact just the midway point. Two and a half years after Joseph's birth a sixth daughter was born, on June 21, 1916. They named her Amelia, a variation of Emyla, the first wife, but more specifically in honor of Ethel's mother, Amelia Jane Reynolds. With only one child in seven being a son, it occurred to Joseph Fielding that by the law of averages the next one should surely be a son also, and he was right. In fact the next and last four were sons, nearly evening the count: Lewis Warren was born March 10, 1918, and named in honor of Joseph's first father-in-law, Lewis Warren Shurtliff, Louie's father. George Reynolds was born February 13, 1921, and was named for Joseph's second father-in-law, George Reynolds, Ethel's father. Douglas Allan was born May 5, 1924, and named after a couple of family friends. Milton Edmund was born March

Smith children in front of the family home on North Second West. On the donkey, Emily, Naomi, and Lois. Oldest sister Josephine is holding baby Joseph.

4, 1927, and was named after Milton Ross, a handball partner of Joseph Fielding, and after Dr. David G. Edmunds, the doctor who delivered him. "I'm glad that my father and his wives had 11 children," Milton later commented, "because I'm the 11th one."

So in less than 19 years of marriage Ethel bore nine children.

From the beginning of her marriage, with little Josephine and Julina to care for, and then others of her own, she had her hands full. Joseph Fielding never ceased to be amazed at her ability as an organizer and manager. She not only worked hard herself, but assigned specific tasks to each child as she or he got old enough to assist with the household chores and yard work. Joseph was delighted to see this, for it not only helped make for a smooth running family, but gave the children important training in responsibility and taught them how to do things. Another trait he liked about Ethel was her complete fairness and impartiality in dealing with the children. She never favored her own children in preference to Louie's two daughters. She always respected Josephine's position as the oldest child in the family and gave her due preference as the oldest.

When Ethel occasionally accompanied Joseph on a trip, Josephine was left in charge of the family, and each of

Five daughters as young children—back row, Julina and Josephine; front row, Naomi, Lois, and Emily.

the younger children knew that they were to look to Josephine. Joseph Jr. recalls one such instance when he was a youngster: "My father and mother had gone east on one of father's assignments. My sister Josephine was in charge of the family. The first O. P. Skaggs store was located on the west side of Main Street just two or three stores down from South Temple. They had a special on bananas. As I recall they were selling for about three pounds for ten cents. My sister sent each one of us to this store, six blocks away, to buy a limit of bananas. About five of us went separately to make the purchase. My sister Julina has never liked bananas, however, the rest of us had bananas for every meal for days—in pie, on cereal, and in other ways."

Josephine's frugality in the mass banana purchase reflected the careful training she had received. Rearing a family of 11 youngsters on the modest salary of an apostle of the Church was no easy job. It required the most careful management and the cooperation of all family members. L. Garrett Myers, who became a son-in-law, recalls that, "Not long after Emily and I were married, we were invited to spend the Christmas holidays at the family home. Sister Smith (Ethel) was a great organizer and executive. With a family of 11 children, order had to be maintained and a routine established which would enable the family to take care of the household duties with the greatest possible efficiency. Breakfast was served at 7 o'clock in the morning. By that time each task would have been completed. Every child had an assigned responsibility— cooking, scrubbing floors, vacuuming, making the beds, dressing or getting the younger ones ready for school, and performing the myriad of other little or big jobs which one could expect to find in the membership of such a large household. I assumed, however, that during the holidays the rules would be suspended or relaxed to a point that breakfast would be postponed until 8 or 9 o'clock at least. However, long training and habits firmly established are not easily broken, and I was embarrassed to have been the only one to appear at the breakfast table after the dishes had been cleared away to eat by myself, much to the amusement of my wife."

Joseph Jr., who as the oldest son in the family took on added responsibilities, remembers the need of each child making his or her contribution to the success of the family. "I earned most of my spending money. I worked at jobs continuously from the age of 12. While still a youth on Second West I spent my summers dusting, cleaning, oiling machines, and piling stock at the Salt Lake Knitting Factory on First North. . . . At age 14 I worked at the Utah Motor Park on Saturdays, and sometimes after school, as well as summers, for three years. After that, I spent summers cutting eight lawns a week until the time I left for a mission. This is just an example. Other members of the family had special jobs for their spending money. We all had chores at home to do as well. Every morning I made the beds in our room, vacuumed the upstairs hall, and down the steps. On weekends I had to scrub the front porch and also the side basement steps. I used to run and hide when sightseeing buses came down Gilmer Drive because I didn't like to be seen washing front steps. I also watered and cut our lawn, sometimes twice a week.

"One sister prepared breakfast each morning as well as caring for her bedroom. Another had to wash the bathrooms. The younger boys helped a sister wash the dishes. Another vacuumed and cleaned the front rooms, dining room, etc., each day. Another made our lunches each morning. Still another helped mother cook supper. Then occasionally their cooking assignments and some other assignments were switched. Mother, however, was the organizer of all chores. She was a great organizer. Emily disliked cleaning under the old bathroom tub on Second West—the kind with legs, because Naomi or one of the others would regularly let stray cats in the house and they were not housebroken. They seemed to hide under the bathtub."

When Joseph Fielding was appointed to the Council of the Twelve, as mentioned earlier, he made the an-

nouncement to his family by telling them he would have
to sell the family cow because now he would not have
time to take care of it. Fortunately his sister Mamie and
her husband Alfred Peterson who lived next door had two
cows, and the Smiths were able to get their milk supply
from them at a modest cost. The cows were kept in a barn
behind the Peterson and Smith yards, near Grandfather
Smith's former home. Two old stagecoaches parked in the
barnyard made it a rather intriguing area for the youngsters. A family vegetable garden was less intriguing, but
helped to reduce the produce bill.

"My father was very frugal and extremely careful
with church money," recalls Joseph. "He tried to save on
church expenses, and on home expenses. However, whenever we really needed money for school expenses or for
clothes Father always met our needs. But we never had
excessive money or allowances."

One expense that President Smith felt was well
worthwhile at home was the payment of incentive money
to his youngsters to encourage them to read the standard
works of the Church and other good books. A great student himself, he naturally desired that his children develop
good study habits, and especially the habit of reading worthy books. Joseph Jr. recalls, "He was always encouraging
us to read the scriptures and to study. I remember as a boy
of approximately 13 years, I received five dollars which
was offered for reading the Book of Mormon." With 11
children taking the book reading offer seriously it became
quite a financial challenge to the family head to meet all
the payments.

As any writer with a family of youngsters, Joseph
Fielding faced the problem of a conflict of interest—
youngsters take time, writing takes time; youngsters need
your attention, writing needs your attention. There are
never enough hours in the day to devote all the time and
attention one could wish to either youngsters or writing.
So you divide your time and attention, giving a certain
amount to each and wishing you could give considerably
more to both. To write, a person must secure a certain

amount of isolation from distraction, and with a house full of youngsters this is no easy problem to solve. Part of the problem is an emotional one. Writing is a lonely sort of business at best. You do not really wish to isolate yourself, especially not from the little ones who are anxious for you to get home in the evenings, and whose presence in the house is one of the great joys in life. So you get up earlier and you stay up later, to get in some writing time. And you designate an area in the house for your writing effort —a place to keep typewriter, books, papers, erasers, pens —and hope that it will be respected by other members of the family, and not carried off as though caught in a tornado.

Joseph Fielding wisely decided to reserve a room for his study, and for storage. He chose an upstairs room so as not to interfere with the busier traffic lanes in the house. To make sure that his writing materials were not disturbed he kept the room locked. This was an effective but dangerous step. A person can get by with locking a bathroom door and not create any feelings—unless he keeps it locked too long. But to lock another room in the house, no matter how worthy the reason, is a bold step indeed— and one that every writer should risk. Here behind locked doors manuscript paper could rest secure upon the desk without being confiscated for grocery lists or English themes. Come evening, pens and pencils would still be lying exactly where they had been laid in the morning, rather than unaccountably getting into a wife's purse or a young scholar's pocket with no one knowing how they got there nor where they went. Elder Smith had another good reason for keeping the room locked: from his father he had inherited a sword, a desk, two trunks and some letters and other items that had belonged to the Patriarch Hyrum Smith, brother of the Prophet. He had also inherited letters and books that had belonged to his father, President Joseph F. Smith. These precious historic items he kept locked in this room.

As might be expected, as soon as he locked the door to the room there developed an aura of mystery about it among the small fry. Conjecture grew as to what lay hidden behind the locked door in this forbidden room. To young Joseph Jr.'s mind came exciting thoughts of Bluebeard and his dark secrets. This much was known for certain by the youngsters: their father spent a good deal of time in the room, usually in the early morning and late evening. Another thing: he had more than just literary and historical property in there. In the suspenseful days before Christmas that is where packages were hidden away for safe keeping. And at any time of year Father's room became the depository for tasty perishable goods—especially perishable if they were not locked up. Crates of oranges, sacks of bananas, packages of cookies, boxes of candy were sometimes shut up in the mystery room, and the tantalizing aroma emanating from under the door was enough to drive you up the wall with excitement.

Not all the produce could be stored in this room of course. The upstairs back screen porch was the major produce storage center. Apples, flour, potatoes, tomatoes and other garden truck generally were stored here, and the honor system prevailed: youngsters were entrusted to use wisdom and discretion in what they took to eat.

As a student of the gospel in the dispensation of the fullness of times, Joseph Fielding saw in each new invention and development further fulfillment of God's purposes in the earth, and took a delight in them. For instance, when the first radio crystal sets came on the market, he was one of the first to purchase a set. It was great fun as a family to gather around this pioneer model with the earphones and acorn-like speaker, to hear voices coming through the ether.

Of even greater interest and worth to the Smiths was the automobile. Joseph Fielding had traveled so much by train and street car—and by horse and buggy—that it was a genuine pleasure to be able to drive an automobile, even though it had to be cranked to start and tires blew out after a few miles and had to be changed by hand. Some of the older children have a vague recollection of the Model "T" Ford being the first car in the Smith family. But the one that is best remembered was the Reo bought in 1916. It was a seven-passenger, one of the larger touring cars then available. It was high, with big-rimmed tires, running boards and celluloid windows that hooked onto the sides to give protection from cold and storms, but could be taken off to allow more air in good weather. Many fond memories are associated with that old Reo: picnic and camping trips into the nearby canyons, and even as far away as Strawberry Reservoir. If the whole family went, a table board across the two jump seats accommodated all the children. Sometimes it became a choice of who went and who stayed at home. A tent housed them for the two or three nights they camped out at a time.

Joseph Fielding found little time for recreation. He, Ethel and the children took occasional rides in their automobile, sometimes out to the Smith Brothers Jersey Dairy Farm, which especially interested the children. His brother George managed the farm. In August, 1916, he notes in his journal that he had "made arrangements to purchase an automobile and to sell my small one. I have just had some Deseret Building Society stock mature which will enable me to do so." It was the seven-passenger Reo he bought, that he and Ethel and their youngsters had looked at and admired. September 5 was a day of excitement for the Smith family, for it was on that day that they received their "Reo machine." There was only one problem: the Reo was too large for the garage. Two weeks later Joseph Fielding notes that he has had to enlarge his "automobile house."

One summer day Elder Smith was asked to attend a church service at the Girls' Home in Brighton, high in the mountains east of Salt Lake City. President Heber J. Grant was also to be there. Joseph Fielding decided to take some of his youngsters along for the outing. Joseph Jr. recalls, "It was a real struggle for our family to get the Reo to respond. Every few yards in the steep area of Big Cottonwood Canyon, the car would begin to boil. Numerous waiting periods were necessary as we permitted the car to cool and fed the radiator more cold water from the

An early picture of Joseph Fielding Smith's six daughters at home on North Second West. From left to right, Josephine, Julina, Naomi, Emily, Lois, and Amelia.

The sons of Joseph Fielding Smith who were born at 165 North Second West with home in background—Lewis, Joseph, Reynolds and baby Douglas in arms of his father.

stream nearby. President Grant had a chauffeur who drove his big Pierce Arrow. Finally we had to abandon our Reo and ride with President Grant in his Pierce Arrow. It presented quite a sight with the extra load."

It was not just in mountain climbing that the Reo had its problems. One cold, snowy day as Elder Smith was driving on the streets of Salt Lake City, a tierod broke loose between the steering wheel and the front wheels. It was necessary for one of the youngsters to get out and trot along by the front side of the car, kicking the wheels straight while Joseph Fielding endeavored to drive it to a spot of safety where he could stop.

Although the Reo had become almost like a member of the family, the day came in the 1920's when Joseph Fielding felt they must part company. Yale Ward, where the Smiths then lived, was having a fund raising drive to build a new chapel. Elder Smith gave the Reo to the bishop for resale. There were feelings of nostalgia as the old automobile was driven away for the last time. Ironically, this act of generosity resulted in criticism of Joseph Fielding: although he had already paid a sizeable cash assessment to the building fund, some busy-body who put two and two together and got ten, spread the story that Elder Smith was pretty cheap because all he gave to the ward was an old automobile.

In later years when some of the children were grown and gone, but the younger ones were still at home, the Smiths bought a cabin from Taylor Merrill in Millcreek Canyon. Two of Joseph's sisters had cabins nearby. In the heat of the summer Elder Smith sometimes retired to the cool of the cabin to work on his books or other writing projects. But after a few years he decided the cabin was more bother than worth, and resold it.

With growth, the personality of cities and of neighborhoods changes. When Joseph and Louie built their house on Second West Street in 1902-03, it was an ideal place to live. But by the mid-1920's it was no longer an ideal place to live. The area was fast becoming commercialized, and the traffic had increased manyfold. Clearly, in the years ahead the commercialization and the traffic would intensify still more. Then too, the family had outgrown the house. More room was urgently needed. It was with reservations that Joseph Fielding and Ethel decided to build a new house on the east side of the city and then sell the Second West house. A house even more than an automobile becomes a sentimental part of one's life. It is not easy to say goodbye. Here the children had been born and spent their youth. Here too was the old Smith homestead. The old home where Joseph Fielding had been born and spent his childhood still stood just through the backyard. Several close relatives still lived on the block. But up east was virgin country, where meadow larks still sang in the cool of the morning, quail were abundant in the brush, and no steady string of traffic polluted the air with noise and gas fumes. Hyrum G. Smith, a favorite cousin, had built on Yale Avenue, and urged Joseph Fielding to come up and join him. There were few houses in the area when the Smiths dug the foundation for their home in 1925 at 998 Douglas Street, near Ninth South and Thirteenth East. It would be a large, stately brick house, with a much larger yard than the family had been able to have on Second West. Here Joseph Fielding would build a tennis court and have a horseshoe pit, to help encourage his children in sports, and find some recreation himself.

During the several months that the house was under construction, it was fun to drive up the several miles distance to it and see it taking shape. Finally it was done and

The home built for the Smith family at 998 Douglas Street.

the time came for the big move. Numerous trips back and forth in the Reo were necessary to transport the accumulated wealth of years, despite the extensive discarding that typically accompanies a move. The old house on Second West was sold to the Backer family from Germany. For many years now the house has been the site of the West High Bakery. A rolltop desk that Joseph Fielding left behind is still used in the bakery.

Perhaps it is rather fitting that the house was converted into a bakery, for Joseph Fielding Smith himself was quite a connoisseur of pastries. His mother had taught him to bake bread and pies, and while on his mission to England as a young man he had abundant opportunity for practicing the culinary arts. It was a happy day for his youngsters when they saw Dad don an apron and start a wholesale batch of pies. Mincemeat was one of his favorites. He made his own mincemeat filling. But he also ventured into other kinds of pies: apple, cherry, peach and pumpkin. His pie making efforts became a family project as youngsters were sent off in this direction and that to help gather in the necessary tools and ingredients. The savory, tantalizing aroma of pies baking in the big oven made a happy hour of anticipation. A watchful check was kept on them, that they did not come out either too soon or too late. Meanwhile Ethel stirred up a batch of homemade ice cream and the youngsters took turns cranking the ice cream freezer, so that when the pies were brought from the oven, there was a big scoop of ice cream to go on each piece for those who preferred it a la mode.

A freezer of ice cream as well as a big sack of sandwiches and other goodies usually accompanied the Smith family on their trips by train out to Saltair, on the south shore of Great Salt Lake. A dip in the salty brine water was sufficient to whet appetites. It was fun riding the train out and back, but quite a challenge to Joseph and Ethel to get all the youngsters rounded up off the beach in time to catch the train for the return trip. It was always easier to get them down to the train depot in Salt Lake City for the trip out than to get them back. On one visit to Saltair, when Joseph Jr. was about 11 years old, his father sent him to the concession stand to buy some soft drinks for the family. "I brought back some bottles of Coca-Cola. He made me return them, stating that it was not good for us. I never forgot that, and as a result I have never tasted Coca-Cola. Such was the effect of his teaching."

It was not just on pie-making days and on trips to Saltair that the Smith youngsters got homemade ice cream. Joseph Fielding as a youngster had been able to have ice cream only three days a year. But times had changed and he and Ethel were pleased that their youngsters could have it more often. "When we were young," remembers one of the children today, "every Sunday during the month of July was homemade ice cream day. Mother made excellent ice cream. This was the one month Father did not go on assignments. It was vacation time for the general authorities and we were happy to have Father home on weekends. He of course liked the ice cream too."

As to gifts, Christmas had offered pretty slim pickings in Joseph Fielding's youth. His children had it better. "Christmas was always an important event around our home," remembers Joseph Jr. "Father enjoyed preparing neat little sections with gifts for each member of the family. He would spread sheets on the long table in the basement recreation room and then neatly proportion each child's gifts on the table. I remember the year my sister Lois and I couldn't sleep too well because of excitement. We decided to sneak quietly down to the basement at 4 o'clock in the morning to get a preview of our Christmas gifts. We had to go past Father's bedroom door which was on the main floor across the hall from the basement steps. He heard us as we were halfway down the stairs. He did not know there were two of us. I was ordered back to bed, but Lois hurriedly scampered on downstairs. About this time, Father decided to get up and he spent some time in the basement admiring the various gifts that he had carefully laid out for each of us. For the rest of the early morning, Lois was hiding under the table, fearful he would see her. But he didn't. By the time the rest of the family appeared Lois was ready to go back to bed."

Getting up at 4 o'clock in the morning was more than just a Christmas day occurrence with Joseph Fielding. He was up every morning at 4 o'clock or shortly after, first to tend to the chore of making the fire in the coal furnace in the cold of winter, or setting hoses for watering lawns in the summer. Then it was up to his study room to work on a book for a couple of hours before breakfast. At six o'clock he awoke his youngsters if they were not already up. "We never got to sleep in, no matter how late we were up the night before," recalled one of the children. Beds had to be made and other chores attended to before breakfast, which was always served promptly at 7 o'clock. But before anyone ate, the family kneeled around the table together in prayer, with Papa Smith either offering the prayer himself or calling on his wife or one of the children. They also held family prayer together in the evening.

Through gathering their youngsters in family prayer, encouraging them to read the scriptures and other good books, taking them to church meetings, holding family gatherings and taking them on outings, Joseph and Ethel tried their best to help their children gain a testimony and love of the gospel—and in this they succeeded wonderfully well, with all 11 children continuing active in the Church throughout their lives. But it was a constant challenge. As in any family, some responded more enthusiastically than others, and each child presented a special case, to be handled in a certain way. The Smiths often chuckled over the response of their third son, George Reynolds, when a neighbor, Alma N. Johnson, approached him one day. "Well Ren," Brother Johnson asked the boy, "how is your testimony today?" "I don't know," replied Reynolds, "Father is out of town."

Being out of town so much on church assignment was one of the special problems Joseph Fielding had as a general authority, in rearing 11 youngsters. He had to rely heavily upon Ethel to keep things running smoothly at home. One would suppose that a man who lives into his 90's must have somehow managed to keep his mind free from worry. But such was not the case with Joseph Fielding. When it came to his wife and children, he seemed to be a natural born worrier. His letters home to Ethel and the family while off on church assignments are filled with anxiety about their welfare. From the moment he climbed aboard the train until he returned home several days later his mind seemed busy with worry about things at home. With long hours of train travel it is only natural that such thoughts of home would occupy much of his time.

In December 1913, for example, while visiting in Mesa, Arizona, shortly before their first son was born, he wrote in part, "I think of you and the cold weather you are having and am sorry you have to be alone. Naomi must be Papa's good girl and not run out in the cold. Tell Emily Papa wants to see her and the other children and our Mama just as much as she wants her Papa. . . . I hope my kiddies are all well. They must be careful and keep warm. The two who go to school must be warm and wear something on their heads to protect them. Why should I write this way? I know you will do all you can to see to these things. I hope you have eaten all the chickens up. I hope you are not suffering any evil effects from your visit to Martha's. . . . The Lord bless our Mama and kiddies and watch over them. I will soon be home with you now, and then will not have to take another long trip for some time, I hope."

The worry when he was traveling was not all his. Ethel and the youngsters at home also worried about him. Especially did Julina. "Someone told me at a very tender age about cannibals," she explains. "Every time father would board a train at night to go to a conference I would worry myself sick for fear he would have to go to cannibal land and would be eaten up. I would always promise myself that as soon as he returned I would ask him if he would ever be sent there, but when he would return safe and sound I would forget until the next conference, usually the following week. I would lie awake and wonder if the Lord would really send so valuable a person to such a forbidden place. But I kept remembering that the gospel had to be preached to *all* the world. This presented quite a conflict, it seemed to me. Finally, after many, many long months of fretting and forgetting, I remembered to ask him about it. He was reading the newspaper when I finally asked. Without even looking up he said 'maybe' in a very casual tone and left me still wondering. But at least I thought that if he wasn't any more worried about it than that, then surely the Lord would take care of him if he was ever sent to the cannibals."

Ethel became especially worried when Joseph Fielding started traveling by airplane instead of by train. The first time was when he reached home a day early from an assignment in California. Josephine remembers, "Mother was so upset that he would fly that she kept saying, 'Promise me that you will never fly again!' She was very worried to think that he would even enter an airplane."

The family usually saw him off on the train, and met him again at the depot upon his return. The deep love that existed in the family could be measured by the sadness of the one experience and the anxious waiting and joy of the other. Ethel, ever thoughtful, would often write a letter to him before ever he left them, hide it in one of his suitcases or coats, and he would find it somewhere along the way. She would also pack special treats for him, such as fruit or homemade candy.

Sometimes Joseph Fielding would take one of the youngsters with him on a trip, especially when he was traveling by automobile. One such trip to Vernal in the Uintah Basin in northeastern Utah was especially memorable for Joseph Jr. because of an unusual incident that occurred: On their way back home they became engulfed in a heavy rain storm and took a wrong turn in the road near Duchesne, leading them off the road to Salt Lake City up into Indian Canyon. The storm became heavier and the road very muddy and slippery, so much so that it was not only dangerous but impossible to travel farther. The heavy mist shrouded the deep chasm off the one-lane dirt road, and young Joseph Jr. and Dr. David E. Smith who were passengers attempted to push and steady the car for fear of its sliding into the deep canyon below. The wheels began to spin in the mud, and eventually the car came to a standstill. Young Joseph recalls that his father said, "We have done all we can. We will call upon the Lord." He bowed his head in prayer, calling upon the Lord to prepare the way that he might right his mistake and get out of the dangerous canyon and proceed on the journey home. He told the Lord that he had important commitments that needed his attention the next day, and that it was imperative that he be back in Salt Lake City. Miraculously, the storm abated, a wind came up, drying off the road sufficiently that they were able to reach Castle Gate and eventually get back onto a highway. No sooner had they reached low ground than the storm settled in again, stalling traffic in the immediate area for several hours. As they proceeded down Provo Canyon headed for Salt Lake City, after many hours of extra travel, they were stopped by a highway patrolman who asked where they had come from. When informed that they had come through Indian Canyon the officer said, "That's impossible! It's reported that all the bridges in that area have been washed out." To their surprise, the headlines of the next day's paper reported 200 cars stranded in the area from which they had escaped.

How do you maintain discipline in a family of 11 youngsters? Joseph Fielding and Ethel achieved it mainly through love and attention to the interests of their children. There was never any harshness. Children were never beaten—lightly spanked perhaps—and seldom scolded. There was firmness. Each child knew he or she had certain responsibilities to fulfill and a certain standard of conduct to meet. Ethel always admonished the children to "remember who your father is." They were given to understand that any misdeeds on their part would reflect on their father and thus on the Church, he being a general authority. Joseph Fielding in turn reminded the youngsters of their responsibility in bearing the name of Smith and honoring the noble lineage that was theirs. Until 1918 their grandfather was president of the Church, and that of course was an important factor to be reckoned with as it influenced the thinking of the youngsters. Joseph Fielding was concerned that they be mindful of their relationship and yet not become conceited or arrogant about it. To help safeguard against the latter he utilized a touch of humor: Smith being so common a name he told his youngsters that in the beginning all men were named Smith, but when they did something wrong they had to change their name! As his daughters grew older and married, he had to allow that there were other reasons for changing one's name from Smith.

Keeping them busy with household chores and money-earning jobs helped to keep them out of mischief. When one of the youngsters did get out of line, Joseph Fielding rather than spanking him might grasp him by the shoulder, look him in the eye and say in his most solemn voice, "I do wish my kiddies would be good!" As they got older he developed a standard line of admonishment, which did not really make any sense and thus was doubly useful. He would look at them sort of in disgust or disappointment and say, "You make my tired ache!"

Several of the children recall that it always made their father feel so bad whenever he scolded them that they tried to behave themselves to spare him the mental anguish he went through in reproving them. "He would always come and put his arm around us afterwards," recalls Lois, "and tell us how sorry he was, and that he loved us. We always felt badly because we had made him feel so bad." Joseph Fielding himself had once been mistakenly punished by his father and it had left an emotional scar. He was anxious not to make the same mistake with any of his children. In several of his letters home while on church assignments he speaks of his regret at having lost his patience at home, and resolving not to let it happen again, but to be a better husband and father. As an old man he still remembered with regret having lost patience with his youngest son, Milton. Speaking of having taken the family on a vacation to the ocean near San Diego, California, he

President Joseph F. Smith and Julina Lambson Smith surrounded by their children and grandchildren. Joseph Fielding's wife, Ethel, is at the extreme left front with her young son Joseph.

said, "That's where Milton lost his shoes. I often think of it and how awful mean I was to him, but I couldn't help it. Poor little kid, just a baby, took his shoes off and waded into the ocean and then the tide started in and . . . covered his shoes and he didn't know where they were. But I scolded the poor little fellow because he lost his shoes, and I have been sorry ever since." Such was the tender heart of President Smith that the incident had weighed on him through the years.

Occasionally the Smith grandparents would visit the home, and this of course was a delight to the youngsters to have grandparents there. "One time when Grandmother Smith was at our place for dinner," remembers Lois, "we sat around the table talking afterwards. Dad was telling some of the things that he had done when he was a boy. He had made the bread, he had taken care of his

THE LIFE OF JOSEPH FIELDING SMITH

brothers and sisters. And, as we all do, he was remembering so many things that he had done as a child. Grandmother looked at him and said, 'Well, Joseph, what did I
do?' And his answer was, 'You just puttered around!' I
guess kids think that is all that mothers do."

Grandfather Joseph F. Smith, president of the Church,
had not only immensely enjoyed his own four dozen children but found similar delight in his grandchildren. And
they enjoyed him, for he would sit them on his lap, make
a fuss over them, and give them little white peppermints
that he always carried in his pocket. His long gray beard
would tickle their faces and was quite a conversation piece
with them.

Several of Joseph Fielding's brothers and sisters had
died while still youngsters. One of the constant prayers of
his heart was that none of his children would die in their
infancy or childhood. Whenever any of them were sick,
and he was at home, he gave them his constant attention,
walking the floor with them, helping to nurse them
through the night, reading to them, even dancing around
the room to music, played on an old Edison phonograph,
or do whatever would entertain them or relieve their suffering and help them get well. Many a time he administered to them, exercising the power of the priesthood in
their behalf. Fortunately none of his children did die in
their youth. At the time of this writing, 10 of his 11 children are still living. His son Lewis was killed in World
War II.

Joseph Fielding was not without a sense of humor,
but he saw no humor in a joke played on him that caused
him to worry about a baby. "The last time I saw Aunt
Emily," says Lois, "she told me a little about my birth.
Grandmother was the midwife and Aunt Emily was the
nurse. I was premature and very small. She said that a day
or two after my birth she and Mother played a joke on
Dad by hiding me under the covers. When Dad walked
into the room he was very concerned because he could
not see me. They got a kick out of his concern, but he did
not think it was a very funny joke and told them never
to do that to him again."

Joseph Fielding also did considerable floor pacing when his children reached the dating age. He generally stayed up until they got home, and if they were not home by the appointed hour he was ready to turn them into a pumpkin, with or without a wand. Like other parents, he found it was easier to tend to children when they were little than when they grew older. But they were all quite considerate of his feelings and those of their mother.

He taught his boys not to kill for pleasure. As his father before him, he was opposed to killing either birds or animals. He did indulge in an occasional fishing trip, when the children were young, and took them fishing. But in later years he even gave up fishing. The only thing he ever encouraged his children to kill were houseflies. He used to pay them a nickel for every hundred flies they killed.

He did encourage his children, especially his sons, in sports. Joseph Fielding himself was a great swimmer and handball player, and as a spectator enjoyed baseball, football, basketball, and other games. In his youth Joseph Fielding had especially enjoyed playing baseball, and continued in his love for the game. He was a fan of the Salt Lake Bees. Occasionally he played softball with his children. He particularly enjoyed pitching. He was ambidextrous and he would place both hands behind him and then leave it to the batter to guess whether he would pitch right or left-handed. Primarily he was left-handed, but he trained himself to use either hand. He could defeat any of his sons in handball. Reynolds remembers when he and Lewis played against their father in the Deseret Gym, and their father with one hand held behind him soundly trounced them both. He would let the boys designate which hand he could use. He sometimes did a little light boxing with his sons, played tennis with them on their own home court, and horseshoes. He also enjoyed playing chess. Douglas especially remembers playing chess and checkers with his father. All of his sons were sports minded, and Milton as a quarterback on a University of Utah team in the late 1940's and in 1950 became one of

Joseph Fielding Smith ready to throw ball for beginning of M Men Softball Tournament.

the alltime great kickers there. Whenever his church assignments permitted, Joseph Fielding attended games in which his sons were playing, and many other games as well.

He also encouraged his children to develop other talents. Ethel was an excellent pianist and organist, and several of the girls took lessons from her and from other teachers. Lewis took some vocal lessons, Joseph Jr. learned to play the clarinet, and others of the youngsters learned

A friendly handball match between Joseph Fielding and his brother David.

Five sons with their father in backyard of home at 998 Douglas Street. From left to right, Reynolds, Lewis, Joseph, Douglas, Joseph Fielding Sr., and Milton.

Joseph Fielding Smith with picture of son Milton.

other musical instruments. The girls were also encouraged
to learn to cook and sew well.

While living on Second West Elder Smith always
walked to and from work. He had a very distinctive walk,
and the youngsters could spot him a block or two away
as he approached home, and would run to meet him. Ethel
generally had them all tidied up, neat and clean, to please
him. He was always very prompt and punctual about leaving for work by 7:30 in the morning and returning home
by 5:30 or 6 o'clock in the evening, so as not to keep the
others waiting for supper. When the youngsters were old
enough to go to school, at the old Lafayette School located
across the street from the site of the new Church Administration Building on North Temple Street, they would walk
with their father. The first time or two they found it diffi-

240

cult to keep up with his fast pace, but soon got in the habit of walking rapidly. As they parted company he would always kiss each of them goodbye, right out in the open on the street, and they found this a bit embarrassing. But kissing hello and goodbye was an old Smith family custom.

Joseph Fielding and Ethel taught their youngsters respect and consideration for others. They were never allowed to speak in too familiar of terms about the general authorities of the Church. For instance, Heber J. Grant must always be referred to as "President Grant." A member of the Council of the Twelve must be addressed as Elder so and so. And you should be just as considerate of those who did not hold high position or authority. Never a Christmas came but what the Smiths had a gift or special treat for their newspaper boy, the mail carrier, the garbage collectors and others who served the daily needs of the family. Joseph Fielding was always as courteous to the person in a lowly station as to him in a high one, and taught his children to be likewise.

How kind the Smiths could be was demonstrated in the case of their newspaper carrier, Stanley Dixon. When Stan was about 12 years old he was orphaned. His father had been killed two years earlier upon falling from a ladder while cleaning ceilings in the Salt Lake Temple. Now the boy's mother died of cancer, leaving him and several brothers and sisters. Relatives took charge of the other youngsters, but Stan was invited to come live with the Smiths, which he did for several years until reaching maturity, when he moved to California. Counting Stan, Joseph Fielding and Ethel reared an even dozen youngsters, six girls and six boys. It was one of the great experiences of life, and one of their most successful ventures.

Chapter 12

*"The man I know is a kind,
loving husband and father"*

The Death of Ethel

As the campfire grew dim and only the coals remained, the night air became noticeably colder. Though weary from traveling all day, Joseph Fielding lay awake long into the night. He glanced over at the sleeping forms of his companions with whom he was camping in West Yellowstone on their way home to Salt Lake.

Ten days earlier on August 13, 1937, Joseph had traveled by train to Lethbridge and Cardston to attend stake conferences and to handle other church business. Fern and Harold B. Lee and Lanora and Charles S. Hyde had traveled to Canada by car, combining church assignments with a vacation to Banff Park. To arrive home a day sooner Joseph had gratefully accepted the invitation of Brother Hyde to travel home with them.

It had been a sad journey for Joseph. Though he had long since come to accept his absences from home, Ethel was no longer able to go to the railroad depot to bid him an affectionate farewell. And he missed the little surprises and love letters that she used to hide in his suitcases to remind him that she missed and loved him too.

Since 1933 his beloved Ethel had struggled with a terrible illness which she could not understand. At times she was plunged into the depths of depression and at other times her mind raced beyond control forcing her exhausted body to do more and more. The tender love and support of her family, prayers, and blessings, even hospitalizations did not seem to help.

In a letter to Ethel's physician, Joseph Fielding poured out his deep sorrow, as he had often done with the Lord. He would give all he had, even his own life, if only his beloved Ethel could be cured of her great affliction.

This wonderful talented woman had been Joseph Fielding's wife and companion for nearly three decades. Besides running a household of twelve children with her husband often away on the Lord's business, she had filled many important church positions. In 1911 she was called as a member of the Relief Society General Board. Never content with mediocrity, whatever she did, she did well. Studying late at night after the children were in bed, she spent hours writing and re-writing her talks. Her children remember her ironing, dusting, or doing other household chores while rehearsing aloud her next talk. "She was a member of more committees than any other one member," reported Julia Lund of the Relief Society Board, "and very few traveled as extensively in visiting the stakes. Whether in consultation, in lesson work, or in public address, she demonstrated the same thoroughness of preparation and clearness of vision. Her brilliant mind and sincere eloquence always made a great appeal."

Amy Brown Lyman, the president of the Relief Society General Board, said, "Sister Smith was one of the most brilliant women I ever knew. I considered her the finest writer and speaker I had on my board."

With the onset of her illness it became increasingly difficult for Ethel to meet her many responsibilities. After 18 years she was released from the Relief Society General Board in 1936 in order to lighten her burdens and hopefully to regain her health. But Ethel did not improve and a broken-hearted Joseph vainly looked for ways to help his beloved companion while uncomplainingly carrying his heavy duties as a member of the Twelve.

Fondly he recalled how she had always been so

loving and affectionate, so careful to please and help him in every way possible. Despite a house full of children, she had somehow managed to look attractive and smiling at night when he had returned from work. Each child had his duties and visitors were surprised to find the house and children so clean and neat. And seldom did she even hint being burdened as a "church widow" with her husband gone so much of the time on church assignments. Her welcome letters were carefully written to let him share in the joys of their home while away without making him worry over problems.

"Joseph Dear, We were all happy when we received your letter this morning. The children were wondering why one had not come before, but I told them they had to be a little reasonable. If we had received a letter any sooner than we did, you would have had to write before you left. Baby [five-month-old Milton, their last child] was delighted to see it, and I had to fight with him to let me have it first. I was glad to have him fight for it though, because he had been quite sick. I would not tell you this if I were not sure that he is much better. For three days he has had quite a temperature, especially at night. After resorting to all the means I knew of without much result I got in touch with Dr. Edmunds, and we both feel that it's only an attack of indigestion and probably some tooth trouble. He is sleeping now with no noticeable fever, and I surely feel relieved and happy. Through it all he has been smiling. He is such a joy. The first day and night he moaned in his sleep so much, but last night and today he has done very little. I do not tell you this to worry you, but because I feel the need of you so much and also your prayers for us while you are away. It's much harder to have trouble when you are away from me than when you are here to shoulder so much of the responsibility. The baby has awakened and seems to be normal, only somewhat cross.

"As you will read if you have not already done so in Joseph's letter, we have had some storm. Friday we had a terrific hailstorm, and it looked for a time like we would have to leave the basement. It ran in the amusement room, and we mopped it up by the bucketful. It came down the chimney and out of the grate, the dirtiest hail I have ever seen, while it was running out of the coal room and also down the back steps into the kitchen. A lot of your flowers were ruined, but I think by the time you come home there will be a great many more out. That reminds me of what Joseph says of you. Saturday morning I told him he was in such a hurry to do his watering that he did it in much less time than you did and he said, 'Oh well, Papa spends most of his time looking at his flowers!' And he said it as if he believed what he was saying. He has been exceptionally good though. He sticks to his job so well, and I don't think he has been outside of the house but to water more than a half dozen times since you left. He has just finished bringing in the baby's diapers off the line and hanging up all of the baby's dresses. Two or three of the children have slight colds, due to the change in the weather, but the rest of us are feeling very well. Your gas bill of $6.74 is the only bill thus far to arrive, but probably before I post this letter more will come. I have not had much chance to use the auto since you left. Then, too, right now I'm not very crazy over buying gas. However maybe I will get the spirit before long.

"Aug. 30—Baby is much better this morning. While rather fussy all night he had no fever and did not moan. He is again smiling and kicking and making everyone happy. Doug insisted on sleeping in his little bed last night and he was so fussy the first part of the night that I finally scolded him. So he tried to quit whimpering and said, 'I'm sick.' He is normal enough this morning though. Two or three days ago I saw him jumping around in that vacant lot across the road by Patrick's, holding up the back of his coveralls with one hand and reaching out with the other. So I went and called him to find out what his difficulties were, and he yelled back, '*Nervy* grasshoppers won't let me catch *nervy* grasshopper, they jump and fly away from me!' He is the cutest, smartest kid with a big vocabulary for a child his age.

"I wish it were easier to get along without you when you are gone. I can stand it a day or two and then time begins to drag dreadfully, and when night comes, I almost choke with lonesomeness even though the house is filled with kids. We just exist until you get back. I think Milton wonders what has become of you. He jumps and looks around if he hears a man's voice. I certainly hope Brother Pratt does not work you too hard and that you get a little pleasure out of your trip. But I wish like everything we were together. You wrote that you read of a woman suing her husband for divorce because he didn't take her to picture shows. I think there would be more cause for complaint if he did. The other night Julina wanted to go, so I went with her. When I came home the children asked me if it were good and I said, 'no,' so Lewis asked me if I ever saw any show that I liked, and I thought that nearly all of them bored me terribly. Joseph thinks I am writing an awful lot, and as I have no more room and my pen has gone dry, I am forced to stop. With much love and then more, Ethel."

The letter, dated Salt Lake City, August 29, 1927, and addressed to Joseph Fielding in care of President Rey L. Pratt at El Paso, Texas, is typical of the dozens of others Ethel wrote to Joseph during the 29 years of their marriage. Yet, like each of her letters, it was very special to him, as his letters were to her. Carefully read, it is so revealing of the character and personality of the woman who was an inspiration to him for nearly three decades. Reflective of her love and devotion is the very fact that she took time to write the letter at all, and a long letter at that, in the midst of caring for a sick baby, looking after the other youngsters, and cleaning up a basement that has been inundated with a hailstorm flood via the chimney and coal room. It is significant, and typical of her, that she did not mail the letter until the next day, when she could report that the baby was feeling much better. Though plagued with worries herself, she did not wish to worry her husband, especially when he was far away on church business. Resourceful, self-reliant, she had done all she could for the sick baby before finally summoning professional help. Although her mind was too creative to be able to enjoy movies, and although she was very busy, yet she had taken time to go to the movie with Julina. Her letter was optimistic, included several subtle touches of humor, and was filled with love for Joseph Fielding. She freely admitted that while she was surrounded by her children whom she dearly loved, she deeply missed her husband even though he had been gone but a few days.

Some talented wives compete with or even deprecate their husbands. But Ethel was secure in her feelings about herself, her love of her husband, and his love for her. "She always held Father on a pedestal," commented one of the children. Thus the children did likewise, and thus Joseph Fielding was much more able to be an influence for good in their lives.

"You ask me to tell you of the man I know," she once responded to a request of a biographer. "I have often thought when he is gone people will say, 'He is a very good man, sincere, orthodox, etc.' They will speak of him as the public knows him. But the man they have in mind is very different from the man I know. The man I know is a kind, loving husband and father whose greatest ambition in life is to make his family happy, entirely forgetful of self in his efforts to do this. He is the man that lulls to sleep the fretful child, who tells bedtime stories to the little ones, who is never too tired or too busy to sit up late at night or to get up early in the morning to help the older children solve perplexing school problems. When illness comes, the man I know watches tenderly over the afflicted one and waits upon him. It is his hands that bind up the wounds, his arms that give courage to the sufferer, his voice that remonstrates with them gently when they err, until it becomes their happiness to do the thing that will make him happy.

"The man I know is most gentle, and if he feels that he has been unjust to anyone the distance is never too far for him to go and, with loving words or kind deeds, erase the hurt. He welcomes gladly the young people to his home and is never happier than when discussing with them topics of the day—sports or whatever interests them most. He enjoys a good story and is quick to see the humor of a situation, to laugh and to be laughed at, always willing to join in any wholesome activity.

"The man I know is unselfish, uncomplaining, considerate, thoughtful, sympathetic, doing everything within his power to make life a supreme joy for his loved ones. That is the man I know."

Joseph Fielding's thoughts dwelt much on Ethel and on their children as he lay under the pines at West Yellowstone that night. The same day that his son Lewis had received his mission call, he had also had his tonsils removed. Through an error, an acidic solution was injected instead of the local anesthesia, but the irritating solution had added to his pain, and Lewis had been very sick when Joseph Fielding had left town. How was Lewis now? Would he heal completely or could this somehow permanently damage his throat? And how was Ethel?

At Cardston, Canada on August 14, 1937, Joseph Fielding had been met by President Edward J. Wood, a man who enjoyed the power of healing to a most remarkable degree. Joseph wished that Ethel and Lewis might be there with him, to receive Brother Wood's ministration.

Joseph had been very busy in Alberta reorganizing, interviewing, setting apart a new bishopric, speaking at meetings. Still he had not been able to keep his mind free from concern for his loved ones, so when his duties were ended, he hurried home with the Lees and Hydes.

He found to his relief that Lewis had almost recovered, but Ethel was no better. Also during his absence, his mother's sister, Melissa Lambson Davis, had died, and Joseph was asked to speak at her funeral to be held in two days. In between catching up on his office work and caring for his family, he prepared the funeral sermon. But Joseph never gave that funeral sermon.

When he had left for the office that Thursday morning of August 26, 1937, Ethel's condition had been stable for some time. But he recorded in his journal, "I was called to the bedside of my wife who was suddenly stricken. . . . [She] continued to grow worse until all nerve centers ceased, resulting in her death this afternoon. . . . She has been ailing for many months, and in spite of all aid passed away at 3:15 today. A better woman could not be found, or truer wife and mother."

Joseph Fielding and his children recognized the fact that death came as a blessing to their wife and mother, giving her release from the intense suffering she had endured for so long. Yet the void that her death left in their lives was a deep one. She was only 47 years old when she died from a cerebral hemorrhage. His own heart broken, Joseph comforted his children and assured them that they would be with their dear mother again someday.

"The funeral services for my beloved wife Ethel were held today [August 30]. The speakers were Bishop T. Fred Hardy, Nettie D. Bradford, Samuel O. Bennion, and President David O. McKay. Music by John Longden, Harry Clark, and Jessie Evans. Organ: Sister Darrell Ensign."

It was the second time Joseph Fielding had called upon David O. McKay to speak at a wife's funeral. Nearly three decades separated the two solemn occasions, and many changes had occurred in Joseph's life. He was a grandfather now. Most of his children were married with only Amelia, Lewis, Reynolds, Douglas and Milton at home. Amelia would be married in just another month or two, Lewis had already received his mission call, so soon only the three younger boys would be left at home.

For 27 years now Joseph had been a member of the Council of the Twelve Apostles. He was no longer a young man, as he had been when Louie died. He was now 61 years old. Yet as President McKay spoke, he could not help but relive for a moment that service in 1908 when Louie had departed this life. He recalled how Ethel had then come into his life, and had brought great joy where there had been only sorrow. But now, she too, was gone. Beautiful, wonderful, thoughtful Ethel, mother of nine, mother to 12, wife, helpmate, companion, gone from this life, surely to a better one. Perhaps even now she and Louie might be conversing together in Paradise, talking about Josephine and Julina, and the other children also, and maybe sharing some views about a man they both loved and would share eternally.

Chapter 13

*"The song of the righteous is a
prayer unto me, and it shall be
answered with a blessing. . ."*

He Marries a Songbird

As Joseph Fielding Smith sat
behind the pulpit waiting his turn to speak at the funeral
service of Jack Dempsey's sister Florence, a flood of
thoughts rushed through his mind. It was not quite two
months since his beloved Ethel had died and her body
had been buried in the ground. Then, ten days ago he
had set his son Lewis apart as a missionary to the Swiss
Mission, a mission for which he himself as a young man
had felt some desire. That same day he had given away
his youngest daughter Amelia in marriage to Bruce Redd
McConkie, personally performing the sealing ceremony.
The following day he had put Lewis on the train and bid
him goodbye, with little hope of seeing him again for
more than two years. War clouds were gathering in that
very part of the world to which Lewis was going. That
same day that Lewis left, Joseph Fielding's daughter
Lois and her son Billie, who had been visiting home
from Chicago for Amelia's wedding, had also bid him
goodbye. He was 61 years old now, and all of his
children except the three youngest boys, Reynolds,
Douglas, and Milton, were gone from home. Life indeed
was transitory, fleeting. As the hymn warned, "for life is
quick in passing, 'tis as a single day."

Seeing Florence Dempsey Standard laid away in the earth on that Saturday, October 23, 1937, and reflecting upon his own situation, helped Joseph Fielding determine to do something he had been pondering for several days: when he got back to his office he wrote a letter of marriage proposal to Miss Jessie Ella Evans, Salt Lake County recorder and famed contralto soloist with the Mormon Tabernacle Choir.

With this proposal he again reminisced. He did not know Jessie Evans well. In fact, he hardly knew her at all. Before Ethel died she requested that Jessie Evans be asked to sing at her funeral service. "If I should ever die before you," she told her husband one day, "I want you to have Jessie Evans sing at my funeral." At her death Joseph Fielding sent his brother-in-law William C. Patrick to Miss Evans to make the request, since he was well acquainted with her and had volunteered his assistance in arranging the funeral service. She had kindly complied and sang at the service. Afterward Joseph Fielding sent her a note of appreciation:

"Words at times are feeble things in conveying the true feelings of the soul. I greatly appreciate your kindness to me and mine in the services yesterday. You have done much on occasions of this kind to comfort and bless those in tribulation, and your willingness to aid in such cases has long been noted by me. You have been kind to the members of my family before, and I wish you to know that the service so given has been fully appreciated by me. I always enjoy your singing, as much as any person I have ever heard. I trust you will pardon me for saying this, for it is a heartfelt expression. May the Lord bless you and reward you with the fulness of his blessings, now and forever. This I humbly pray."

Jessie Evans had responded to his note, expressing her interest in being of any possible help to him. Telephone calls back and forth had followed. She as county recorder and he as church recorder had some points of interest in common. Then, too, he had once been treasurer of the Tabernacle Choir, and had even worked for a few weeks years ago in the City and County Building where she now had her office, though he had not been personally acquainted with Jessie Evans before Ethel's funeral. A letter to Jessie on October 9 reads, "According to my promise over the telephone, I am sending herewith for your files an article which may be of interest and of some value in establishing the real date for the creating of Salt Lake County. It is a great pleasure to me to help you if and when I can. At any time should you desire information which you think may be in this office, please let me know. The pleasure will be all mine to give it if it is possible. I will consider it much more than a mere duty. It was a pleasure to me to know, as you informed me Sunday, that your mother is interested in the books. Should there ever arise in her mind, or yours, any question in relation to what is written there, please let me know. This letter I have made rather personal, not for your files. May the Lord bless you with everything you can seek in righteousness, I humbly pray."

For days thoughts had been churning in his head. Every man and every woman should have the opportunity for a good marriage. It was not good for man to be alone, nor woman either. That had been one of the important arguments in favor of plural marriage. His father's wives had all been very happily married to him. No man and no woman should pass through the mortal probation without the experience of marriage. The Lord had said that this life was the time to enter into marriage. Jessie Ella Evans was 35 years old, and for some reason had never married.

When Louie died in 1908, Ethel had been sent into his life to heal his hurt and sorrow. Now that Ethel was gone, Jessie had been sent to him. . . . Or had she? Perhaps it was just his loneliness that prompted such feelings. Or perhaps it was Jessie's singing. He loved beautiful music, and Jessie sang so beautifully. And she seemed to be such a happy, vibrant person as well. Yet, there was more than 26 years' difference in their ages. Did she really have any personal interest in him, or did he just imagine it? Just wishful thinking?

253

Joseph Fielding folded the letter, put it in an envelope —and tucked it away in his desk, clear at the back of a drawer. For four days he thought about little else. Much of his time he spent in reading proofs on his forthcoming book compilation, *Teachings of the Prophet Joseph Smith.* What would the Prophet Joseph do in a situation like this? Well, what would he do? He would take decisive action. That's what he would do. In this case, he would marry the woman. He would just walk into the county recorder's office and say, "Sister Evans, the Lord intends that you should become my wife. What's your answer?" Joseph Fielding opened his desk drawer, drew out the letter, put it in his pocket, and walked down to the City and County Building, up the stairs, and into the county recorder's office. Jessie Evans seemed surprised and delighted to see him. She invited him into her private office. Joseph Fielding told her he had come to sign a "specially prepared document of historical nature." Miss Evans was curious to know what it was. Joseph Fielding took the letter from his pocket. But before giving it to her he prepared her for it by reviewing his situation and hers and suggesting the importance of kindred spirits finding fulfillment in life together. As he left he handed her the letter, expressed the hope that she would read it in the spirit it was written, and seek the Lord's guidance. Jessie, smiling with pleasure, assured him that she certainly would. He left in high hopes. Two days later he was on a Western Pacific train headed for Oakland, California, to attend a stake conference. The next afternoon he "had the privilege of crossing the great expansion bridge by auto, to San Francisco and return. This bridge is one of the wonders of the world." He found himself wishing that Jessie Evans could be there to enjoy the experience with him. Love was like that great bridge, spanning a vast space, bridging the gap that otherwise would remain a void, a separation.

It was late Monday night, November 1, when he got back to Salt Lake City, and Tuesday he "met Miss Jessie Evans and had [an] *important* interview with her." She had been constantly on his mind throughout his trip, he told her. Now that she had had time to read and ponder his letter, his proposal, he was anxious to know her feelings.

Her feelings were all very favorable, she assured him. She had the highest esteem for him, and was honored that he would wish her for his wife. She invited him to come and spend Friday evening with her and her mother and get better acquainted. He in turn invited her to come and meet his children and get better acquainted with them, and they with her. Sunday evening, November 7, Jessie was soloist on a special program in the tabernacle, and Joseph Fielding was the most appreciative listener in the entire audience. The following Thursday night he attended the weekly choir practice to listen and see Jessie, then took her to his home where they had "a pleasant interview" with Amelia and Bruce.

On Sunday evening, November 21, 1937, "I called on Jessie E. and left her a ring which she was willing to accept." Their dates became more frequent. On Wednesday evening, December 22, he had a "special appointment with Jessie Evans—a very happy and enjoyable time. I have received *her* as a Christmas present, for which I am grateful." Christmas day and the holiday season saw them together often. On December 27, "Josephine, Julina, Amelia, Bruce and I spent the evening at the home of Jessie Evans who entertained us with songs. A very pleasant and enjoyable evening." The next evening it was a repeat performance at Joseph Fielding's home, and the following day, December 29, he "spent the evening with Jessie Evans, this day being her [36th] birthday, and because she has consented to become my *wife*, for which fact the children are happy as well as I. The Lord bless her." New Year's eve was spent at home. "Jessie and her mother were with us. We had a very pleasant night of song."

As Elder Smith welcomed the new year he recorded in his journal, "Jessie Ella Evans, [daughter] of Jonathan W. and Jeanette Buchanan Evans, was born Dec. 29, 1902, in Salt Lake City. With the most *lovely voice—to me*—that I ever listened to, whose music and song have charmed thousands, but *more especially me*. Always willing and ready to bless others, never refusing to sing at funerals and entertainments, if it is possible to accommodate all who make requests. I love her for her goodness, virtue and loveliness; her consideration and care of her mother, and because she loves *me*. May the Lord bless her always, I humbly pray."

Elder Smith not only found Sister Evans a lovely songstress, but a very jovial person, an extrovert, whose outgoing nature was good for him and helpful in his relationship with others. Nor did he ever change his mind about her. In 1970, after nearly 32 years of marriage, he commented, "Sister Smith is very helpful to me. She is such a happy, pleasant person. We enjoy each other and often spend time studying not only scriptures but also history and current events. The wives of the Church leaders should be happy, helpful wives."

With her acceptance of his marriage proposal he became firmly convinced of his earlier feelings that she had been divinely designated to become his wife. In 1963, a quarter of a century after their marriage, he told his son Douglas, "Your Aunt Jessie always belonged to me. I know that the Lord intended it. And the Lord sent her to me when I needed a wife and needed help and somebody in the family to help us and take care of us, and the Lord had raised her up and sent her to me. And oh, how grateful I am, for she has been just as true and faithful as anybody could possibly be, and we all love her!"

It was on January 5, 1938, that Jessie went through the temple for her endowment, prior to marriage. "I spent the evening with her, discussing temple work and other things." They decided to delay their marriage until April 12. "Due to the gossiping of a few 'friends' many rumors obtained circulation yesterday and today," he noted on January 18, "in relation to me and Jessie Evans." Naming a couple of women specifically, he observed that

Jessie Ella Evans, third wife of Joseph Fielding Smith—

As a young girl

As an opera singer

On honeymoon to Hawaii

In later life

they "and others have been very busy. No real damage done." Joseph and Jessie continued their romance, ignoring the gossip.

Because of their prominence, he being an apostle and author and she being the county recorder and a famous singer, their marriage in April was one of Salt Lake City's top society stories of 1938. On April 11 Elder Smith wrote to President Heber J. Grant, "This is to remind you according to my promise, of an appointment with me and Sister Jessie Evans at the Salt Lake Temple *tomorrow, Tuesday morning at 7:15.* I offer my humble apology in asking you to come to the temple at such an hour of the day, but train schedules make it necessary. . ." Several members of each of their families, including some of his children, were present to witness the marriage. "This morning at 7:15 Jessie E. Evans and I were married in the Salt Lake Temple, President Heber J. Grant performing the ceremony." He later noted that President Grant had told him, "Joseph, kiss your wife," and observed, "He said it like he meant it, and I have been doing it ever since."

They left immediately after the ceremony on a wedding trip to the Hawaiian Islands. "After the ceremony Jessie and I left over the Western Pacific for San Francisco." From San Francisco they went by boat to Los Angeles and then by boat to the Islands. For three weeks they combined a wedding trip with a tour of the Hawaii Mission and stake of the Church there, and were feted wherever they visited. "The good people, especially the Hawaiians, covered us with beautiful leis. . . . We were met by the largest, best and most worthy group of any who got off the ship. This night Sister Ralph E. Woolley prepared a dinner in our honor at which the stake presidency, Brother and Sister Oki, Chinese and others were present, and after the dinner we were royally entertained by two groups of Hawaiian women, who came with their ukelelies, guitars and a bass viol and sang for us. . . . Their singing of Hawaiian songs was a delightful thing. Jessie joined in with them, learning one of their songs, and singing at their request. They were delighted with her singing and have made arrangements for her to sing with them at the conference on Sunday. . . ."

And so it went through their three weeks on the islands, making a most delightful wedding trip. They visited craters, pineapple plantations, beaches and other points of interest, and were entertained with song and dance and treated to sumptuous feasts, Hawaiian style. They returned home the latter part of May, reaching Salt Lake City by train on May 21, and found that his children and her mother had a big dinner awaiting them. Looking back on their visit to the islands Joseph Fielding noted in his journal, "Everywhere we went we were royally entertained by the Hawaiians. We received 283 leis, and attended five or six luaus. We have held numerous meetings, met many hundreds of members, and I hope were able to do some good. Jessie's singing won the hearts of the people and we have made many friends."

The wedding trip set the pattern for their life for the next 33 years: they traveled together, he speaking and she singing at church conferences. She cared little for housekeeping or cooking meals, and he did not seem to care that she did not care for it. Louie had traveled with him not at all; Ethel had traveled with him some; Jessie Ella hardly let him travel without her, and he loved having her with him. While he was primarily a speaker and she a singer, they each did some of the other as well: she sometimes spoke as well as sang, and by and by he began singing duets with her, singing the alto part in his second-tenor voice. The congregations loved it. Once in awhile they would sing one of the songs that he had written. One of the songs they sang most frequently together was "If I Knew You and You Knew Me." They thoroughly enjoyed singing together, and spent many a pleasant hour at home practicing and singing for their own amusement, as well as singing in public.

Jessie continued as a featured singer with the Tabernacle Choir and also recorded some albums of songs. She sang at several dozen funerals every year and was

A familiar scene—President Joseph Fielding Smith and his wife Jessie sing a "do-it or else."

generous with her talents in singing at other occasions also. Busy with his own schedule of meetings and other assignments, Joseph Fielding nevertheless took time to go with Jessie to events where she was to be the featured singer. When the Tabernacle Choir scheduled a tour to California in 1941, with Richard L. Evans as commentator, Joseph Fielding composed a hilarious letter to Evans charging him with the care and protection of Jessie on the trip: "You are hereby authorized, appointed, chosen, designated, named, commanded, assigned, ordained and otherwise notified, informed, advised and instructed, *two wit:* . . ." the letter began, and several paragraphs of nonsense later, "To see that the said Mrs. Jessie Evans Smith, is permitted to travel in safety, comfort, ease, without molestation and that she is to be returned again to her happy home and loving husband and family in the beautiful and peaceful State of Utah and to her anxious and numerous kindred. . . ."

Richard L. replied in part, "Your masterful document of August 15 has cost me a good deal of brow-wrinkling and excruciating concentration. I think without question it will go down in history with the Bill of Rights and the Magna Charta. The remarkable thing about it is, as my legal staff and I have studied it over, that it conveys to me no privileges that I did not already feel free to take and imposes on me no responsibilities that it was not already my pleasure and intention to assume. However, it is a good idea, as many men can testify, to have the consent of a husband before traveling two thousand miles with his wife. . . ."

One day in 1970 when President Smith accompanied Jessie to choir practice, Richard P. Condie, conductor, said, "President Smith, we consider you a member of the choir." Condie was hardly prepared for the President's reply. He asked, "Then why don't you let me sing in the choir?" So Condie assigned him a seat in the choir and Joseph Fielding spent the evening singing.

Both Joseph Fielding and Jessie enjoyed a colorful cast iron plaque that hung on the kitchen wall of their apartment, stating, "Opinions expressed by the husband in this household are not necessarily those of the management." One time when she was assisting him in his office, when his secretary was on vacation, he tapped her on the shoulder as she sat at the typewriter, and said, "Remember, Mama dear, *over here you are not* the Speaker of the House!" She tended to be quite solicitous of his affairs, including his financial affairs, and it became something of a game between them as to how close a check she was able to keep on his income. At the time he became president and moved offices his aides found several thousand dollars in desk drawers, money which obviously did not fall under Jessie's careful accounting. Joseph Fielding had little regard for money as such. In earlier days when he was rearing a large family he had to be very careful in its expenditure. As the family at home dwindled in size and his income increased there was no such squeeze on his financial resources.

Jessie had been a close friend of Brigadier General Alma G. Winn of the Utah National Guard, and through this friendship Joseph Fielding took up the hobby of flying. For several years he flew in jets with General Winn and others of the National Guard. Once in the air he often took over the controls. Jessie apparently did not know this until one time she took a ride with the two of them, Joseph Fielding and Alma Winn, and saw her husband at the controls. "You're not going to let him fly it, are you?" she asked Winn, somewhat alarmed. "Why not?" said Winn. "He's done it before!" Such flying became one of the great delights in Elder Smith's life, from about 1955 to 1965, when at the urging of his friend President J. Reuben Clark he finally gave it up. During this period he also served as sort of a chaplain of the Utah National Guard, headed by Major General Max E. Rich. From time to time he met with guardsmen for Sunday services, preaching sermons to them. He became an honorary brigadier general in the guard and had his own uniform. The flying and other guard activities gave another pleasant dimension to his life. In 1964 he was given the Minuteman Award by the Utah National Guard.

Jessie's standing in the world of music also brought Joseph Fielding into contact with other interesting personalities and situations. The Smiths were patrons of the Valley Music Hall and were adopted as second parents by some of the performers who appeared there. Through the Smiths they received a good introduction to the Church. When the Music Hall's production of "Sound of Music" was in the planning stage, Jessie was offered one of the lead roles, that of the Mother Superior in the convent. She declined the role, feeling it would not be a very appropriate one for the wife of the president of the Council of the Twelve Apostles!

Jessie enjoyed doing fine needlepoint work, and as she got older she felt the need of using a magnifying glass

Joseph Fielding Smith tries his hand at the controls of an Air National Guard jet while Col. Alma G. Winn and Major Gen. Maxwell E. Rich give instructions. Later, Colonel Winn was promoted to brigadier general.

to help her see better. She invented a "no hands seeing aid"—a neck-strap magnifying glass that allows the use of both hands for sewing, reading, knitting, crocheting or whatever. She called it the "Magna Vu," applied for a patent, arranged for it to be manufactured in Japan and sold in the United States.

In 1966 Brigham Young University conferred upon Jessie its David O. McKay Humanities award, and in 1967 Ricks College followed suit, conferring upon her a distinguished achievement award, both of them primarily in recognition of her many years of service as a singer.

Joseph Fielding found satisfaction in these achievements and recognitions of Jessie, even as she did in his. He

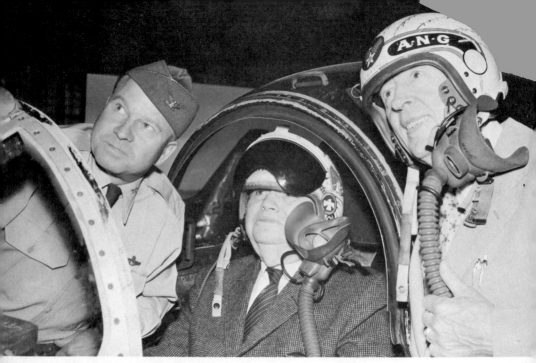

Left to right: Col. Alma G. Winn, President J. Reuben Clark, Jr., and President Joseph Fielding Smith inspect an F-86 Saberjet and its instrument panels and equipment.

traveled with her to such events even as she traveled with him to his numerous assignments. They usually traveled in a small American Motors car, a Rambler or Hornet, with Jessie doing the driving. She liked to drive fast and he had to keep a careful watch on the speedometer. She claimed to have a special permit from the Utah Highway Patrol granting her the right to travel at excessive speeds— another bit of the nonsense she liked to engage in. She also began telling stories of how she and Joseph Fielding had been childhood friends and that he had been a home teacher in their home when she was a girl. These tongue-in-cheek tales were taken seriously by undiscerning writers who either did not know or forgot that there was 26 years' difference in their ages. It was a source of amusement to Jessie to see them quoted in print.

If Joseph Fielding ever felt concerned about her antics he never said so. "In father's eyes Aunt Jessie could do no wrong," commented Milton one day in 1971. There was only one time anyone could remember of his ever deny-

The accomplishments of Jessie Evans Smith—

As a musician and vocalist

As a recorder

As an inventor

As a quilter and crocheter

ing her a wish: Joseph Fielding had inherited his father's pocket watch, and the day came when Jessie wished to make a brooch of the watch. This he refused. But feeling bad about denying her the wish, he had a brooch made up especially for her from some costly gem stones.

He was solicitous of her health and happiness. As the years passed she fell into poor health and had to be hospitalized a number of times. He spent hours and days sitting by her side in the hospital. During a 1969 illness he became particularly worried about her. He was then in his 90's yet was still showing the same concern and attention he always had. Thinking to alleviate his worry and tension, his son-in-law Bruce McConkie suggested to him one day, "Why don't you read from the Book of Mormon for awhile?" With some annoyance he replied, "I've read the Book of Mormon!"

Jessie Evans Smith surrounded by numerous items showing her handiwork.

The day came when his children were all married and gone, and the Smith house on Douglas Street seemed excessively large for just the two of them. Somewhat reluctantly they sold the house in 1952, and moved to an apartment in the Eagle Gate apartment house just across State Street east from the Beehive House. Here they lived for 19 years. The spacious ground floor apartment included a large living room, dining room, kitchen, bedroom, a study and hallway. A baby grand piano, a desk, a typewriter, shelves of books, a portrait of his father, furniture and mementos from near and far adorned their quarters. Here they spent many happy hours, and years, together, until her death in August of 1971, 11 months before his death.

Undoubtedly her presence in his life, her wit, her music, her outgoing personality, had helped to keep him young and happy, and useful beyond the usual span of years. She in turn enjoyed a life rich and full beyond what she could ever have had otherwise, had she not become the wife of Joseph Fielding Smith. Although she had no children of her own, she took a great interest in his children, especially the younger ones still at home when she joined the family: Reynolds, Douglas and Milton. To his children she was "Aunt Jessie," and she took a delight in being such. Her mother lived with them until her death January 1, 1957, and tended to the cooking and other domestic duties that Jessie had little interest in.

Of course it was a thrill to Jessie to become the first lady of the Church in January of 1970 when Joseph Fielding became the president of the Church. At the close of 1970 she commented, "It has been a very busy and exciting year. I've tried to be the best wife I could be to my husband and I hope that together we can do things pleasing to our Father in Heaven." Life with Joseph Fielding she had found pleasant beyond her fondest dreams. "He is the kindest man I have ever known," she often declared. "I have never heard him speak an unkind word." To which he would respond with a smile, "I don't know any unkind words."

Chapter 14

"The Lord has decreed that the wicked shall slay the wicked"

Turning Out the Lights in Europe

Sitting on the veranda of their hotel room in the colorful city of Florence, Italy, Joseph Fielding and Jessie Evans Smith looked down upon the nearby Arno River. By moonlight it seemed especially beautiful and peaceful. But early the next morning, the Fourth of July, 1939, they were awakened from sleep by the tramp, tramp, tramp of Benito Mussolini's soldiers marching by on the street below. "It gave us a terrible feeling."

A few days earlier, on June 22, they had traveled from Switzerland to Milano, Italy, and "visited the church where [Leonardo] da Vinci's original painting of the Last Supper is shown, and it was wonderful. We then went to a display of his works and also the beginning of television. From there we went to the famous Milano Cathedral which looks like lace from the outside. . . ." A week later they were at the Vatican City and "visited the Church of the Capuchin Friars where seven rooms are decorated with the bones of dead Friars and you see thousands of them." The next day in Rome they saw the tomb of Caesar Augustus and the "Mussolini Forum where 4,000 boys are in training from the age of 15 years until they are 21. The grounds and buildings are magnificent."

On the romantic Isle of Capri, just off the coast of

Italy, they watched the moon come up over the mountain and the moonlight shimmer enchantingly upon the waters of the Mediterranean Sea. Boat riding in Venice and touring in other picturesque cities of Italy, they found interest in the ancient cathedrals, the statuary, the hand-carved doors, the art galleries, the marble shops, the market places. And the people seemed warmly friendly. Yet spiritually they found not only Italy but all Europe deccorated with the bones of dead Friars. Writing from Denmark to his son Lewis, a missionary in Switzerland, near the close of their six-month stay in Europe in the summer of 1939, Joseph Fielding, faced with the reality of World War II, commented, "As I have traveled by train, by auto or by boat in this land I have been impressed with its beauty everywhere. The landscape has appeared so peaceful and beautiful with vegetation, cattle peacefully feeding, etc., and I have wondered how with such beautiful surroundings the hearts of men could be filled with greed, hate and evil and the desire to possess all out of harmony with the surroundings."

On July 24, Pioneer Day back home in Utah, the Smiths concluded a visit to Czechoslovakia, which had been betrayed into Hitler's hands that spring by Prime Minister Neville Chamberlain of England and Premier Edouard Daladier of France, in their futile effort to avert World War II. From Prague, Czechoslovakia's capital, they traveled to Berlin, where Jessie was invited to sing on Germany's largest radio station, and was paid 60 R marks for it. Agents of the Nazi party kept watch on their movements but did not interfere with them. In Danzig, the quaint city on the Baltic shore of Poland, the Smiths were luncheon guests of the government and attended an open air night time staging of Richard Wagner's opera, "Siegfried," on July 27. Danzig at the moment was the most discussed city in the world, for on threat of war Hitler demanded that it be given to Germany along with a wide strip of land across the Polish Corridor that divided Germany and East Prussia.

The following Sunday, July 30, the Smiths attended

LDS services in Berlin, and as they entered the chapel 650 German saints sang, "We Thank Thee O God for a Prophet." At services in nearby Chemnitz later that day the hymn was repeated by 900 German saints. At each service Joseph Fielding and Jessie both spoke and sang duets to the appreciative congregations. Nazi SS troopers roamed the nearby streets, while German youth were indoctrinated into hatred of parents and home, God and religion, and industrialists happily manufactured guns to conquer the world and gas ovens in which to burn to death Europe's several million Jewish men, women, and children.

From May through October, 1939, Joseph Fielding and Jessie Evans Smith toured Europe: England, Scotland, Belgium, France, Switzerland, Italy, Czechoslovakia, Austria, Germany, Sweden, Norway, Holland, and Denmark, visiting the missions of the Church, preaching and singing and conferring. But what started out to be a tour to strengthen the missions became in the end an emergency operation to help direct the evacuation of nearly all missionaries from Europe, except from the British Isles.

While Hitler, Mussolini, and Stalin were each plotting the enslavement of various European countries, Joseph Fielding conducted a conference of all European mission presidents at Lucerne, Switzerland, in early June. Mission presidents giving reports at the conference included Thomas E. McKay, brother of David O. McKay, and president of the Swiss and East German Missions, Mark B. Garff of the Danish Mission, Frank Murdock of the Netherlands Mission, Hugh B. Brown of the British Mission, Joseph E. Evans of the French Mission, M. Douglas Wood of the Swedish and West German Missions; John A. Israelson of the Norwegian Mission, and Wallace F. Toronto of the Czechoslovakian Mission. Each man there was deeply concerned about the spectre of war that threatened Europe.

Yet despite the mounting tensions in Europe, it was generally a pleasant summer for the Smiths. It was as a second honeymoon. Wherever they visited they were royally welcomed, given sight-seeing tours, dinners, bouquets of flowers, jewelry and other gifts, as the missionaries and local Saints expressed their appreciation for the visit of a general authority and his songstress wife. At each meeting Joseph spoke and Jessie sang, and usually the two of them sang duets and Jessie also spoke. Throughout Europe, day after day and week after week the same soul-satisfying schedule was followed. Though there were no branches of the Church in Italy several days were spent there in visiting such famous cities and sites as Rome, Venice, Genova, Napoli, the Tower of Pisa, ruins of the ancient City of Pompeii, etc. From the Scottish Highlands to the Swiss Alps, to the blue Danube, to the glaciers of Norway, to the tulip fields in Holland, they saw nearly every site of worth to see throughout Europe.

Making the visit to Switzerland doubly enjoyable for the Smiths was the presence of Joseph's son Lewis, who as a missionary there served as a reporter at the mission presidents' conference, and a month later became private secretary to President Thomas E. McKay. It was the first that Jessie and Lewis had met, although they had previously corresponded.

Since coming to power in 1933 Hitler and his Nazi henchmen had been building Germany into a war machine, and by 1938 it was apparent to many that he and Mussolini in Italy were ready to plunge the world into war if need be to achieve the political domination they sought. Austria had been annexed to Germany in April 1938, and Czechoslovakia in March of 1939, while Italy annexed Albania.

In April, 1939, the presidency of The Church of Jesus Christ of Latter-day Saints, Heber J. Grant, J. Reuben Clark, Jr., and David O. McKay, assigned Joseph Fielding to make an inspection tour of its European missions and conduct the mission presidents' conference. To Lewis he wrote April 11, 1939, "If Mr. Hitler and Mr. Mus— whatever his name is and he is a muss, will just keep cool for a few more weeks and not cause another world war, I will be with you in June. . . . I may be in Europe in May and June and even later. . . ." And a week later, "In three more days, Friday the 21st, I will be on my way to Europe. We will go from here to New York, perhaps stopping on the way at Palmyra and the Hill Cumorah. . . . So I will be in England shortly after this letter reaches you. We will sail [from New York] on the 29th [of April]. I suppose that Aunt Jessie and I will be kept very busy when we arrive in Europe, and there will be many things to be done. It is now 40 years, or will be on the 12th of May, since I left home for my mission to England. There have been many changes, no doubt, in that land since that time, and also in all of Europe. I hope that things will remain quiet for some time to come. . . ."

As late as August 18, 1939, the Smiths, nearing what they thought to be the end of their mission tour, could note in Denmark, "It is very quiet and peaceful here." But Hitler was massing his troops on the Polish border, and England and France promised to aid Poland if she were invaded. Writing to Lewis in Switzerland from Copenhagen, August 16, Joseph Fielding reported, "From here we will go to other parts of Denmark, and then we have to go back into the West German Mission to finish our labors. As far as Germany is concerned, we would just as soon go to Holland and France. If we had the same freedom in Germany it would be better. However, we got along well when we were there, but we had to be more guarded in our remarks and were watched by secret agents. These things do not add to your peace of mind. However, we are prepared to do our duty. There was a great contrast in the meals of Germany and Sweden. In Germany we got much synthetic food, but in Sweden we had a good supply of the very best. Good butter and cream were furnished us in Sweden in abundance and also good bread. Then again they give you a square meal before they serve you the meal you order. You have the privilege of going to the table and helping yourselves as often as you like, and it is all good too. In Norway they give you good things to eat, but they are not so elaborate with it. We have yet to learn about Denmark as we have been fed at the mission quarters since we arrived."

The Smiths moved from Denmark back into Germany and had planned to leave for home the fore part of September. As late as August 24, writing to Lewis from Hannover, Germany, Joseph Fielding could say, "We are hoping now that nothing will arise to interfere with the program as it has been arranged, and we will be permitted to finish the work as it has been arranged for us. We have had a very pleasant and we hope successful visit in Sweden, Norway and Denmark, where we were well received. Our meetings here have also been successful. We have found some very good faithful people and they have been delighted with our visit."

Joseph Fielding Smith, Jessie Evans Smith, Evelyn N. Wood, and President M. Douglas Wood in Nuremburg, Germany, railroad station where they made arrangements for evacuation of some of the missionaries.

President Wallace F. Toronto, Jessie Evans Smith, and Joseph Fielding Smith on a Czech train during evacuation.

But later on that very day, President Wood of the West German Mission received a telegram from the church presidency in Salt Lake City "to be prepared to move upon immediate notice."

"It was quite exciting," recorded Jessie in her journal of August 24. "The feeling is very tense. We held meeting that night and had a very splendid service, but everyone was still wondering about conditions." The following day they "received word from President [Thomas E.] McKay that he was sending his elders to Denmark [from East Germany]. We decided we better return to Frankfurt [Germany], so we took the train arriving there at 3:30. We went to [mission] headquarters and things were surely popping. Phone calls, telegrams and cablegrams, and everyone busy packing. We received a cablegram from [the church] presidency stating that all elders be removed from Germany immediately, and that we were to make headquarters in either Holland or Denmark until we received [further] word. We were going to Basel [Switzerland], but Joseph immediately went down and got tickets to Holland. They were the last two on the train, so we were very fortunate for everyone and everything was in turmoil and a terrible feeling. The train left at 12:05 a.m. [Saturday, August 26]. We were on the train all night, and about 4 a.m. the train stopped at the station Kologne for one hour and a half, and that wasn't a very pleasant feeling. We could see many people running and making a lot of noise, a lot of baggage, and we thought sure they were letting the troops through and that we could not get through. That was a terrible feeling. We didn't sleep. We could see through the train windows soldiers out in fields putting up guns and soldiers lined up along the way. It was a terrible feeling. When we reached the border we didn't know whether we were going through or not, but we had our boat tickets and were saved. . . ." (Their having boat tickets was evidence that they did not plan to remain in Holland and thus were allowed to come in.)

In Holland the Smiths learned that "we were the last to cross the border [from Germany into Holland], because one hour after we received a phone call that they wouldn't let any of the elders across, so we were surely in a fix," noted Jessie. "They were on the border with no money. We called Brother Wood and he sent a man with money to one border, and Brother Murdock sent a man to his border. By that they were taken care of and sent on to Copenhagen, so we then decided to go to Denmark. We also decided to fly. Brother Murdock called, and we couldn't get a thing until Wednesday. It took 18 hours by train, but in a few minutes they called and said they had two places that day so we took them, leaving Holland at 5:30, arriving in Copenhagen at 7:30, and were they glad to see us."

During the next two months the Smiths assisted in

the transfer of more than 200 missionaries from the war-threatened countries back to the United States. Still demanding a corridor across Poland, the Germans invaded that unfortunate land on September 1 and completely crushed it in a month's time. Russia also invaded it before the month was over. England and France both declared war on Germany September 3, and the following year Germany swept through Denmark, Holland, Norway, Belgium, and France, while Russia invaded Finland, and soon many of the nations of the world were engulfed in World War II.

In a letter to Lewis from Copenhagen on September 1, the day Germany invaded Poland, Joseph Fielding, apparently still unaware of that invasion, reported his experiences as a visiting apostle in Germany, Holland and Denmark in that fateful last week of August 1939: "Our tickets took us through Germany. . . . We left Aalborg [Denmark] with some misgivings, because the American ambassador in Copenhagen stated to President Garff and me two days earlier that he would give us one week before the break between the powers would come [Germany vs. England, France and Poland]. Following closely German propaganda he felt he could judge somewhat accurately how many days it would take. Of course we hoped that he was wrong and took a rather gloomy look at the situation, but we could not help being impressed. When we reached the German border we saw no indications of excitement and the same day moved on to Kiel. . . . While there I went with some of the missionaries on a ride through the harbor and saw some of Germany's great war machines. We held our meeting and then moved on to Hamburg. By this time the papers [German newspapers] had increased their accusations against Poland, and some of the missionaries said that this was a regular stage in the propaganda, and it would not be many days before trouble would come. The next morning it was reported that the Poles were pulling ugly faces at the Germans across the border and were massing for an attack. We continued on to Hannover. At this place while we

were holding a meeting with the missionaries in the afternoon word was received from the First Presidency giving
instructions that all missionaries should immediately pack
and be prepared on a moment's notice to leave Germany.
We held a good meeting at night. I spoke on the second
great commandment and told [why] strife and bitterness
prevailed in the world and nothing but the gospel of
Jesus Christ could cure the ills. I got away with it not-
withstanding the fact that there is much agitation now
against the Hebrew scriptures. There is agitation to this
effect, 'we got rid of the Jew and now his book must go.'
We have a photograph showing anti-Christian literature
and attacks upon the Jews displayed in a bookshop
window.

"Early the next morning word was received for
everybody to clear out of Germany. The Woods left for
Frankfurt by plane, and we went by train, arriving there
in the early afternoon. There was great commotion in
trying to reach all the missionaries and put things in shape
for the departure. I had my ticket to Basel [Switzerland],
but word came from the presidency relayed from London
for me to move on either to Holland or Denmark and set
up headquarters and take charge of the situation. Our
plan was that all East German missionaries should go into Denmark, and all from West Germany into Holland.
Instructions were given to this end, and our army [of
missionaries?] commenced moving onto the Holland borders. We took the night train and after some delays
reached the border the next morning where we found stiff
resistance on the part of the Dutch who were determined
not to let foreigners into their land. As we had our ticket
for the journey home on the *Manhattan* they permitted
us to squeeze through. We went to The Hague where I
intended that we should remain, but the Dutch government refused to let the missionaries enter except some
who had tickets beyond the borders of Holland and
turned them back. These missionaries had no funds.
Brother Murdock sent two missionaries to the border
with money to try and reach the stranded elders and

give them tickets to Denmark. We also contacted Brother Wood and had him send an elder with funds to the other border, and in this way we finally contacted these elders after very great difficulty and turned them towards this more hospitable land [Denmark]. Finding that the majority of missionaries would be in Denmark we felt that it was necessary to leave Holland for Denmark also. We were able to get passage on the airplane that same afternoon [Sunday] and in a little more than two hours were in Copenhagen. Since arriving here we have been kept extremely busy trying to reach the different missions and with communications from and to the First Presidency. From the reports we received conditions are getting more grave and communications more difficult. . . . We are both well but kept constantly near the telephone and typewriter. We still have one worry, in addition to the many others, as President Toronto and his missionaries have not arrived [from Czechoslovakia]. We hope they will be here tonight."

At first it was planned to reassign many of the missionaries from Germany and Czechoslovakia to Holland, Denmark, Sweden and Norway, but the plan was soon changed, and they were sent back to the United States. Only Denmark was willing to receive any and soon she also refused. "We have been kept very busy ever since we landed in Holland. We felt, when Holland shut her gates against us and turned the missionaries back into Germany, that the proper place for us was here in Denmark," Joseph Fielding wrote to Lewis from Copenhagen September 8. "We have asked the Lord to bless this little country for her hospitality to the servants of the Lord who have come into her borders. Both Sweden and Norway have tightened up and will not let foreigners enter now, but they did at first. Under the conditions we have not sent missionaries there as we first decided to do, but are returning them all to the United States—all who came out of Germany from both missions—except eleven who have been sent out to labor in Denmark. We feel comparatively safe up here, although bombs have been dropped on Esbjerg and within a short distance of our meeting-house. . . . We hope that the bombers will not get in this land again.

"We sent 40 missionaries out on a freight boat, the *Mormachawk* and 60 on the *Scanyork*. They were furnished cots in the hold instead of freight in the space they occupy. Each boat carried about ninety passengers. . . . They were all happy and seemed to be very comfortable. We are sending the group who remain out this coming week, and then we will have all of them, except the eleven, homeward bound, including Presidents Toronto and Wood, but they will not leave until about the 19th on a Swedish boat. . . .

"Each morning we have had the missionaries together in meeting, and I have given them one hour to one hour and a half in which they have asked questions. I think they have learned more, at least some of them, in that period than they learned all the time they have been in the mission field. I hope, at least, that we were able to clear up some of the funny notions some of them had, and the more I think of it the more I become disgusted with some of our so-called educators.

"Well, things are beginning to ease up for us somewhat. I will be glad when we have things so well in hand that there will be no necessity for us to be here, but we could not go under fire. We had our ticket for the *Manhattan* which was to have sailed from Southampton today, and which sailed a week ago and is now in New York. I let a missionary and his wife from West Germany have the tickets and sent him home. We have no idea when we will be permitted to leave. Perhaps when most of the missionaries are out of Europe. Tell President [Thomas E.] McKay we have taken good care of his missionaries and made them as comfortable as we could when we sent them home. . . . After this week all will be gone except the forces of these Scandinavian missions, and we hope they will be reduced. It will be a pleasure when we learn that those in France are out and homeward bound."

By the latter part of September a great majority of

the European-assigned missionaries were on their way home. Lewis was one of the few who remained on the continent, and that was because as private secretary to Thomas E. McKay in the Swiss Mission he had some assignments to handle after the others were gone. Joseph Fielding and Jessie had hoped to get a ship from Denmark by October 10 and were restless to be on their way inasmuch as there was nothing more for them to do. To Lewis on October 7 he wrote from Copenhagen, "I am willing to remain here indefinitely, but cannot see anything more that I can do. I am no help to you in Switzerland, and cannot assist you or the missionaries in France or Holland to get away. We have no missionaries here in Denmark, except the three secretaries. There is only one in Norway and three in Sweden, and they will be leaving from Sweden shortly. As I cannot pass from one land to another I am of little value, and we feel that our work is about over so far as any help is concerned."

The Smiths finally sailed for home from the Netherlands in the last week of October. The boat they had been waiting for in Denmark had not shown up by October 15, and they had an opportunity to take passage aboard the *Zaandam* from Holland along with the missionaries still in Holland. To Lewis he wrote from The Hague on October 18, "We had received so many invitations to come to Holland and leave with the missionaries from here that finally we accepted the invitation and came. . . . We have found the past two weeks very trying because there has not been anything to be done. I have held my hands or spent [my time] walking the streets or reading while Aunt Jessie has knitted."

Elder and Mrs. Smith arrived in Salt Lake November 12, 1939, six days after arriving in New York aboard the *SS Zaandam*, carrying the last group of missionaries to leave the war area. Three mission presidents and 11 missionaries, including his son Lewis Warren Smith, were left in Europe to carry on the work of the Church, he reported.

What were Joseph Fielding's feelings in regard to the

causes of the war, the saints left behind to suffer in Europe, Europeans generally, and the principle of gathering to Zion as it touched on this tragic situation in Europe in 1939? In three letters to his son Lewis, two of them in October shortly before leaving for home and the third after reaching home in November, he made some candid remarks regarding these matters:

"If these foolish and frightened nations realized *what* and *who* we are, they would beg to have the missionaries remain in their lands rather than ask that they leave their borders. When the priesthood is withdrawn and that because they [these countries] have indicated that those who bear it must leave their borders, then they are placing themselves where they are not entitled to the protection that they would otherwise receive. Of course the members of the Church who remain may be a force for good and a means of protection, but of this there is some uncertainty. We have thousands of members in Germany. Some of them are as faithful as any that can be found in any land, but I fear they will have to suffer. . . . I have felt very keenly that I would, if I had the power, pick them up in one body—all who are faithful— and transplant them somewhere in Zion, or on the American continent, for that is the land of Zion. Unfortunately I do not have this power.

"As I traveled from place to place in Germany and especially when we were in Danzig and Konigsburg I realized that it was only a matter of time, and a very brief time, when this trouble would come. We could feel it in the air. We could see it on every side and we realized that Germany was preparing to take over all the [Polish] corridor and very soon, peaceably if possible but at any cost. When she made her agreement with Russia [on August 24, 1939] then we knew that the time had come. My heart was sick every time we held a meeting and shook hands with the people at its close. They all greeted us warmly, and their [friendship] meant more to me than they perhaps realized. Some of them shed tears and said they were looking for grave trouble, and we would never meet again in this life. I feel sorry for them now, and pray each day that the Lord will protect them through this dreadful time.

"I am very thankful that I have not taken the responsibility upon me to counsel anyone to remain in this land, in any of the nations, if he had a chance to go to America, in any part of that choice land. I never have been able to do that and have argued this point because I do not know when the Lord reversed his commandment (D&C 29:8 and 133:1-16), that his people should be gathered out from Babylon. It is true that our nation has made restrictions [on immigration], with which I have never agreed. . . . We do, however, have opportunities and people can get into the United States. If they cannot get on the quota to go there they could have gone to other lands, and any place in America, in my judgment, is better than this land of turmoil and strife. . . . Europe has always been a place of turmoil and strife and principally so in Germany. . . .

"I believe with President Murdock, when all of the missionaries are out of these lands then it will be just too bad for these nations. They have not appreciated the message which was sent to them. They did not want us and are glad to see us go, and I think the Lord will remember them for their works and the rejection of the message of salvation which was sent unto them. Read Sec. 133 [of the Doctrine and Covenants]. The answer the Lord will make to the nations is that they shall lie down in sorrow because when he came they heard him not. When he spoke again they refused to hearken and rejected his servants. While the Lord has said the wicked shall slay the wicked, yet I think he will remember the bandits and gangsters who have brought this trouble upon the world. . . .

"We have preached the gospel as the Lord has commanded us to do and have borne witness to these nations for over one hundred years of the restoration of the gospel. We have tried to convince them that the Lord has again spoken from the heavens and that he has sent his servants forth with the message of salvation as it has again been revealed in this dispensation of the fulness of times, but they seemingly do not want our message and will not heed the warning. We have been crying repentance among the nations for all these years as the Lord commanded us to do, but steadily and persistently the nations have been growing more corrupt and more ungodly year by year. . . . The Lord has decreed that the wicked shall slay the wicked, and this will go on until eventually the earth will be cleansed of its evil and wickedness when Christ shall come in glory to take vengeance upon the ungodly who shall be as stubble and burned. That day is not far away. . . ."

Chapter 15

*"We cannot be too humble, prayerful
and diligent in our work"*

Missionary and Soldier Sons

It was late at night and the streets were but dimly lit, with the lights on the street corner posts casting eerie shadows across the snow for a few feet then fading into darkness. The houses along Salt Lake's Douglas Street stood silent and forboding, like grim sentinels. Through the dark and cold of the night a lone figure came walking down the street, his footsteps so silent in the snow that they could not be heard. When he reached the corner house, he turned up the walk without pausing and onto the porch, where unlit Christmas lights hung. Quietly he tried the door, but found it locked. Without any noise whatever he walked around to the side of the house and tried the kitchen door. It too was locked. He then tried pushing up a window next to the door, and after some little effort managed to get it up far enough to slip an arm through, reach around and unlatch the kitchen door.

Joseph Fielding Smith sleeping in the bedroom next to the kitchen was awakened by the noise. He got up from his bed and carefully opened the door into the kitchen and quickly flipped on the lights. There stood a young man in a soldier uniform. Tears welled in Joseph Fielding's eyes. He rushed across the room and embraced his son Douglas.

Two days earlier, on December 21, 1942, Joseph Fielding had suffered the traumatic experience of seeing his son and other young men in Salt Lake City loaded into an army truck like so many head of cattle and conveyed to Fort Douglas for induction into the army. He had little hope of seeing him again for several months or even years. But after two days of processing, the draftees were allowed to return to their homes for the Christmas holidays. Douglas, not living so far from Fort Douglas, had chosen to walk home, but it was late at night when he had been allowed to leave. Years later he remembered that moment in the kitchen as one of the most joyous experiences of his life. He said he fully realized for the first time just how much his father really loved him, as he wept and embraced him.

Having five sons it was inevitable that Joseph Fielding was going to become deeply involved in America's effort in World War II. How great a sacrifice he would be called upon to make he did not realize until that terrible day of January 2, 1945, when like a thunderbolt there came from the War Department a telegram: "We regret to inform you . . ." His son Lewis Warren Smith had been killed!

The same day the telegram arrived, a card had been received from Lewis, sent from the Holy Land.

Reeling from the shock, Joseph Fielding reached for his journal, again seeking the balm of expression: Turning its pages back to Friday, December 29, 1944, the day on which Lewis had died, he recorded. "My son Lewis W. was killed today in the service of his country. He was returning from an appointment which took him to India. He spent Christmas day in Bethlehem and, from all we know, was on his way back to his base somewhere in Western Africa when the plane crashed. . . ." He later learned that the plane had exploded in mid-air. Cause was unknown but sabotage was suspected. Lewis was in the Army Intelligence Service, and his assignments were of a highly confidential nature. He had been in the military service since March 4, 1942, and was expected back in the United States soon. He was 26 years old, Joseph Fielding's second oldest son, and held the rank of staff sergeant.

Lewis Warren Smith, killed in the service of his country Dec. 29, 1944.

"This word came to us as a most severe shock as we had high hopes that soon he would be back in the United States. We had felt that he would be protected as he has escaped several times before from danger. It was hard for us to realize that such a thing could happen," Elder Smith noted in his journal.

Grieved though he was he found comfort in the fact that Lewis had lived a clean life and thus was qualified for a place in the celestial kingdom. "If Lewis ever did or said a mean thing I never heard of it. His thoughts were pure as were his actions. . . . As severe as the blow is we have the peace and happiness of knowing that he was clean and free from the vices so prevalent in the world and found in the army. He was true to his faith and is worthy of a glorious resurrection, when we shall be reunited again."

President Smith soon received letters from his son's commanding officer, a Lieutenant Garland F. Smith, and from several of his buddies in the military, each praising his character and expressing their sorrow at his death. Joseph Fielding took great comfort in the letters. Writing to his daughter and son-in-law, Lois and William S. Fife, several weeks later he said, "We got further word about Lewis from one of his companions, Gene F. Walburn. He gave us the information regarding the accident to the plane and said the bodies were taken to Maiduguri, Nigeria, and buried in a 'beautiful military cemetery' there. One thing that helps us is the fact that each of the men who has written to us has testified to Lewis' clean life, his high principles and his integrity to his religion. When each writes this way, without any consultation, it is a great tribute to our boy, son and brother. . . . Such words as these are comforting, and each has testified in the same manner about him. The beautiful thing about it all is that it is so true. A better boy could not be found. A more worthy one could not be taken. We are sure that he was called to some work on the other side."

This latter thought he had expressed in more detail in a letter to Miss Anabel Monroe, a friend of Lewis' living in Great Falls, Montana. In response to a letter of sympathy from her Joseph Fielding wrote a lengthy reply, stating in part, "You can imagine the severity of the shock which came to us, for we had built up high hopes that Lewis would return to us again. There had been some very remarkable experiences through which he had passed which led us to believe that he was to be protected. He had written in the latter part of November that he was appointed to go to India, and when he returned he would be privileged to return to the United States. . . . And then the news came that stunned us, and it was difficult for us to believe that an error had not been made. We are reconciled to the condition because it all has the appearance, to us, that he was called to the other side, there to engage in some labor far more important than his service here. We feel sure that he has some mission and has been taken by divine command. To think this is comforting. We realize that there is a great work that has to be done over there in preparation for the coming of the great day of righteousness, and that some are called to labor there in preparation of that great event. . . . With the assurance which the gospel brings, we feel that all is well with Lewis and we know that we will see him again. We know that he went out of this life clean, and is entitled to every blessing that exaltation can give, for these blessings shall be his. . . . We know that we are in the last days and it will not be long before the great change will come, the earth will be cleansed, the graves will be opened, the righteous will come forth, peace will reign and wickedness will be found no more. . . ."

It was five years before the government returned Lewis' body to Utah. Joseph Fielding tells of it in a letter to his son Milton who was then completing a mission to Argentina: "Friday morning, December 2nd [1949], the body arrived with an escort, a sergeant named Strange came with it and remained until the services were over. The same day we met in the Larkin Mortuary, the family and some friends, and had prayer, Elder Richard L. Evans offering the prayer, and then we went to the cemetery. It was a beautiful day just like spring, and for this we were grateful. At the grave Bishop Joseph W. Bambrough made a few remarks, also Richard Gunn who was with Lewis in India and the last member of the Church to see him. Then Bruce [McConkie] made a very fine talk which was impressive. We had no singing. Uncle Roy Taylor dedicated the grave. Then the military honors were paid him according to the custom in the army, and we laid his body away. Now we feel much better knowing that it is here and we are happy because we know he was clean and was worthy in every respect and entitled to every blessing that can be obtained."

When word of Lewis' death had reached Joseph Fielding, he had two other sons in the service: Douglas, a private, was serving as a military policeman in France, and became a veteran of the Battle of the Bulge, one of the famous campaigns in World War II. George Reynolds was a specialist third class in the navy, in training at a school in Kansas. Being the father of three children, Joseph Fielding Jr. was exempted from military duty. Milton, the youngest son, was still too young to be in the service at that time but went later. He served in the navy on a minesweeper out of San Francisco.

All five of the Smith boys served on missions for the Church: Joseph Fielding Jr. in England, 1933-35 where he served as president of the Liverpool District for the last 16 months of his mission; Lewis in Switzerland, 1937-39; George Reynolds in Argentina, 1940-43; Douglas in the Northwest (and Alaskan) Mission, 1947-49, and Milton in Argentina, 1947-49. Milton also served as president of the Central American Mission, 1968-71. Two of the Smith girls served as mission matrons, wives of mission presidents: Emily, whose husband Louis Garrett Myers was president of the North German Mission, 1962-66, and Amelia, whose husband Bruce R. McConkie was president of the Southern Australian Mission, 1961-64.

At one time two of Joseph Fielding's sons were separated in their missionary labors almost pole to pole. Milton was laboring on the island of Chubut off the southern tip of Argentina while Douglas was in far off Alaska.

All five sons were set apart to their missionary field of labor by their father. The tone of these blessings is exemplified in the blessing given to his son Lewis:

MISSIONARY BLESSING GIVEN TO
ELDER LEWIS WARREN SMITH BY HIS FATHER
JOSEPH FIELDING SMITH

Lewis Warren Smith, my beloved Son, by virtue of the holy priesthood I lay my hands upon your head and set you apart to labor in the Swiss-German Mission or unto such field as you may be assigned in that land. Go forth in the spirit of faith with a desire in your heart to magnify your calling, for it is a responsible duty which has been assigned you and a great privilege. It is in fulfillment of the promise made by our Lord that this gospel of the kingdom should be preached in all the world as a witness before the end of

The four serviceman sons of Joseph Fielding Smith

Milton Edmund Smith—navy

Douglas Allan Smith—75th Infantry, army

George Reynolds Smith—navy

Lewis Warren Smith—Army Air Force Intelligence.

unrighteousness shall come. All men are to be warned so far as they may be reached by the message of salvation, for the Lord grants unto every soul the privilege of hearing the truth. They who have not heard it and will not hear it in this life, shall have the opportunity in the spirit world.

Your duty shall be to warn all men and to seek in the spirit of prayer and faith to find those of the House of Israel who will hearken. Do nothing without first asking the Lord for guidance in humble prayer. I bless you that you may be protected from every evil influence, for Satan will lie in wait to destroy. But if you hearken to the counsels of the priesthood and will magnify your calling and seek the Lord in prayer you shall be protected. Be sober and diligent, and I bless you that your mind may be quickened and your understanding enlarged by the Holy Spirit, and through your faithfulness that your tongue may be loosed. If you are faithful you shall have the gift of language so that you may speak to the people in power in their own tongue. Remember your covenants, be faithful unto them, honor the priesthood which you bear and honor your parents.

O Father in heaven let thy spirit go before this thy young servant, protect him, grant unto him the blessings of health and strength and wisdom and power to serve thee in the name of Jesus Christ, Amen.

The contrast in feeling which Joseph Fielding had toward his sons being in the military service and being on church missions was well expressed in a letter to Milton shortly after he left for his mission in April, 1947: "Once more we have had the occasion of seeing one of our boys off on a long journey and with a seemingly long period before him before he can return. We watched the train as far as we could see it, and you standing on the back platform with thoughts in your mind which we can only surmise. I think I know quite well what you were thinking, for I have passed through a like experience, and it seemed that the time ahead of me was to be so long that it could hardly come to an end. . . . The best way to help the time to pass is to have your mind on your work and diligently labor to accomplish all for which you have gone forth. This is the cure for that strange feeling which all missionaries get in the beginning. To keep the mind occupied with the duties which are required is the most satisfactory cure for that longing feeling, and then will come a real satisfaction in accomplishing the work which is assigned. . . .

"I stated that our feelings were very tender when you left and we left with some tears in our eyes, but withal it was not a case of tears of sadness or misgivings, as was the case when our boys left once before to enter the service and to be required to do we knew not what. It is a joy to be in the service of the Lord, but not to be in the service of his adversary, or be called upon to contend by force of arms against the Lord's adversary. We were very blue when we turned our boys in each instance over to Uncle Samuel, not knowing what the end would be, or whether they would return or not. We will never forget how Douglas was forced into a truck and taken to Fort Douglas with such a crowd that they had to stand for lack of room. He went away cheerful enough, but we went home very sad indeed. So it was with you and Lewis and Reyn. But now we are sending another boy out to serve the Lord and the feeling we have is very different; it is one of rejoicing that we have sons worthy to engage in such a work, for there is no greater work than to be in the service of our Lord and endeavor to bring souls to him. The Lord will bless and protect you if you will be true to him. . . ."

Despite his extremely busy schedule, Joseph Fielding Smith found time to write frequently to his sons while they were in the service and while they were on church missions. When he was on his mission in England as a young man at the turn of the century he learned the worth of letters from home. His wife Louie and his father President Joseph F. Smith had been particularly faithful about writing to him. He desired to be just as faithful in writing to his sons. In a testimonial for President Smith in 1971 his youngest son Milton humorously recalled that his father's letters, both those written to him in the service and on his mission, were "more preachy than newsy," but nevertheless he had greatly appreciated getting them. Indeed his letters to all his boys tend to be full of admonition, constantly urging them to be true and faithful, to keep themselves clean and unspotted from the sins of the world, to do what is right. But if a father does not concern himself with such counsel to his sons, who will? Or who better should?

Douglas and Milton were on their missions at the same time, and in the course of his mission in Argentina, Milton, or Mitty as he had come to be known in his college days, felt the need of purchasing a horse on which to travel through the rural areas to which he was assigned. Joseph Fielding remembering that he had nearly always walked while on his mission in England, questioned Milton's need for a horse, and wondered about the problem of his taking care of it. Nevertheless he sent the funds to finance its purchase. Sometime later he was asked, "Brother Smith, are you supporting anyone in the mission field?" To which he replied, "Yes, two boys and a horse!"

When Joseph Fielding and his brother Joseph Richards were on their missions to England 1899-1901, their father President Joseph F. Smith several times answered questions one or the other had raised regarding principles of the gospel, such as whether there were daughters of perdition. Now Joseph Fielding in turn answered in letters to his missionary sons questions that one or another of them posed in letters to him. In these letters then there is a wealth of commentary upon doctrine, commentary which makes for some choice reading for anyone with a serious interest in LDS theology. There are also some delightfully candid comments upon politics, religion, science and other issues.

Joseph Fielding offers it as his opinion, for instance, that glorified beings live on the sun. It was a hot summer day in Salt Lake City, July 18, 1948, the day before his 72nd birthday anniversary, when he was writing to Milton in Argentina, and his interest had turned to the sun: "The weather here for several days has been really warm. . . . We have no complaint coming, however, for we depend upon the sun for most everything. If it were not for the sun we would have no rain, no water to drink, for it is the sun which draws the water up into the sky and then lets it down again. The grass would not grow; the trees would not bloom and there would be no fruit. Everything would wither up and die. . . . We know that we could not exist if we did not have the good old sun to warm us and provide us with what we have. . . .

"But there is something still more important than all of this about the sun. Contrary to the teachings of the astronomers and men of science—these great men who think they know it all—the sun is not gradually throwing off its heat and eventually after eons of years it will [not] become a cold dead world like the moon. I do not know just how dead the moon is, but that is another question. . . . It is my judgment and belief that the sun is a celestial body. It has previously passed through its death and had its resurrection, just as it is decreed that this earth shall do. No man ever saw the face of the sun, so far as I know, for it is surrounded by a cloud. This cloud is what the astronomers see. It is very apparent during an eclipse, but the sun is veiled so that we cannot see its surface. Moreover, I believe that it is inhabited. Why not? If we ever have the privilege of dwelling on a celestial earth—and this earth will become such—we will have to endure 'everlasting burnings.'

"If you have a copy of *Teachings of the Prophet Joseph Smith* turn to page 347 and read what the Prophet said. The Lord dwells in 'everlasting burnings.' If we are worthy of celestial glory we will do the same. In Hebrews 12:29, we read 'For our God is a consuming fire.' This means that anything mortal, corruptible, could not endure his presence. Joseph Smith could not have stood the presence of the Father and the Son, when he saw them in glory, except he was protected by the Spirit of God. It was the presence of that power that protected the three companions of Daniel when they were thrown into the fiery furnace. Moses said that if the Spirit of the Lord had not been with him he would 'have withered and died in his presence, but his glory was upon me; and I beheld his face, for I was transfigured before him.' (Moses 1:11.)

"Of course the scientists *know* so much about this earth and the universe, so much more than the Creator of them knows, that all this is foolishness to them, but I tell you, son, what I have written is true. . . . We know nothing of the spiritual forces and conditions existing in the spiritual world, or existence, except that which the Lord has revealed. But we know this, that eventually, based upon the atonement of Jesus Christ, everything which is now mortal will after the resurrection become spiritual. Beings that become celestial will also shine like the sun and they will radiate energy from their bodies, not like radium, but with a radiation that will never end. This is the condition of the sun. It radiates energy, but that energy is not diminishing and will endure forever. After the resurrection our bodies, if we are faithful, will radiate and have a luster that would be blinding to mortal eyes, unless the power of the Lord protected them." He then quotes rather extensively from Brigham Young regarding the celestial state of the earth in a distant day, and adds the comment, "Well, son, such doctrine is foolishness to the wise men of this world, but it is true!"

These comments by a latter-day prophet suggest additional meaning and significance in the revelation received by the Prophet Joseph Smith known as the Olive Leaf, or Section 88 of the Doctrine and Covenants: ". . . This is the light of Christ. As also he is in the sun, and the light of the sun, and the power thereof by which it was made. . . . And the light which shineth, which giveth you light, is through him who enlighteneth your eyes, which is the same light that quickeneth your understandings; which light proceedeth forth from the presence of God to fill the immensity of space—The light which is in all things, which giveth life to all things, which is the law by which all things are governed, even the power of God who sitteth upon his throne, who is in the bosom of eternity, who is in the midst of all things. . . . Behold, all these are kingdoms, and any man who hath seen any or the least of these hath seen God moving in his majesty and power. . . ."

Douglas had inquired about resurrected bodies, and received this explanation, in 1948: In regard to the resurrection read Alma chapter 11, and especially the last five or six verses. When the body at the time of the resurrection comes forth it will have *all* of its parts, or as Amulek states, will be restored to its perfect frame. Deformities will disappear. In speaking of the perfect frame, the prophet does not mean that it will come forth free from all sin, for if the person has been wicked and filthy he will be filthy still. (Alma 41:10-15.) Remember that some who have received the resurrection were beheaded, such as John the Baptist. When he received his resurrection following the resurrection of our Savior, his head was in its proper place, he was not carrying it under his arm. There was a special reason for the wounds to appear in the hands of the Savior after his resurrection; this is not a criterion by which we will be guided. When he comes again to the Jews at the Mount of Olives he will then show the same prints of the nails and the spear to the unbelieving Jews, but the Savior is not going around all the time with unhealed wounds in his body. Babies will come forth the same size as they were when they were laid away, but will grow afterwards. Bodies do not grow in the grave, but they may grow to the full stature after the resurrection and to the perfect frame. President Brigham Young has said that the righteous who are worthy to enter the celestial kingdom will be perfect, and all their petty smallness which so many of us manifest here will be removed. Then husbands and wives who seem to have difficulty here will be able to love each other, for they will not be looking through a glass darkly, but shall know as they are known. This is very fortunate. If we wish to enter that kingdom, then we should begin right now to overcome our weaknesses, keep our bodies clean, free from every evil practice and strive to draw as near to the Lord as we can that we may have the guidance of his Holy Spirit."

Many wonder about the eternal state of those who failed to marry in this life, and about marriages where either the husband or wife has been unworthy. Douglas also posed these questions to his father, in 1948, and received this reply: "You ask will one who fails to marry in this life have a chance in the life to come, or later? That depends. If a man has refused to marry because of selfishness he may not. Every righteous woman will have that opportunity even if deprived here. Every young man like Lewis, who was cut off before the opportunity came, yes. During the Millennium the work will be done for all for whom we are unable to do it here. Those who would have married but were deprived will have the opportunity, the work being done for them by proxy. If a man and a woman are married for time and all eternity and one of them 'misses the mark' as you put it, meaning that he proves unworthy, he will be denied, but the faithful wife will go on to the fulness. She will be given to a faithful man for eternity. The reverse is also true. If the wife is unworthy, then she cannot keep the man back and he will go on. You mention Emma Smith. She is in the hand of the Lord and he will do right by her. The Doctrine and Covenants declares that if she was untrue, she should be cut off. See Sec. 93:48-49. and 132:54. I think these passages answer your question."

The answers to questions in letters to his son Joseph formed the basis and inspiration for his writing his book, *Religious Truths Defined*, several years later. Samples of these answers from letters follow:

"You are evidently troubled over the statement of the Lord to the brother of Jared: 'And never have I showed myself unto man whom I have created, for never has man believed in me as thou hast. Seest thou that ye are created after mine own image? Yea, even all men were created in the beginning after mine own image.'

"When Adam was in the Garden of Eden and before the fall, he was in the presence of God the Father as well as the presence of Jesus Christ. He walked in the presence of the Father, for he was free from sin and was not subject to the mortal conditions which came upon him after his fall. The fall brought the first, or spiritual death upon Adam, and he was shut out of the presence of the Father and was subject to the ministrations of angels sent from the presence of the Father.

"Because of the fall, Jesus Christ became the Mediator between God the Father and man in his fallen state. It is true that Jesus appeared to the prophets before the flood, but not in person as he appeared to the brother of Jared. These early prophets only saw him in the heavenly vision as he appeared to the brother of Jared before he saw his finger. If you read the account in the Book of Ether carefully, you will discover that the brother of Jared went into the mountain and prayed asking the Lord to touch the sixteen stones. Now the Lord talked to him and they conversed together. This was an appearance such as the appearance in former, or earlier times. On this occasion the faith of the brother of Jared was so great that he actually saw the finger of the Lord and thought it to be of flesh and blood.

"He had talked with the Lord before on several occasions, had evidently heard his voice, and could have said with truth that the Lord had appeared to him although he did not see him in person. Now, however, it was because of his faith that the Lord showed him his body just as he was and he saw him in the full stature of his person and most likely in his glory, or such portion as he was able to bear. Before this time no prophet had been privileged to receive such a personal visitation.

"It is true that Enoch 'walked with God' but he did so just as the brother of Jared did before this manifestation, and just as Moses did when he saw the burning bush. I firmly believe that there have been very few times in the history of the world, before the birth of Jesus Christ, that any of the prophets actually beheld him in his full person and conversed with him. They saw him in vision usually and not in person, or when seeing him it was not to discover him as completely as did the brother of Jared on this occasion. It is very likely that Moses saw him. After his resurrection, of course, many have seen him, but for some reason including lack of faith to see him as did this Jaredite prophet, the ancient prophets did not behold him in such detail.

"This must be true, or the Lord would not have said it."

In 1934 he wrote to Joseph:

"In regard to your question pertaining to the work of Jesus Christ, who created many worlds under the direction of his Father, I will say that you should read carefully the Lord's instruction to Moses. (Moses 1.) While the Lord was willing to reveal this truth to Moses, yet he told him that he would limit his knowledge to the earth upon which he stood. Because of our lack of faith and obedience, the Lord has withheld knowledge from us concerning other worlds, other than that they are his and he has peopled them with his children. When we reach the state of full faith, then he will make these things known to us. See 2 Nephi 27:7-10, 3 Nephi 26:6-10, and Ether 3:21-28, and 4:5-7.

"Jesus Christ is the creator of many worlds, yet he did not have a body of flesh and bones until he was born in Bethlehem about two thousand years ago, 1934 years, to be exact. It is sufficient for us, until we are prepared by faith to believe and understand greater things, to confine our study to the salvation of men and the dealings of the Lord with us here and now. Until we can comprehend the simple things of the gospel and put them into practice, we better not try to get off on some other world. If we do we may get lost in transit. See D&C 101:32-34.

"If any investigator or member of the Church desires to know these things, tell them that they better learn the simple truths and how to live them first. It is foolish to attempt to teach children of the primary grade higher mathematics. We must first master each rung of the ladder, we cannot reach the top in one jump from the bottom. Let your attitude be for the present the same as the Psalmist: 'Such knowledge is too wonderful for me; it is too high, I cannot attain unto it.' (Ps. 139:6.)

"Jesus Christ is our Redeemer, he came into the world to repair a broken law—to restore and make whole. He came to give us the resurrection and conquer death; to grant us forgiveness from our individual sins on the conditions of our repentance and acceptance of his truth and on no other ground. See D&C 19:15-19. I know these things are true, and if I will be faithful and obedient to him and his work, keeping his laws in all diligence and faithfulness, I will be saved and exalted in his kingdom with all who become members of the Church of the First-born and who are partakers of the fullness of his glory. If I refuse to hear him and to keep his commandments then I shall be shut out from his presence and will not have these exalted blessings. We cannot be obedient unless we know that is his will and what is plainly written in the scriptures. See D&C 93:1-3, 88-83, also verses 63-65."

Joseph Fielding's son George Reynolds, known in the family only as Reynolds, served his mission in Argentina during the Second World War years. Censors read all his mail. Letters from his father "usually contained 90 per cent gospel and 10 per cent news," according to Reynolds. Whenever Joseph Fielding quoted from the standard works he would give the quotation including the reference such as D&C 4:1. The censors would cut out all quotations. When Reynolds wrote his father that his letters looked like confetti, he then began to write more doctrinal quotes on doctrines of salvation and informed the censors it was for their benefit.

When leaving for his mission in Argentina the visas for missionaries in Reynolds' group were not ready. They were diverted to Palmyra, New York, for the annual Hill Cumorah Pageant. "We did all the dirty work, and I was assigned the 'outhouse' at the Sacred Grove," Reynolds reported. His complaints to his father brought the rebuke, "Son, you should be grateful that you have been called to clean the filth from a sacred spot."

On January 24, 1934, Joseph Fielding Smith wrote a letter to his young son Lewis, then 15 years of age:

"My Dear Lewis:—

"I have just written a letter to your oldest brother who is in England, and I thought that it would not be out of place for me to write a letter to you also, for you, being at home, do not get many letters. I was thinking that we have sent one boy away to try to teach the gospel to people in the world, and that the people here at home need it just as much as do the people in foreign lands. The world is full of theories, philosophies, and all kinds of doctrines, and people are being led astray. I wonder if I am putting forth the proper effort by example and by precept, to instruct my own children so that they will understand the truth and have the power to overcome the temptations and sins of the world. An ancient prophet said that in these last days the devil would rage in the hearts of the people; that he would be stirred up to anger against that which is good. Some people he would lull away into false security until they were bound by the chains of hell. (See 2 Nephi 28.) The Lord told Joseph Smith that there were many spirits abroad in the land (D&C 50:1-3.) and that some spirits or doctrines are the commandments of men and others of devils. (D&C 46:7.)

"Another ancient prophet said that in the last days men would be lovers of pleasure more than lovers of God; they would be disobedient (2 Tim. 3:1-7) and they would be ever learning and never able to come to a knowledge of the truth. They would be sent 'fables' because they would not receive the truth, and 'strong delusions.' (2 Tim. 4:3-4.) They would have their consciences seared with a hot iron (1 Tim. 4:1-2.) and would follow seducing spirits and doctrines of devils. (Thessalonians 2:11.) In this manner, and there are many other passages containing prophetic sayings of this kind, the Lord has warned us so that we may escape from all these things if we will only treasure up his word. (Pearl of Great Price page 47.) The light of the Spirit of the Lord will keep us in the path so that we shall have power to recognize evil and segregate it from the truth if we will only do the will of the Lord. He who will not do his will is deceived until the time comes when he is bound by the chains of hell.

"Now, I am somewhat concerned over the school work of my children, for I know that they are taught all kinds of theories, as we never were taught before, which have a tendency to destroy faith and make people deny the power of God. You cannot be too careful in matters of this kind. I want to protect you and each of the children from these attacks and cunningly laid plans of Lucifer to destroy faith in the Son of God and the redemption of man.

"I sense keenly the dangers which confront my children and all other children at this day. You do not sense it because you have not had the training and experience, so I want to help you. Let me say that I KNOW that Joseph Smith spoke the truth. It is not a question of guessing or belief, just as you know that 2 added to 2 will equal 4. I know that Jesus Christ is the Only Begotten Son of God, and the Redeemer of the world. What a glorious thing it is to know this! How soul satisfying it is! What peace and comfort it brings to me! I want *you* to know it also, and you may if you seek.

"I want you to be true to your priesthood, and one day you will have the higher priesthood conferred upon you. I want you to live to be a teacher of men in the everlasting truth, not the truth which the world knows, and which is mixed with error. The pride, wisdom and prudence of the great men of the world will have to pass away; but the *truth* which comes from God will never pass away for it is eternal.

"I am depending on you to learn these things for yourself and teach them to your younger brothers. I depend upon you, you must not fail me! What ever else you do be true to your Father which is in heaven. Have I ever set you an example in unrighteousness? Have you ever known me to lie? to steal? to wilfully bear false witness? to be unclean in body and in mind? I want you to remember that you have descended through the lineage of prophets! Your fathers before you, not counting your own father, have been mighty men of God. Your grandfather was always true, and would have laid down his life for the gospel. He gave his life *to* it, and would have given it *for* it, in fact sacrificed his time and comfort for it. Your great-grandfather not only suffered persecution, trials and tribulations, but he did give his life for the gospel truth. These were noble men. I want you to so live that you will be a credit to them, and if you can an improvement on your father.

303

"Now, you may not fully appreciate this letter *now*. I want you to save it and someday you may read it with greater care and understanding. Be true to me, true to your mother, true to the Church and true to God! . . ."

Repeatedly Joseph Fielding admonished his missionary sons to read and reread and give heed to Section 4 of the Doctrine and Covenants, which declares,

"Now behold, a marvelous work is about to come forth among the children of men. Therefore, O ye that embark in the service of God, see that ye serve him with all your heart, might, mind and strength, that ye may stand blameless before God at the last day. Therefore, if ye have desires to serve God ye are called to the work; For behold the field is white already to harvest; and lo, he that thrusteth in his sickle with his might, the same layeth up in store that he perisheth not, but bringeth salvation to his soul; and faith, hope, charity and love, with an eye single to the glory of God, qualify him for the work. Remember faith, virtue, knowledge, temperance, patience, brotherly kindness, godliness, charity, humility, diligence. Ask, and ye shall receive; knock, and it shall be opened unto you. Amen."

Frequently he admonished his sons to remember that the blood of the prophets flows in their veins and that they should strive to live worthy of their honorable heritage. He also warned them repeatedly of Satan's tremendous power. "If you are humble and diligent you will know the truth and love it," he told Milton in a letter, in 1948. "Satan is as busy as he can be with his hosts that follow him. He is raging in the hearts of the people in all parts of the earth. He is determined to rule or ruin, and he has made a thorough job of ruining humanity since the beginning. We cannot be too humble, prayerful and diligent in our work, and thus leave no loophole that he can enter. He will do all in his power to destroy the missionaries and especially my boys, and the other descendants of the Patriarch Hyrum Smith. He has obtained the mastery over the sons of the Prophet and this is being carried on in the second and third generations among them. I hope that soon some of them will be able to remove the scales of darkness from their eyes and see the truth. Well, son, be diligent, prayerful and seek the guidance of the Lord in all that you are called on to do."

Much to Joseph Fielding Smith's satisfaction, each of his five sons, Joseph Jr., Lewis, Reynolds, Douglas and Milton, completed honorable missions for the Church.

Chapter 16

*"Send forth the elders of my church unto
the nations which are afar off . . ."*

President of the Council of the Twelve

Out on the blue Pacific somewhere between Hawaii and Japan the ocean was wonderfully calm and the day balmy, just right for cruising. Joseph Fielding, his wife Jessie and 18 Latter-day Saint missionaries were aboard the *President Wilson*, along with many other passengers, headed for the Orient. There was a spectacular sunset that evening, as the ship's passengers sat down to a delicious Italian style dinner. The waiters were smartly dressed in Italian motif, and the tables were covered with attractive red and white checkered cloths. Each person was handed a bib to wear for the meal, adding to the novelty of it. The day was July 19, 1955, and just before dessert was served a message was broadcast over the ship's loudspeaker, announcing that it was the 79th birthday anniversary of a distinguished passenger, Joseph Fielding Smith, president of the Council of Twelve Apostles, The Church of Jesus Christ of Latter-day Saints. All the ship's passengers and crew joined in singing happy birthday to him, after which the head waiter came to his table carrying a large birthday cake. In the middle of it was one candle, which he lit, made a wish, blew out, and then the cake was cut and shared with other passengers. In the midst of the festivities came a cablegram from Salt Lake City announcing the birth of a grandson that same day, later named Richard Fielding Smith, son of Joseph Fielding Jr. and wife Zella.

It was an auspicious beginning to a successful mission tour. For several weeks the Smiths toured the Far East, dividing the Japanese Mission to form the Northern Far East and the Southern Far East missions, and dedicating Korea, Okinawa, the Philippines, and Guam for the preaching of the restored gospel of Jesus Christ. Thousands of orientals and United States servicemen saw and heard President Smith and his wife as they visited various cities and army bases, meeting with groups of church members, investigators and others who seemed greatly pleased to have a high official of the Church of Jesus Christ in the Far East. Harold Grant Heaton was appointed as president of the Southern Far East Mission, and he and his wife and child accompanied the Smiths on the ocean trip. His mission included Formosa, Hong Kong, the Philippine Islands, and Guam. Hilton A. Robertson, previously appointed president of the Japanese Mission, would now be president of the Northern Far East Mission, including Japan, Korea and Okinawa.

Upon their arrival in Tokyo, the first stop, they were feted at a reception at which a group of Japanese singers entertained them. Jessie was also invited to sing, and did one song in Japanese. After a day of meeting with military officers Joseph Fielding was flown back to mission headquarters in a helicopter, affording him an opportunity to see Tokyo and the Japanese countryside by air. As the Smiths met with one enthusiastic group after another they must at times have thought of the pleasant contrast between the reception they enjoyed and the discouraging times that Heber J. Grant had suffered there half a century before when he attempted without success to preach the gospel in Japan. No one it seemed wished to hear the gospel message then, but now thousands were anxious to do so.

It was the feeling of some of the brethren and others that Satan in stirring up the hearts of men to war in Korea had unwittingly hurt his own negative purposes.

LDS servicemen gathered outside the Munsan-ni, Korea chapel after one of the LDS servicemen's conferences held at Munsan-ni, August 3, 1955. Front row, left to right, President H. Grant Heaton; Rodney Fye, supervising elder for Korea; Lt. Col. Schleisser, 24th Infantry Division chaplain; President Hilton A. Robertson, President Joseph Fielding Smith, and Lt. Col. Robert H. Slover, LDS Far East Service coordinator.

Through the war faithful Mormon soldiers had introduced the restored gospel to that strife-torn country, and greatly increased its influence in Japan and elsewhere, even as Hitler's famous Berchtesgaden retreat in the Bavarian Alps became the site of a Mormon missionary gathering. Many of the meetings that Joseph Fielding conducted on the tour were primarily with servicemen. Typical of the comments in Jessie's diary of the trip is this one of July 31, 1955: "Meeting was held in the servicemen's chapel. It was packed [375 present], the chairs being in the isles. The authorities were sustained. Brother [Robert] Slover [a Mormon colonel in the armed forces stationed in Japan and chairman of the LDS Servicemen's Coordinating Committee in the Far East] spoke and told that they had

40 organized groups and seven organized branches. All districts were present [represented?]; there are 1500 or 1600 [LDS] servicemen; that they had made contributions of $26,000. . . ." At each meeting Joseph Fielding spoke and Jessie sang, and sometimes spoke also. She had learned a song or two in Japanese, which particularly pleased the congregations there. From Japan President Smith and several other brethren went to Korea for two days, then returned to Japan. He, Jessie and others next traveled in turn to Okinawa, Formosa, Hong Kong, just five miles from Communist China, and the Philippines, then homeward via Guam and Wake Islands, then to Hawaii for a stake conference, and finally home again on September 3. Their five-week visit had given a fine stimulus to missionary work and church growth in eastern Asia.

Telling of his visit to Korea, where the women were not allowed to go, President Smith reported that on "August 2, 1955, we held the first session of conference. Forty-one were present, and at the close of the services, I, with President Grant Heaton, President Hilton A. Robertson and a small group including Colonel Slover, went to the top of a hill near the monument for the dead soldiers, and I dedicated Korea for the preaching of the gospel. There was a large pole on the outside of the grounds and they had a radio attached, and the voice of Sister Smith came over it [they had brought along one of her records], singing, 'The Heavens Were Opened,' and it was a thrill to hear her voice although she wasn't there.

"I came down off the hill after the services and there was a little boy standing there with the magazine, The Children's Friend, and it had the story of me in it, and the young boy showed it to me and said, 'See, I can read all about you now, and you ordained me a deacon last night and now I can help with the gospel.' I put my arms around him with tears in my eyes and thanked the Lord for the privilege of being in that land with those wonderful people."

As president of the Council of the Twelve Apostles

for nearly two decades Joseph Fielding had primary responsibility for missionary work throughout the world, and personally did considerable traveling as well. His tenure of office as council president was one of the longest, if not the longest, in church history. He became acting president of the Twelve in October 1950, following the death two months earlier of George F. Richards. David O. McKay, at that time second counselor to George Albert Smith in the presidency of the Church, was ordained president of the Council, being the senior apostle next to George Albert. But inasmuch as he was a member of the presidency, it was deemed proper to designate Joseph Fielding, the next in line, as the acting president.

Half a year later, during the April conference in 1951, George Albert Smith died, thus elevating David O. McKay to the presidency. Joseph Fielding Smith then became the senior apostle next to President McKay and as such became president of the Council of the Twelve. He continued in this position until January 23, 1970, when he became president of the Church upon the death of President McKay. When he was called to be a counselor to President McKay October 29, 1965, it might have been expected that the next man in seniority, in this case Elder Harold B. Lee, would have been called to serve as acting president of the Council of Twelve, the pattern that had been followed several times in the past, even as with President Smith himself in October of 1950. But this was not done, and so Joseph Fielding for more than four years served both as active president of the Twelve and as a counselor in the presidency; perhaps the first man in church history to do so.

Those appointed to the Council of the Twelve before Joseph Fielding, who died while he was a council member, 1910-1970, were, by sequence of appointment: Francis Marion Lyman, John Henry Smith, Anthon H. Lund, Rudger Clawson, Reed Smoot, Hyrum Mack Smith, Charles W. Penrose, George F. Richards, Orson F. Whitney, David O. McKay, and Anthony W. Ivins, and those appointed after him, who exited by death or, in one case by excommunication, while he was still a member of the council: James E. Talmage, Stephen L Richards, Richard R. Lyman, Melvin J. Ballard, John A. Widtsoe, Joseph F. Merrill, Charles A. Callis, Joshua Reuben Clark Jr., Alonzo A. Hinckley, Albert Ernest Bowen, Sylvester Q. Cannon, Matthew Cowley, Henry D. Moyle, Adam S. Bennion, and George Q. Morris. Clark did not actually serve in the Council, being a counselor in the presidency, but he did have rank in the Council. Richard L. Evans died after Joseph Fielding became president of the Church. So President Smith outlived 16 apostles appointed to the Council after he was.

Others who served with him in the Council and who survived him are: President Harold B. Lee, Spencer Woolley Kimball, Ezra Taft Benson, Mark Edward Petersen, Delbert Leon Stapley, Marion G. Romney, LeGrand Richards, Hugh B. Brown, Howard W. Hunter, Gordon B. Hinckley, Nathan Eldon Tanner, and Thomas S. Monson.

For Joseph Fielding it was an interesting, challenging climb to the top, being daily engaged in the work of the Lord and associated with men for whom he had the greatest esteem and friendship. Although he did not always agree with the policies and decisions of the presidency and others, he always felt a loyalty to the brethren and tried to work in unity and harmony with them. As he gradually moved up the ladder from youngest to oldest member of the Council, his influence and responsibilities in the Council naturally increased accordingly. Sometimes they involved even more than what might have been expected.

When President Heber J. Grant died, on May 14, 1945, after years of poor health, Joseph Fielding in his journal observed an interesting coincidence: "One strange thing about his going is the fact that it occurred just one week after the surrender of Germany [World War II], and my father passed [died] just one week after the armistice in 1918 [World War I]." As was true in the death of several of the other brethren, Joseph Fielding was appointed to a committee of the Twelve to help arrange the funeral services for President Grant.

George Albert Smith, distant cousin of Joseph Fielding, served as president of the Church from May 21, 1945, to his death on April 4, 1951. The high esteem in which Joseph Fielding held him is reflected in his journal comment, "He was greatly beloved by all members of the Church and by a host of friends without. He came nearer to loving his neighbor than anyone else that I know and will be mourned by people all over the United States." Again Joseph Fielding was on the committee to plan the funeral arrangements. Interestingly, among the speakers was John F. Fitzpatrick, publisher of *The Salt Lake Tribune*, a choice that clearly reflected the change from antagonism to friendship which had gradually been effected between Mormons and non-Mormons in Salt Lake City. He also noted that Israel A. Smith, president of the Reorganized Church, attended the funeral service and a session of conference, and was impressed with the unity and orderliness that prevailed.

Because of George Albert Smith's death April conference was extended a day or two, with David O. McKay being sustained as president of the Church, Stephen L Richards as first counselor, J. Reuben Clark Jr. as second counselor, and Joseph Fielding Smith as president of the Council of the Twelve. President Smith was voice for the ordination and setting apart of President McKay. In turn President Smith was set apart by President McKay, as were Presidents Richards and Clark. Six months later Marion G. Romney, an Assistant to the Twelve, was promoted to the Council to fill the vacancy created by Elder Richards' advancement to the presidency—Elders McKay and Clark had already been serving in the presidency.

Although nearly 76 years old at the time of his appointment as council president, Joseph Fielding did not spare himself in stake conference travel assignments as he developed the schedules of visits by the brethren. He noted in his journal a time or two that the Church was growing so fast, and so many of the authorities were being called by the presidency to preside over missions or to fill other assignments, that it was difficult to meet all the stake conference assignments. In fact the day came when the Church recognized the impossibility of always having one of the general authorities in attendance at each of the stake conferences. Nor did President Smith limit his own travel to the nearby stakes, but continued to take his regular turn to those in Idaho, Arizona, California, and other distant areas, even to Alaska and Texas. Usually Jessie went with him, serving ever more as his chauffeur as he got older, as well as participating in the conference sessions as a singer and sometimes as a speaker.

President Smith's assignment to the Far East in the summer of 1955 was his first major mission tour as president of the Council. Three years later, in September, 1958, he and Jessie accompanied President McKay and several other general authorities to the dedication of the Latter-day Saint temple near London, England. The Smiths also visited for several days the Swiss-Austrian Mission, where his son Lewis had served, and spoke to several groups of missionaries. They also took a sight-seeing trip to the Alps and other points of interest which they had visited 19 years before, in 1939, just before the outbreak of World War II. Upon their return to London he was invited by President McKay to dedicate the mission home adjacent to the temple.

In mid-November, 1958, a few weeks after returning from England, the Smiths flew to Australia and New Zealand for a tour of the missions there, stopping en route in Hawaii where they visited his nephew Joseph F. Smith, son of Hyrum Mack Smith, and former patriarch to the Church, who had resigned in 1946 after four years in office, and was succeeded by his distant cousin Eldred Gee Smith.

Upon their arrival in New Zealand the night of November 19 the Smiths were given a cordial and interesting welcome, with a performance by Maori and Samoan dancers and singers. "After this greeting and performance we were very happy to retire, it being after midnight," observed President Smith in his journal. At 82 years of age he still showed remarkable stamina in making such a

Officials at dedication of London Temple, left to right, front row, Elder Gordon B. Hinckley, President David O. McKay, President Joseph Fielding Smith, Elder ElRay L. Christiansen; back row, Elder Richard L. Evans, A. Hamer Reiser, Selvoy J. Boyer, and Edward O. Anderson, church architect.

long flight, then attending a three-hour program late into the night. Their tour of the two countries, New Zealand and Australia, was a stimulating experience both for the Smiths and for the church members whom they visited. To have the president of the Council of the Twelve Apostles visit in such far off lands was a rare experience indeed.

After about a week in New Zealand they flew on to Australia, and after not quite a month in Australia they returned to New Zealand for several weeks, spending both Christmas and New Year's Day there. Joseph Fielding was pleased to note that in quite a number of their meetings in the two countries there was considerable interest in the gospel shown by investigators in attendance. It seemed that the future of the Church was bright indeed in this part of the world.

President Joseph Fielding Smith assuming the role of a barber for Jessie Evans Smith at the mission home, Sydney, Australia, December 1958.

Apparently, despite advancing age, the more President and Sister Smith traveled the better they liked it. In 1960-61 they took another major trip, this time a three-month tour of the South and Central American missions, accompanied by A. Theodore Tuttle of the First Council of the Seventy. Flying from Salt Lake City to New York October 13, they left next day by boat for a 10-day cruise down the Atlantic which was, said Jessie, "just as smooth as if we were riding in the air. We had to go out to see if the ship were moving. They treated us wonderfully." In 1960 the Church had five missions in South America: the Brazilian, with headquarters at Sao Paulo, with William G. Bangerter as president; the Brazilian South, with headquarters at Curitiba with Asael T. Sorenson as president; the Uruguay, with headquarters at Montevideo, and Arthur M. Jensen as president; the Argentine, with headquarters at Buenos Aires, and Lorin N. Pace as president; and the Andes Mission, with headquarters at Lima, Peru, and James Vernon Sharp as president. This latter mission also included Chile. The Central American Mission headquarters were in Guatemala, with Victor C. Hancock as president.

Their tour was described by a *Church News* reporter as "a succession of conferences with members, special meetings with missionaries, banquets and entertainment furnished by members in branches of the missions." They helped select sites for new buildings and broke ground for one new chapel. Meetings were held in several recently constructed chapels. There was every indication of an upsurge in acceptance of the gospel by Latin Americans, which subsequent years proved indeed to be the case. "It was gratifying to see how the members were feeling their responsibility," commented President Smith, "and assuming duties formerly done by missionaries." Members traveled as far as 500 miles to meet the three visitors.

At several meetings Jessie sang two songs in Spanish, "Behold 'Tis Eventide," and "Secret Prayer," as well as several in English. Capacity congregations filled the chapels wherever they went. In many places it was the first time that an apostle had ever visited, and it stimulated considerable interest in the Church. At 84 years of age President Smith seemed unbelievably youthful, maintaining a strenuous schedule of travel, meetings and other engagements.

An interesting instance of healing by President Smith while touring in Brazil was related in the *Ensign* by Richard D. Proctor, a missionary there at the time. It seems that a certain woman in Canoas had recently joined the Church and was eagerly looking forward to President Smith's visit to nearby Porto Alegre. She got so excited about it she suffered a heart attack and had to be hospitalized. When informed of her condition, and of her keen disappointment in not being able to meet him, "President Smith decided personally to visit her and administer to her. When he entered the hospital room, the woman gave a cry of joy, exclaiming, 'Now that he has come, I'm sure to get well!' Then President Smith placed his hands upon her head

President Joseph Fielding Smith and Jessie Evans Smith visit on horseback while traveling in Ecuador.

and commanded the sickness to depart from her. From that time on there were no symptoms of the woman's heart attack. Later she explained that when President Smith placed his hands upon her head and began to speak, the pain immediately left her. The physicians, amazed and uncomprehending, found her medically sound and released her the following day. The sister continued faithful in the gospel, testifying to many of this miraculous healing. It was an added witness to her of the divinity of the gospel of Jesus Christ."

With his son-in-law Bruce R. McConkie of the First Council of the Seventy serving as a mission president in southern Australia in 1963, and his daughter Amelia as mission matron, it seemed a likely time to Joseph Fielding to return for another visit to that far away land. He and Jessie left Salt Lake City on November 20. After a fueling stop in Hawaii, they reached Sydney, Australia

Jessie Evans Smith with Koala bear, Lonepine Sanctuary, Brisbane, Australia.

the next day, where they spent a week in the Australian Mission with President Morgan S. Coombs. From Sydney they flew to Brisbane and attended stake conference, then returned to Sydney where they spent Thanksgiving Day with the Coombs family and attended Sydney Stake conference. The Smiths next flew to Melbourne, on December 2, where they had a joyous reunion with Amelia, Bruce and family. They spent the next 10 days with them in the Southern Australian Mission home and visited the missionaries, local members and investigators. President Smith dedicated the mission home there on December 6 and presided at a Melbourne Stake conference the following two days. Leaving Melbourne December 12 they were back in Salt Lake City two days later. It was a question as to which was the more remarkable, the speed of travel in this space age or the endurance of this 87-year-old apostle to make such a lengthy trip with such ease.

One of President Smith's most time-consuming assignments was as a member of the missionary committee. Along with missionary work he of course had many other concerns. Another was serving as chairman of the executive committee of the Brigham Young University board of trustees during a period of rapid growth at that school. Each week nearly, and sometimes more often, he conducted committee meetings, generally with BYU President Ernest L. Wilkinson present, to review progress and to make plans. Consolidation of the church school system had been decided upon in 1953, with Wilkinson to have overall direction, at the time of the retirement of Franklin L. West as church commissioner of education. So rapid was the growth of the studentbody and the campus at Brigham Young University that on one occasion, May 26, 1954, there was a dedication of 22 buildings at once, with President McKay, President Smith, Elder Harold B. Lee and others participating.

That summer Elder Lee conducted a seminar at Brigham Young University for institute and seminary teachers, and President Smith gave several talks at it. The difficulties that he had experienced in earlier years with some of the teachers in the church school system surfaced again a number of times in the 1950's. A political science teacher at the Brigham Young University objected to President Smith's book, *Man: His Origin and Destiny,* published in 1954, "to protect our youth, particularly, against the false doctrines of the modern scientific world," he explained in his journal. Following an interview with this man President Smith noted in his journal, "I was not pleased with his attitude. . . . Evidently this young teacher does not accept all that is written in the standard works." That was putting it kindly, for this teacher was openly ridiculing the idea of the saints one day returning to Jackson County, Missouri, and other important aspects of church teachings.

319

In interviewing teachers and other members of the Church President Smith discovered there were so many misconceptions and so much ignorance about gospel principles and church history, that he accepted an invitation from his neighbor, Richard L. Evans, editor of the monthly *Improvement Era* (now *The Ensign*) magazine to conduct a question and answer column, entitled "Your Question," which began in May of 1953 and was continued for nearly 14 years, until March 1967. This became probably the most popular feature of the magazine. The questions answered by President Smith with the addition of several from personal correspondence were later published in five volumes, *Answers to Gospel Questions*, from 1957 to 1966, compiled and arranged by his son, Joseph Fielding Smith, Jr.

Frequently in his journal through these years President Smith noted the tremendous amount of time it was taking to conduct this column. In 1963, for instance, after 10 years at it, he observed, "Since I accepted the invitation of the *Era* to answer questions I have been flooded with them. Some are good interesting questions and many are not. I do not endeavor to answer them all. . . . I receive a great number of letters containing all kinds of questions. Some of them are worthy of answers, and many are not. This takes a great part of my time. Some of the questions I ignore when they are unworthy. I am troubled by some young mothers frequently who want me to endorse the use of contraceptives because they do not want children. Of course this practice I do not endorse. Many are pertaining to the word of wisdom and proper *amusement* on the Sabbath day. . . . Some are asking for explanations of mysteries or things that are foolish or at times that a small child should be able to answer." Along with answering a constant flood of mail he spent many hours each month in counseling visitors who came to his office seeking guidance on personal problems. Several times in his journal he lamented the fact that many church members neither study the scriptures, heed carefully the church authorities, nor use their power of reasoning. After satisfying three young men who felt upset about the church policy regarding Negroes, he commented in his journal, "The ignorance of many—far too many—members of the Church is almost unforgivable."

On June 4, 1951, two months after becoming president of the Council of the Twelve, Joseph Fielding was awarded an honorary Doctor of Letters degree from Brigham Young University for his "spiritual scholarship," and two years later he as well as President McKay was awarded an honorary Master M-Man pin at the annual MIA June convention breakfast at the Hotel Utah. June 3, 1960 he received a distinguished service award at Brigham Young University commencement, and on June 29, 1968 he was awarded a plaque from the Boy Scout committee of the YMMIA General Board "for six decades of ardent service to the boys of The Church of Jesus Christ of Latter-day Saints."

It was while serving as president of the Council of the Twelve that Joseph Fielding became keenly interested in flying, thanks to Jessie's friend Colonel (later General) Alma Winn of the Utah National Guard. It began on June 9, 1954: "Colonel Alma Winn invited me to take a ride with him in a jet plane, which I did. It was a wonderful experience to travel in such a plane at about 500 miles per hour." So delighted was he with the experience that from then on Colonel Winn and eventually others of the guard frequently invited him to take such rides. Two weeks later he commented on a ride, "We could see in all directions, into Idaho, Wyoming, Nevada and as far south as lower Utah or beyond. It was a wonderful sight." On November 13: "This is my father's birth anniversary. I went up in a jet plane with Colonel Alma Winn, and General Maxwell Rich of the Utah National Guard [went] with Colonel Roland R. Wright in another plane. We pierced the dark heavy clouds up into the clear sunshine. It was the most beautiful scene I can remember, as the top of the highest peaks penetrated the clouds like islands. The clouds on top were perfectly white, [and those] below extremely dark, with some rain falling later."

Four years later on his 80th birthday anniversary—
80 was the age his father had reached just a few days
prior to his death—Joseph Fielding was feted at parties
given by his family and by employees of the Church
Historian's Office, the Genealogical Society and other
church office groups, at which President McKay and
President Clark spoke. But it was no surprise to any of
his family or associates that a highlight of his anniversary
was a jet ride with Colonel Winn. Through much of the
afternoon of July 19 they rode high up in the blue, from
Salt Lake down over Fish Lake in southern Utah, back
up to the Utah-Idaho border and around, with President
Smith at the controls much of the time.

That same year, 1958, there was another ride, of an
entirely different nature, that Joseph Fielding particularly
enjoyed. For years he and Jessie had kept a cabin in Millcreek Canyon east of Salt Lake City, generally using it
several days each year through the heat of the summer.
President McKay meanwhile had kept as a retreat the
old McKay homestead in Huntsville, up through Ogden
Canyon, and was fond of going there whenever his
schedule permitted. With obvious pleasure President
Smith recorded in his journal for Saturday, October 4,
1958: "This afternoon early, Jessie and I took President
and Sister McKay up Millcreek Canyon. This was the
first time they had ever been in this canyon. The leaves
on the sides of the highway and the mountain sides were
beautiful in all their fall beauty. President McKay admitted
it was far more beautiful than Ogden Canyon. He was delighted with the beauty. The following day the frost set
in and the leaves began to fall."

Much as he enjoyed flying, President Smith questioned
the wisdom or worth of the government's expensive efforts to place men on the moon. In recent years the rumor
has circulated around the Church that President Smith
once prophesied that men would never reach the moon.
The falsity of this report is apparent from the fuss that
was raised back in 1962 when he commented on the
moon venture. In his journal for May 1 and 2, 1962, he

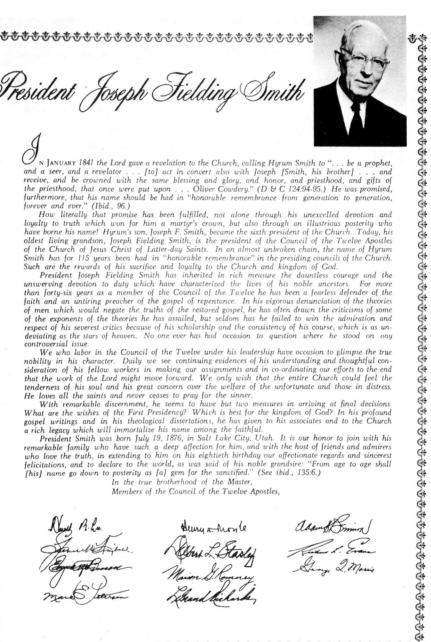

President Joseph Fielding Smith

*I*N JANUARY 1841 the Lord gave a revelation to the Church, calling Hyrum Smith to ". . . be a prophet, and a seer, and a revelator . . . [to] act in concert also with Joseph [Smith, his brother] . . . and receive, and be crowned with the same blessing and glory, and honor, and priesthood, and gifts of the priesthood, that once were put upon . . . Oliver Cowdery." (D & C 124:94-95.) He was promised, furthermore, that his name should be had in "honorable remembrance from generation to generation, forever and ever." (Ibid., 96.)

How literally that promise has been fulfilled, not alone through his unexcelled devotion and loyalty to truth which won for him a martyr's crown, but also through an illustrious posterity who have borne his name! Hyrum's son, Joseph F. Smith, became the sixth president of the Church. Today, his oldest living grandson, Joseph Fielding Smith, is the president of the Council of the Twelve Apostles of the Church of Jesus Christ of Latter-day Saints. In an almost unbroken chain, the name of Hyrum Smith has for 115 years been had in "honorable remembrance" in the presiding councils of the Church. Such are the rewards of his sacrifice and loyalty to the Church and kingdom of God.

President Joseph Fielding Smith has inherited in rich measure the dauntless courage and the unswerving devotion to duty which have characterized the lives of his noble ancestors. For more than forty-six years as a member of the Council of the Twelve he has been a fearless defender of the faith and an untiring preacher of the gospel of repentance. In his vigorous denunciation of the theories of men which would negate the truths of the restored gospel, he has often drawn the criticisms of some of the exponents of the theories he has assailed, but seldom has he failed to win the admiration and respect of his severest critics because of his scholarship and the consistency of his course, which is as undeviating as the stars of heaven. No one ever has had occasion to question where he stood on any controversial issue.

We who labor in the Council of the Twelve under his leadership have occasion to glimpse the true nobility in his character. Daily we see continuing evidences of his understanding and thoughtful consideration of his fellow workers in making our assignments and in co-ordinating our efforts to the end that the work of the Lord might move forward. We only wish that the entire Church could feel the tenderness of his soul and his great concern over the welfare of the unfortunate and those in distress. He loves all the saints and never ceases to pray for the sinner.

With remarkable discernment, he seems to have but two measures in arriving at final decisions. What are the wishes of the First Presidency? Which is best for the kingdom of God? In his profound gospel writings and in his theological dissertations, he has given to his associates and to the Church a rich legacy which will immortalize his name among the faithful.

President Smith was born July 19, 1876, in Salt Lake City, Utah. It is our honor to join with his remarkable family who have such a deep affection for him, and with the host of friends and admirers who love the truth, in extending to him on his eightieth birthday our affectionate regards and sincerest felicitations, and to declare to the world, as was said of his noble grandsire: "From age to age shall [his] name go down to posterity as [a] gem for the sanctified." (See ibid., 135:6.)

In the true brotherhood of the Master,
Members of the Council of the Twelve Apostles,

Tribute paid to President Joseph Fielding Smith on his eightieth birthday.

observed, "When in Tulsa, Oklahoma, I was interviewed by a reporter. He asked me about the endeavor to place men on the moon. I answered that they might, but evidently if so he might have difficulty to get back again. This was sent out as a dispatch to newspapers all over the U.S., and I am flooded by letters in relation to it, with some editorial criticisms. Why such a fuss? . . . This remark apparently disturbed a great many people. The fact is, however, although I did not say it, man—mortal man—has no business trying to get on the moon, for earth is a probationary state and in mortality we are expected [to stay on] this earth." He did not say whether the letter writers were upset because he said that man might get on the moon, or because he said they might have a difficult time getting back. Perhaps there was some criticism from each side.

In addition to taking him for jet rides Colonel Winn and his associates in the National Guard had President and Sister Smith as guests at their annual military ball March 25, 1955, and conferred upon him the honorary rank of colonel in the guard. Seven years later, on August 17, 1962, in a program at Camp Williams, he was advanced to the honorary rank of brigadier general and given a general's uniform, "which I did not expect." The Smiths and Winns did some socializing together through the years, and President Smith a number of times delivered Sunday sermons to the Utah guardsmen.

As others, President Smith of course was delighted to see the ever accelerating rate of growth in the Church. Yet he could not help but have some misgivings about a couple of related matters. Several times in his journal he expressed concern about the amount of money the Church was spending on various building projects. And the other concern was over the growing practice of the Church to establish stakes in other parts of the world instead of urging converts to move to Zion. In August, 1962, for instance, he observed, "Our spending everywhere is to me alarming, but I have nothing to say. . . . The Church is spending enormous sums in building all

President Joseph Fielding Smith admires the Minuteman Award given to him by the Utah National Guard. (1964)

over the world. We are constantly creating stakes in Europe, the islands of the Pacific, and on the American continent. I wonder if we have forgotten the commandment to gather. To come to Zion." Yet, eight years later as church president he approved of the organization of such stakes and spoke of the importance of The Church of Jesus Christ of Latter-day Saints becoming a world church.

Despite advancing age President Smith continued to take keen interest in the nation's political affairs and in scientific and other developments. His journal contains frequent mention of these matters, for instance the explosion of an atomic test bomb in Nevada on March 17, 1953. "This was a marvelous sight, both the scene of the explosion and the fact that we could see it sitting in our own home. . . . Surely the world is preparing for its destruction." He was much disgusted with the New Deal and Fair Deal administrations of Franklin Roosevelt and Harry Truman, and expressed great relief when the Republicans finally regained control of the federal government. Nevertheless when President John F. Kennedy spoke in the Tabernacle September 27, 1963, just a few weeks before his death, President Smith at 87 years of age dutifully attended the meeting, sitting on the stand next to Stewart Udall, Kennedy's Secretary of Interior. Udall recalled as a boy in southern Arizona when President Smith visited in their home while on a stake assignment.

By the early 1950's all of Joseph Fielding's children were gone from home. In January of 1953 he made a tough decision: "Placed my home for sale. . . . This becomes necessary as all of our children are now married and in their own homes, and I am unable to take care of the place and be away from home so much as I have been required to be." He was then 76 and a half years old. A month later, on February 23, 1953: "With the help of my sons, Joseph, Douglas and Milton, I commenced moving from my home to an apartment in the Eagle Gate Apartments." He then "entered into agreement with Asael Richardson, to sell the home." For the next three weeks

Four generations of Josephs, left to right, Joseph Fielding Smith, Jr., President Joseph Fielding Smith, painting of President Joseph F. Smith, and Joseph Farr Smith. The picture was painted during World War I, and had been in the possession of Joseph Fielding Smith since the death of his father in November, 1918.

he with the help of his sons and two grandsons was intermittently engaged in moving, finally completing it by mid-March. There was not room in the apartment for all of his hundreds of books, so at the time of the move he "disposed of most of my library among members of the family." The Eagle Gate Apartment, just across east from the Beehive House, would be his and Jessie's home for more than 18 years, until her death in 1971.

Even after they moved into the apartment President Smith continued to take the lead in a long standing practice of the Smith family, that of getting together—as many as possible of them—to study scriptures and socialize. "Today we held our family meeting at the home of Douglas," read a typical entry in his journal, "where we studied Section 10 of the Doctrine and Covenants." They also had special get-togethers occasionally, such as on June 15, 1953, when he noted that at a family party at his daughter Naomi Brewster's place, "we had all the members of the family present for the first time in a number of years." To President Smith having continued family unity was a most important achievement.

Through the years President Smith maintained a torrid work pace. At one time he held seven major positions simultaneously, plus his writing efforts: (1) apostle; (2) church historian and recorder; (3) president of the Salt Lake Temple; (4) chairman of the church committee on publications—the reading committee; (5) president of the church Genealogy Society; (6) chairman of the Melchizedek Priesthood committee; (7) chairman of the executive committee of BYU board of trustees. He was also a member of several boards of directors of church subsidiary businesses, and the missions committee.

In 1963 Joseph Fielding Smith was 87 years old. To realize the sort of a schedule he was maintaining at that advanced age, consider a few of his activities: except when out-of-town he was daily at his office during the week, writing letters, preparing his column for the *Improvement Era*, counseling visitors seeking advice, conducting meetings of the Twelve and other groups, and tending to various business matters. He spoke and sang at several stake conferences, traveling to them by automobile as far away as the panhandle of Idaho. He participated in the dedication of a pioneer monument at Independence, Missouri; dedicated the visitors' center housing Liberty Jail, and visited other historic sites there. He attended President Kennedy's speech at the tabernacle. He set Thomas S. Monson apart as a member of the Council of the Twelve. He presided at the laying of the cornerstone of the Oakland Temple. He made a three-week trip to Australia where he presided at stake conferences and dedicated a mission home. He reviewed his life's history in a taped interview with his son Douglas. He visited President McKay and others who were hospitalized. And on New Year's Eve, December 31, 1963, he wrote in his journal, "The year is rapidly drawing to its end. I hope I have accomplished *some* good during the year and helped to make someone happy."

Chapter 17

"Gather unto yourselves wise men, experienced and aged men, to assist in council . . ."

Counselor in the Church Presidency

The several hundred miles between Lewiston, Idaho, and Salt Lake City seemed even longer than usual as Joseph Fielding and Jessie Evans Smith drove homeward with a nephew, Elmer J. Smith, and his wife Marian on a Sunday evening in the 1960's. Ordinarily they refrained from traveling on Sunday, but a long distance phone call that morning had informed them that President David O. McKay had been hospitalized and had requested that Joseph Fielding Smith administer to him. Apparently he was unaware that President Smith was on a stake conference assignment in Idaho's panhandle. They had traveled to Lewiston in Elmer's car. As soon as the morning session of the stake conference was ended the Smiths left for Salt Lake City with Elmer Smith as chauffeur. If President McKay wished to be administered to by Joseph Fielding Smith, so it would be. All afternoon and evening the Smiths drove, and on into the night, mile after weary mile, finally reaching Salt Lake City and the hospital at 3 o'clock in the morning. "As these two old friends and life-long servants of the Lord met, they embraced and kissed, repeating each other's name affectionately," reported an observer in the *Improvement Era.*

By the fall of 1965 President McKay at 92 years of

Presidents David O. McKay and Joseph Fielding Smith were associates in the ranks of the general authorities for 60 years.

age was failing fast in health and strength, after having enjoyed excellent health and vigor for the first 90 years of life. His poor health plus the increasing work load of the presidency, commensurate with the rapid growth of the Church, persuaded him that it would be well to add to the membership of the church presidency. Both Joseph Smith and Brigham Young had at times had more than two counselors, so there was good precedent for the decision. Joseph Fielding Smith as the first in line to the office of president seemed a logical choice. His appointment would not only increase the capabilities of the presidency but would afford him an opportunity to be even better prepared to succeed to the president's office upon the death of President McKay. Besides President Smith, President McKay decided to add Elder Thorpe B. Isaacson to the presidency. Isaacson was an assistant to the Council of the Twelve, and for many years had been a counselor in the presiding bishopric. Next to President Nathan Eldon Tanner he was possibly the most capable of the general authorities in the field of financial administration, an area of vital importance in a church with a multi-million dollar expense account. So it was that on October 29, 1965, President McKay announced to the Church that he was appointing Joseph Fielding Smith and Thorpe B. Isaacson to be his counselors, along with Hugh B. Brown and Nathan Eldon Tanner. On April 6, 1968, he added a sixth man to the presidency, Alvin R. Dyer, who like Isaacson had been serving as an assistant to the Twelve. He also ordained Elder Dyer an apostle, although there was no opening in the Council of the Twelve. President McKay had earlier lost three counselors through death: Stephen L Richards, J. Reuben Clark Jr. and Henry D. Moyle.

At the time of his appointment as a member of the presidency, Joseph Fielding was 89 years old. He was the oldest man ever to be so appointed. Lorenzo Snow had become church president at the age of 84; Wilford Woodruff at 82; John R. Winder a counselor to Joseph's father at the age of 80, and Charles W. Penrose a counselor to Joseph's father at the age of 79. The Prophet Joseph had spoken of the worth of having older men in counsel, and most of his counselors had been older than he, including his father, his uncle John Smith, his brother Hyrum, Frederick G. Williams and Sidney Rigdon.

Upon his appointment as a counselor, Joseph Fielding became the fourth generation of his family to serve in the presidency of the Church: His great-grandfather, Joseph Smith Sr., father of the Prophet Joseph, had served as an assistant counselor and member of the presidency with his son. Joseph Fielding's grandfather, Hyrum Smith, had served as assistant counselor, then second counselor, then assistant president to his brother the Prophet. And Joseph Fielding's father, Joseph F. Smith, had served as a counselor to four presidents and then became sixth president of the Church.

This, however, was not the first instance of four

generations in one family serving in the presidency of the Church: the Prophet's Uncle John Smith served as an assistant counselor to the Prophet. Uncle John's son George A. Smith served as first counselor to Brigham Young. George A.'s son John Henry Smith served as second counselor to Joseph F. Smith. And John Henry's son George Albert Smith became the eighth president of the Church, and thus the fourth generation of that family to serve in the presidency.

President and Sister McKay lived in an apartment on the eighth floor of the Hotel Utah, midway between the Temple and the Church Office Building and convenient to both. Because of his old age and poor health, President McKay spent most of his time in the apartment during the last few years of his life, and most of the presidency meetings were held there during the four years and three months that Joseph Fielding was a counselor in the presidency. President Smith usually was in meetings with President McKay and the other counselors at least two days a week and often three or four days. Tuesdays and Wednesdays were the most frequently used days for the meetings in his hotel apartment, though sometimes Mondays. On Thursdays the presidency and Council of the Twelve met together in the Temple, though President McKay was not always to these meetings. On Fridays the presidency and presiding bishopric met together in the church offices. Mondays were often used by President Smith for correspondence, though sometimes he was returning on Mondays from stake conference visits. Saturdays he had decided to take off, remain at home, except when traveling to stake conferences. He and Jessie generally went grocery shopping on Saturday afternoons. If he did not have a stake visiting assignment on Sunday he usually would attend his own Eighteenth Ward services. Living only a block from the McKays he and Jessie a number of times made social calls on them. Being largely confined to his apartment, President McKay was especially appreciative of such visits. Occasionally he and his wife would still get up to their beloved home in Hunts-

President Joseph Fielding Smith conducting a session of general conference as a counselor in the First Presidency. Presidents N. Eldon Tanner, David O. McKay, and Hugh B. Brown listen attentively.

ville, and at least once President Smith notes in his journal that the weekly meeting of the presidency was held at the Huntsville home.

As a counselor in the presidency Joseph Fielding of course was a participant in most if not all major decisions in regard to church government during this period of 1965-1970, a period of rapid growth and development. The missionary program was always a prime consideration. President McKay's slogan, "Every member a missionary," had caught the popular fancy in the Church and seemed to stimulate considerable interest in home missionary efforts. The missionary force sent into the world was also greatly increased, and the rate of conversions and church growth jumped until it was estimated that at the time of President McKay's death half the Church population had known no other president than him. President Smith continued to devote considerable time to the Church school system also, as chairman of the executive committee of the board of trustees of Brigham Young University, where the student enrollment, the faculty, the curriculum and the campus all continued a healthy growth.

As president of the Council of the Twelve Joseph Fielding was called upon ever more frequently for the dedication of various buildings and monuments. In 1965, for instance, though nearly 90 years old, he had dedicated the new Deseret Gymnasium in Salt Lake City, the Franklin S. Harris Fine Arts Center and the Ernest L. Wilkinson Center at Brigham Young University, the Olympus Stake Center, Zion's First National Bank and other structures. And the year before, in May of 1964, he had participated in dedication of the Mormon Pavilion at the New York World's Fair. As a counselor in the church presidency he was in still more demand for dedicatory programs.

President Smith had long felt considerable interest in historic church sites. On the morning of May 24, 1966, just a few months after his appointment to the church presidency, he was sitting in a meeting of the committee on expenditures when he was informed that President McKay would like to see him immediately in his apartment at Hotel Utah. Upon his arrival at the McKay apartment he was asked if he would be willing to accompany President McKay on a visit to Adam-ondi-Ahman and other historic sites in Missouri. President Smith was delighted at the invitation, and pleased that President McKay, now in his 90's, was finally going to visit those places, having never yet done so.

So, a week later, on June 1 and 2, 1966, these two venerable leaders, one nearing 93 and the other just two months short of 90 years old, took a flight to the land of the Missouri and back. They were accompanied by Elder Alvin R. Dyer, an assistant to the Twelve who had made arrangements for the visit, and by David Lawrence McKay, the president's eldest son. Several local church officials also accompanied them on the tour.

At Independence, Missouri, "the party stopped in front of the small frame Church of Christ chapel (Hedreckite) on River Boulevard," reported Elder Dyer, "where in plain view to the left, about one half block away, stood the auditorium of the Reorganized LDS Church. Across the street to the east of the auditorium is the 23-plus acres of temple land which belongs to our Church. While in front of the Hedreckite Church I pointed out that this particular spot was the high point of the some 63 acres of the original 'inheritance' or 'Temple Land' property and where the Prophet Joseph Smith dedicated a temple site, which is destined to become the Temple of the New Jerusalem. . . .

"Crossing over the Missouri River the party arrived shortly thereafter at Liberty, Missouri. . . . Reaching the Liberty Jail Bureau, the party got out of the car. President McKay, with President Smith near his side, walked up the steps and into the bureau at Liberty Jail. . . . In the rotunda which encloses the restored Liberty Jail, the historic events [were reviewed] that led to the Prophet Joseph and his brother Hyrum and four others, without just cause, being placed in this crude and barren enclosure 14 feet square with a dungeon and upper room for approximately four months in the winter of 1838-39. Here in the depths of sorrow and abject persecution, the Prophet sought God the Father for guidance and assurance. . . .

"President Joseph Fielding Smith told of his having dedicated this building including the jail [in 1963], and so far as he knew [that was] the only time a jail was ever dedicated. He also referred to the fact that his father, Joseph F. Smith, who became president of the Church, born near Far West, Missouri, was brought to the jail where his grandfather [Joseph F's. father] saw him for the first time. . . .

"From this hallowed place the entourage went directly to Adam-ondi-Ahman. The rolling hills, the many trees, hedges and completely green countryside were beautiful to behold. The Missouri River which flows from

President Joseph Fielding Smith addresses crowd before dedication of visitors center housing old Liberty Jail. Thickness of jail wall is shown.

the vast northwest on its relentless flow to the Mississippi River was crossed several times during the day with the reminder, as exclaimed by the Prophet Joseph Smith, [while confined in Liberty Jail] 'that [as] well might man put forth his puny arm to stop the flow of the mighty Missouri [as] to stop God from pouring down blessings upon the heads of the Latter-day Saints.' . . .

"The valleys and hills of Adam-ondi-Ahman . . . were never more beautiful. The early growth of the farmers' crops, mostly corn, was in evidence, and the trees and shrubs on uncleared land were dense and seemingly impenetrable. The party passed the farm homes of Henry and Joyce Dustman, (Old Di-Ahman Farms) of Elmore and Estes, having driven through the Daviess County seat of Gallatin, a place significant in Church history. . . .

"Passing Dustman's Di-Ahman Farms we crossed over a creek bed bridge and ascended the hill on a narrow road to Tower Hill. The party stopped here and President McKay, President Smith, and the rest of us got out of the cars and stood close to the spot of the ruins of the old Nephite and Adamic Altar of prayer. Elder Dyer narrated some of the events of historic significance that transpired at this place, which concerned the many visits of the Prophet Joseph Smith and of his designating the altars and how they were used by the ancients.

"Elder Dyer identified the two pieces of property totaling 140 acres [for which] options to buy had been obtained from Dustman by the Church. The one piece contained the bluff area of Spring Hill where once many of the homes at Adam-ondi-Ahman were erected, including also the ruins of the storehouse located in the center block in this old city, together with the temple site and the altar site where sacrifice was offered by Adam. . . .

"To get a better feel of the area the car with President McKay and President Smith [in] was driven down the narrow cobblestrewn road from Tower Hill, and passing the remains of Lyman Wight's home, into the large valley of Adam-ondi-Ahman. . . . The 'high point' of Spring Hill was pointed out to the President. It is upon this high part of the bluff where the temple site was dedicated and near to this is the site of the Altar of Adam. President McKay remarked that all this was most important land, and a very sacred place. . . ."

The party next drove to the Far West temple site. "At the site our car turned east so that the temple excavation baring the four cornerstones was to our immediate left and the site of the city square, now a cornfield, was to our immediate right. . . . Four of the brethren stood one each on the four cornerstones of the temple excavation. This enabled President McKay to judge the outline of the temple. . . .

"Elder Dyer related to President McKay that the two counties, Caldwell, of which Far West was the center of gathering for the saints, and Daviess, of which Adam-ondi-Ahman was the center, had been created largely for the

'Mormon settlers' through the efforts of the Honorable Alexander W. Doniphan of the Missouri legislature. . . .

"Caldwell County in 1836 was a wilderness. By the spring of 1838, it had a population of 5,000, 4,900 of whom were Mormons. The city of Far West at one time had 150 houses, four dry goods stores, three family groceries, half a dozen blacksmith shops, a printing establishment and two hotels. A large and comfortable school served as a church and courthouse. . . .

"As President McKay gazed out at the temple site with thoughtful contemplation, President Smith got out of the car and walked the short distance to the temple site. Elder Dyer told of the persecution of the saints at that time, which reached a climax at Far West. To the right of the car, once the city square, is where the exterminating order of Governor Boggs was read. . . .

"President Smith told of his father being born somewhere just west of the temple site. He lived to become the sixth president of the Church.

"At Far West we all stood amazed at the fact that there remained nothing of Far West except the four stones of the temple excavation which at one time was dug and cleared by 500 brethren in preparation for a house of the Lord. President McKay seemed pleased and elated at the fact that the Church owns 80 acres at Far West, including the dedicated temple site. He seemed visibly affected in the reflections of that which transpired at this hallowed and sacred place designated by the Lord as most holy. . . .

"It was a momentous and historically important trip. All marvelled at that which had been accomplished in just a little over one day. President McKay was in fine spirit and had been all during the trip. . . . President Smith too was feeling fine and enjoyed the visit, speaking of his happiness that President McKay had visited these historically sacred places in Missouri. . . ."

Elder Dyer, whom President McKay subsequently ordained an apostle and later set apart as a counselor in the church presidency, offered some interesting afterthoughts on Far West:

"In connection with President McKay's visit at Far West, it is to be noted that while there the President appeared somewhat overwhelmed. The place made a deep impression upon him; so much so that he referred to Far West a number of times in the ensuing days as a place of deep impression.

"The feeling that President McKay had at Far West registered upon me once again, but now with greater impact. The events that transpired there are significant: (a) The Lord proclaimed Far West a holy and consecrated land unto him, declaring to Joseph Smith that the very ground he stood on there was holy. (b) The Prophet Joseph Smith contended with the devil face to face for some time, upon the occasion of the power of evil menacing one of his children in the Prophet's home just west of the temple site. Lucifer declared that Joseph had no right to be there, that this was his place. Whereupon the Prophet rebuked Satan in the name of the Lord, and he departed and did not touch the child again. (c) The overwhelming feeling that President McKay had when he visited this sacred place.

"*The Answer:* I have often pondered the holy significance of Far West, and even more so since President McKay's visit. The sacredness of Far West, Missouri, is no doubt due to the understanding that the Prophet Joseph Smith conveyed to the brethren, at these early times, that Adam-ondi-Ahman, the place to which Adam and Eve fled when cast out of the Garden of Eden, is where Adam erected an altar unto God, and offered sacrifices, and that Far West was the spot where Cain killed Abel.

"This information tends to explain why the Lord declared Far West to be a holy consecrated place; and no doubt explains why Satan claimed that place as his own, as it was here that he entered into a covenant with Cain, resulting in the death of Abel, the first of mortal existence [to die] upon this earth.

"It would appear that President McKay while there felt the spirit and significance of this holy place."

Monuments erected on the Far West temple site with references to revelations given in Far West. Left to right, Bishop Victor L. Brown, Elder James A. Cullimore, Elder Alvin R. Dyer, Jessie Evans Smith, and President Joseph Fielding Smith.

One reason President McKay chose to tour the Missouri historic sites was to gain impressions helpful in making decisions in regard to further church expenditures for buildings and monuments in that area. He gave his approval to construction of a half million dollar visitor center near the temple lot site in Independence and to monuments and improvements at and near the Far West temple lot site. On August 3, 1968, two years and two months after their tour of these areas with President McKay, President Smith and President Dyer returned to Missouri, accompanied by their wives and by Elders Harold B. Lee, Mark E. Petersen, James A. Cullimore and Bishop Victor L. Brown, for dedication of monuments and improvements at Far West and for ground-breaking services for a visitor center at Independence. This was on the 137th anniversary of the date that the Prophet Joseph Smith dedicated the land at Independence for the erection of a temple, August 3, 1831. President Smith conducted the program and prayed at Far West in the morning, and gave the dedicatory speech and prayer at Independence, in the afternoon. Jessie sang.

On the printed program at the ground-breaking were published two pertinent statements regarding the destiny of that area. The first was by the Prophet Joseph in his prayer of dedication in 1831 when he declared, "I now pronounce this land consecrated and dedicated unto the Lord for the possession and inheritance for the saints, and for all the faithful servants of the Lord to the remotest ages of time, in the name of Jesus Christ, having authority from him." The second statement was by President Joseph Fielding Smith, who obviously was not disturbed by the fact that nearly a century and a half had passed without fulfillment of the area's destiny:

"Over 100 years have passed since the site of Zion was dedicated and the spot for the temple was chosen, and some of the members of the Church seem to be fearful lest the word of the Lord should fail. Others have tried to convince themselves that the original plan has been changed, and that the Lord does not require at our hands this mighty work which has been predicted by the prophets of ancient times. We have not been released from this responsibility, nor shall we be. The word of the Lord will not fail. If we look back and examine his word carefully we will discover that nothing has failed of all that he has predicted, neither shall one jot or tittle pass away unfulfilled. It is true that the Lord commanded the saints to build to his name a temple in Zion. This they attempted to do, but were prevented by their enemies, so the Lord did not require the work at their hands at that time. The release from the building of the temple in 1833 did not, however, cancel the responsibility of building the city and the house of the Lord, at some future time. When the Lord is ready for it to be accomplished, he will command his people, and the work will be done."

In his dedicatory sermon President Smith again affirmed these historical pronouncements. He also gave somber warning of the need for taking the prophecies seriously and getting one's house in order:

"Many things have taken place during the past 138 years to impress faithful members of the Church with the fact that the coming of the Lord is near. The gospel has been restored. The Church has been fully organized. The priesthood has been conferred upon man. The various dispensations from the beginning have been revealed and their keys and authorities given to the Church. Israel has been, and is being, gathered to the land of Zion. The Jews are returning to Jerusalem. The gospel is being preached in all the world as a witness to every nation.

"The words of the prophets are rapidly being fulfilled, but most of us fail to see it. One wonders if we are not now seeing some of the signs in heaven? Do we not see airships of various kinds traveling through the heavens daily? Have we not had signs in the earth and through the earth with the radio, railroad trains, automobiles, submarines and satellites, and in many other ways? There are yet to be great signs.

"Daniel said, 'And in that day many shall run to and fro, and knowledge shall be increased.' Are not the people running to and fro today as they never did before in the history of the world? Is not knowledge increased? But sad to say, the words of Paul are true: the people are 'ever learning and never coming to a knowledge of the truth.'

"Have you ever tried to associate the outpouring of knowledge, the great discoveries and inventions during the past 138 years with the restoration of the gospel? Do you not think that there is some connection? Because God has willed it so in our generation. Yet men take the honor unto themselves and fail to recognize the hand of the Almighty in these things.

"The gospel was restored in America, rather than in some other land, because the Lord willed it.

"Have we not had numerous rumors of war—such wars as the world never saw before? Is there not today commotion among the nations—rulers troubled? The whole earth is in commotion. Earthquakes in divers places. Yet the old world goes on about its business paying very little heed to all the Lord has said. Men harden their hearts and say that 'Christ delayeth his coming until the end of the earth.' Pleasure and the love of the world have captured the hearts of the people, and they have no time to worship the Lord or give heed to his warnings. The Lord as well as Elijah gave us warning, also Joseph Smith.

"And so the people refuse to heed the warnings the Lord so kindly gives to them, and thus they fulfil the scriptures. Peter calls attention to the destruction of the world in the flood and says, at the coming of Christ, which scoffers would postpone or deny, there shall come another cleansing of the earth, but the second time by fire. In the Pearl of Great Price it says, 'Verily I say unto you, this generation, in which these things shall be shown forth, shall not pass away until all I have told you shall be fulfilled.' Shall we slumber on in utter oblivion or indifference to all that the Lord has given us as a warning? I say unto you, 'Watch therefore, for ye know not what hour your Lord doth come, but know this, that if the good man of the house had known in what watch the thief would come, he would have watched and would not have suffered his house to be broken up. Therefore, be ye also ready, for in such an hour as ye think not the Son of Man cometh.'

"May we heed this warning given by the Lord and get our houses in order and be prepared for the coming of the Lord, I humbly pray, in the name of Jesus Christ our Redeemer, Amen."

As if the Missouri trip were not sufficient travel in one week for a man of such age, three days later President Smith, accompanied by Jessie, was in Palmyra, New York, attending for the first time the annual Hill Cumorah Pageant. "It was excellent, magnificent!" he declared. "We heard every word, and the lighting was perfect. It brought tears to our eyes."

Due to ill health President McKay had been unable to attend either of these events that year and in fact was no longer able to do any major traveling. His health and strength continued to decline, and by 1969 he was very weak. Several times at his request Joseph Fielding Smith administered to him. President Smith was ever solicitous of his welfare and happiness. Since childhood when it was a rare treat Joseph Fielding had always been especially fond of ice cream. Thinking that some might taste good to President McKay he sent a carton to him at Christmas time, 1969, as a gesture of friendship. In the first week of January, 1970, President and Sister Smith received what must be one of the very last letters sent by President McKay, and signed in a labored hand, dated December 31, 1969, just 18 days before his death. To 93-year-old Joseph Fielding Smith and his wife, 96-year-old David O. McKay wrote:

"It was indeed kind and gracious of you to send to Sister McKay and me that delicious and refreshing ice cream which has added much to our happiness during the Holiday Season.

"Thank you, and may God bless you and yours during this season and in all days that are to come! Affectionately, David O. McKay."

Chapter 18

"A posterity as numerous as the sands
of the seashore . . ."

On Being a Grandfather

When Dr. Silas S. Smith, the
family physician, arrived at the home of Joseph Fielding
Smith on Douglas Street to check on Amelia's baby, he
found the infant being carried about the house in the arms
of its grandfather, who felt greatly concerned about it.

"Joseph, what are you doing?" Silas asked.

Joseph Fielding looked steadily at his brother and replied, "Silas, I have been caring for sick infants for three
generations now!"

And such indeed was the case. As the oldest boy in
his mother's family he had helped with the other youngsters in illness. As a father he had spent many a sleepless night caring for his sick children. When he became a
grandfather his concern with sick youngsters did not end.
Rather, he spent considerable time in helping to care for
the little ones, whether at his home or by visiting the homes
of his children. Four of his children, Josephine, Lois,
Joseph, and Amelia, lived for a time in his home after
their marriages, and remember well the keen interest he
took in their children, and his solicitous concern whenever
they were ill.

"I went back home with my two little boys when
Bill did his internship," recalls Lois, "because interns did
not make enough to support a family. Richard was a small

baby when I came home. I used to put him on his teeter-babe on the kitchen table while I got dinner ready, and it was just about this time of night that Aunt Jessie and Father would come home from work. The minute Dad would walk into the house, that baby would start teasing for his grandfather to pick him up. He would get so excited when he would see his grandfather." And grandfather was just as excited to see the baby!

"I was also living at home at the time that my first baby was born," remembers Lois. "Father was very concerned and worried abut her when she was at the hospital. She was then six months old. He had administered to her, but he told me afterward that he had not felt good about the situation, and he had known that we were probably going to lose her. The night that we were called to the hospital—Bill and I—because she was dying, Father stayed at home and wrote a letter to me. 'My Beloved Daughter Lois: I am writing this that it may be a comfort to you at this time and throughout all your life. . . . That we have been privileged to come here and take bodies is the greatest blessing bestowed upon the spirits of men. . . . It matters not so far as the ultimate end is concerned whether we stay here long or a short time, after we get our bodies. Every little child which is taken away will be saved in the celestial kingdom. . . . Jesus redeemed all little children. They are saved, and no power can prevent them from obtaining a place in the celestial kingdom. Then we know that the time will come when they will receive the resurrection and will grow to maturity in holiness without the ills of mortality. They will also be entitled to the fulness of glory. No blessing will be taken from an infant who is not spared in this life, but the Lord will make up to them all things even to the fulness of exaltation. . . .'"

At the time of his death in 1972 President Smith had 11 children, 59 grandchildren, (29 grandsons, 30 granddaughters), and 99 great-grandchildren, (56 great-granddaughters and 43 great-grandsons). Surprisingly there were not yet any great-great-grandchildren. But his many de-

President Joseph Fielding Smith with a group of his young grandchildren.

scendants had the makings of a posterity "as numerous as the sands of the seashore," which greatly pleased Joseph Fielding.

For many years the Smith children and their families gathered together on Joseph Fielding's birthday anniversary, July 19, at Liberty Park or at some other park in Salt Lake City for a family outing. It was a proud and happy occasion for the family patriarch. Small gifts were purchased for the youngsters and Grandfather would hand these out to the little ones. At the picnic lunch "Happy birthday dear Grandfather!" was sung before anyone started eating. At least that was the rule. A softball game was a traditional feature of the festivities, and Grandfather played along with everyone else, until he got into his mid-80's, when he decided he better umpire instead.

Joseph Fielding took particular joy in the fact that all

of his children married in the temple—all 10, with only Lewis not having the opportunity of marriage—and that they and their families have all continued active in the Church. He delighted in being able to say, as he often did, "I am the father of 11 children, and to this day every one is a faithful member of the Church, and all are active, for that is the way they were taught, and they were obedient. They will belong to me forever and are the foundation stones of my kingdom."

Briefly, the family of Joseph Fielding Smith is as follows:

Josephine Smith Reinhardt of Bountiful, Utah; widow of Henry M. Reinhardt; married May 28, 1927. He died October 27, 1946. She has one daughter, Maxine Hodson, and four grandchildren. She is retired.

Julina Smith Hart of Rexburg, Idaho; wife of Eldon Charles Hart; married June 8, 1938. They have four children: Eldon Charles Jr. (deceased), Julina Hokanson, Mildred Andrus and Lewis Warren, and 12 grandchildren. She and her husband both teach school, he at Ricks College and she in the public schools.

Emily Smith Myers of Salt Lake City; wife of Louis Garrett Myers; married November 26, 1931. They have five children: Louis Garrett Jr., Janice Louise Neill, Douglas Smith, Evelyn Calder, and Wallace Warren, and 17 grandchildren. Her husband was a supervisor in the Church's Genealogical Society for 27 years and presently is manager of national sales at Mountain States Bindery.

Naomi Smith Brewster of Salt Lake City; wife of Hoyt William Brewster; married September 1, 1932. They have six children: Myrle Stoker, Barbara Amott, Hoyt William Jr., Karen McMillin, Anne Neeley, and Fielding Craig, and 19 grandchildren. Her husband is executive director of Utah State Medical Association.

Lois Smith Fife of Sacramento, California; wife of William Stewart Fife; married June 22, 1934. They have nine children: Dorothy Elayne (deceased), William Smith, Richard Stewart, Joseph Allen (deceased), Marian (deceased), Keith Reynolds, Roger Layne, Kathryn Thomas, and Bruce Fielding, and seven grandchildren. Her husband is an M.D., psychiatrist.

Joseph Fielding Smith Jr. of Salt Lake City, whose wife is the former Zella Farr; married May 16, 1933. They have nine children: Joseph Farr, Diane Groneman, Lane Farr, Carolyn Read, Zella Jeanne Jensen, Lewis Farr, Louise Spencer, Susan Davis, and Richard Fielding, and 28 grandchildren. He is an author and senior account executive at Deseret News Press.

Amelia Smith McConkie of Salt Lake City; wife of Bruce R. McConkie; married October 13, 1937. They have nine children: Bruce R. Jr. (deceased), Vivian Adams, Joseph Fielding, Stanford Smith, Mary Ethel Donoho, Mark Lewis, Rebecca, Stephen Lowell and Sarah Jill, and 11 grandchildren. Her husband is a member of the Church's First Council of the Seventy.

Lewis Warren Smith (deceased); did not marry.

George Reynolds Smith of Salt Lake City, whose wife is the former Marilyn Poulton; married November 17, 1949. They have four children: Vicki Ann, Stephen Reynolds, Michael George, and Donald Glen. He is a loan officer with the Small Business Administration.

Douglas Allan Smith of Salt Lake City, whose wife is the former Roberta Carlquist; married December 10, 1951. They have five children: Allan Douglas, Janet, Robert Carlquist, Sue, and Valerie. He is assistant secretary of Beneficial Life Insurance Company.

Milton Edmund Smith of Orem, Utah, who has been married twice. His first wife was a distant cousin, Donna Smith, a sister of Eldred G. Smith, patriarch to the Church. They were married March 31, 1950, and had three children: Terri Lyn Ballstaedt, Randall Milton, and Ruth Lynette. Donna died May 11, 1956. His second wife is the former Valoy Frandsen; married June 6, 1958. They have four children in addition to the earlier three: Lori, Scott Douglas, Rebecca, and Mark Allen, and one grandchild. He is an instructor in business management at Brigham Young University.

Through visits, phone calls and letters Joseph Field-

President Joseph Fielding Smith with his children on his 95th birthday. Back row left to right, Lois S. Fife, Julina S. Hart, Josephine S. Reinhardt, Emily S. Myers, Amelia S. McConkie, Naomi S. Brewster. Front row, left to right, Joseph Fielding Smith, Jr., George Reynolds Smith, President Smith, Douglas Allan Smith, and Milton Edmund Smith.

ing and his children and grandchildren kept in pretty close touch through the years. He of course was fortunate in having so many of his children living in or near Salt Lake City. Despite his busy schedule he took time to occasionally call on his married children and grandchildren. Sometimes he and Aunt Jessie even sang and played for them—she played the piano.

All of Joseph Fielding's children received some college education and most of them received bachelor degrees. Three, Julina, Reynolds, and Milton, received master's degrees. Most of the grandchildren have a similar interest in education, which was pleasing to President Smith. As chairman of the executive committee of Brigham Young University board of trustees for many years, he was especially conscious of the importance of a college education, although he himself had not received such.

Like most grandfathers, Joseph Fielding continued to exercise the right to give his children and grandchildren advice as he saw they might benefit by it. Joseph Fielding did not believe in long courtships for his children. Douglas recalls that after he had been courting Roberta for a few weeks his father one day asked him how he was getting along with his courtship, and then told him, "Either marry that girl or leave her alone!"

Sometimes Joseph Fielding's advice was a bit surprising. "After we first moved here to Sacramento," writes Lois, "I was asked to substitute in the Relief Society for the literature lesson one week. And as things go, once you start substituting, you are in. A short time later I was asked to work in the Primary, to teach a class. I thought Father would be very pleased when he heard of my activity, so I wrote and told him all that I was doing. When he wrote back, all he said about this was, 'Remember your family comes first.' I have heard him since give the same advice to the Relief Society general conference."

When Joseph Fielding's church assignments took him into an area where one of his children or grandchildren lived, away from Salt Lake City, he usually paid them a visit. On one of his visits to Lois and Bill Fife in Sacramento he decided to go for an early morning dip in their swimming pool, being very fond of swimming. But he was in for an embarrassing surprise. Lois tells what happened: "One morning he woke early, as has always been his custom. I don't think it was even light. It was about 4 a.m. He decided to go out and take a little swim before anyone was awake, and without bothering anyone. That year we had an awful lot of ducks, more than 50 of them, I believe. Dad no sooner got out into the pool and dived into the water when every one of those ducks started quacking at the top of their lungs and came around the back where we have the pool. He had been found out. He couldn't take his swim in silence. The ducks were telling on him."

Two other amusing experiences occurred at Lois' place while Joseph Fielding was visiting there: "I will never forget one little boy who came over [to our place]," says Lois. "His older brother was being married, and the family had asked to borrow my silver punch bowl for the reception. The father came over to pick it up and brought his youngest son with him. I brought them in and introduced them to Father. The father very solemnly told his son who he was meeting—'this is President Joseph Fielding Smith, president of the Quorum of the Twelve,' etc. The kid just looked up at his father and said, 'Who ya kidding?' . . .

"Speaking of family prayers I will have to tell you something that happened here once. I have chuckled over it many times but I have not liked to relate the incident because it tells of my neglect. One morning while the folks [Joseph Fielding and his wife Jessie] were here we gathered together before breakfast to have family prayers —all kneeling down by the chairs as we used to do. Bruce [her young son] pipes up, 'We sit on our chairs, we don't smell them!' "

Chapter 19

*"We are and shall be a world church.
This is our destiny."*

President of the Church

As the big plane touched down at the airport near Mexico City, thousands of men, women and children surged forward, anxious to get a glimpse of Joseph Fielding Smith. As he walked up the concourse, the huge crowd burst into song, "Te Damos, Señor, Nuestras Gracias"—"We Thank Thee O God for a Prophet"! Tears ran down the faces of many, and President Smith was deeply touched. Airport officials and other passengers watched in wonderment the elderly stranger who received such an enthusiastic greeting from so many Mexican citizens.

In another week Joseph Fielding would be 94 years old. For the past six months he had been president of The Church of Jesus Christ of Latter-day Saints; recognized by three million members as a prophet, seer and revelator, spokesman for God upon earth, holding keys of the dispensation of the fulness of times. Now he had come to a country, an area, rich in Book of Mormon history. As he met with five thousand Mexican saints in two stake sessions, he declared, "My feelings are to bless you, and to pray our Father in heaven to look down upon you in love and mercy, and give you those things which you need both temporally and spiritually.

"I have been to Mexico many times, but on this visit

I am especially pleased to see the great growth and progress that has come to the Church in your country. When I first came here many years ago, there was just one small mission. Now we have five missions and several stakes in the Republic of Mexico, with many thousands of members. . . .

"There is much work ahead of us. The field is white, all ready to harvest. . . . I think if all men knew and understood who they are, and were aware of the divine source from whence they came, and of the infinite potential that is part of their inheritance, they would have feelings of kindness and kinship for each other that would change their whole way of living and that would bring peace on earth.

"We believe in the dignity and divine origin of man. . . . Because God is our Father, we have a natural desire to love and serve him and to be worthy members of his family. . . . And because all men are our brothers, we have a desire to love and bless and fellowship them—and this, too, we accept as an essential part of true worship. Thus, everything we do in the Church centers around the divine law that we are to love and worship God and love and serve our fellowmen."

It was simple. It was eloquent. It was beautiful: This aged prophet, in his mid-90's, traveling two thousand miles to bring his blessings, his proclamation of peace and goodwill to God's children in a benighted land rich in history but poor in the daily wants of life. Here was a land and a people of destiny due to see in the years ahead the unfolding of God's purposes upon the earth. The old and the young in those congregations would remember seeing this prophet of God, hearing his voice and feeling the inspiration of his presence and his message.

Joseph Fielding Smith was president of the Church for just two and a half years, the shortest tenure of office of any of the first ten presidents of the Church. But that short time, from January 23, 1970, to July 2, 1972, was one of great growth in the Church, both numerically and spiritually. To the surprise of those who had regarded him as a cold, austere individual, President Smith's great plea to the Church and the world was for the cultivation of love and brotherhood among all people—through obedience to God's laws.

Society had never seen anything like it before, a 93-year-old man taking office as president—as president of anything, let alone of a three million-member Church with a multi-million dollar operation and an exceedingly ambitious world-wide program in the saving of souls. Yet here was this man Joseph Fielding Smith who not only took office at 93, but exercised it with surprising vigor. His programs of reorganization, his extensive travels and visits, his sermons and editorials, his daily agenda of work, and his capable grasp of the business at hand were all beyond any reasonable expectation for a man of such age.

Following President McKay's death and burial the first order of business was of course a reorganization of the presidency. As senior apostle and president of the Council of the Twelve it was not only Joseph Fielding's right but responsibility to handle this matter. At the time of President McKay's death there had been five counselors: Hugh B. Brown, N. Eldon Tanner, Joseph Fielding Smith, Thorpe B. Isaacson and Alvin R. Dyer. Obviously one option President Smith had was to leave these other four men in their positions as counselors. A majority of the presidents before him had retained the same counselors as their predecessor. Of these four men, President Smith decided to retain only one, N. Eldon Tanner, to continue as second counselor. President Tanner he had found was not only a financial genius but a spiritual giant, having a rare combination of traits, admirably suiting him for that important position. The other three men were reassigned to their former positions: Hugh B. Brown as a member of the Council of the Twelve, Thorpe B. Isaacson and Alvin R. Dyer as assistants to the Twelve. President Smith had decided to have only two counselors, the same as his father and most of the other presidents had. Nor did it take long to decide whom he wished for his first counsel-

President Joseph Fielding Smith with his counselors in the First Presidency, President Harold B. Lee and President N. Eldon Tanner.

or: Harold B. Lee, next to him in seniority among the apostles and a trusted associate for three decades. Spiritually and doctrinally Harold B. Lee was as solid as the granite walls of the temple. He would be a strong right hand, and the experience as a counselor would help prepare him for the day, obviously not far distant, when he would become eleventh president of the Church.

So it was that on January 23, 1970, the day after President McKay's funeral service, Joseph Fielding Smith was ordained by the Council of the Twelve Apostles as the tenth president of the Church, with Elder Lee being voice in the ordination. President Smith in turn then set apart Elder Lee both as his first counselor and as president of the Council of the Twelve, and Elder Tanner as his second counselor in the presidency. Spencer Woolley Kimball was set apart as acting president of the Twelve, so that President Lee could devote his full attention to his duties as a member of the presidency. Two and a half months later the new presidency was sustained in a solemn assembly at the 140th annual general conference of the Church, April 6, in the Tabernacle. It was an impressive moment as the various quorums of the priesthood arose in turn to give their sustaining vote.

Inasmuch as President McKay had ordained Alvin R. Dyer an apostle, there was naturally some anticipation that he would be appointed to the vacancy created in the Council of the Twelve by Elder Lee's elevation to the presidency. Instead, Boyd Kenneth Packer, another of the assistants to the Twelve, was appointed to the Council. Like President Smith himself, Elder Packer was the father of a large family (ten children), a family outstanding in its devotion to the Church. Three new assistants to the Twelve were also named: Joseph Anderson, long-time secretary to the presidency; David B. Haight of Brigham Young University and William H. Bennett of Utah State University.

Rubie Egbert, President Smith's secretary for more than 52 years, continued as such until retirement on December 31, 1971. D. Arthur Haycock, who had been serving as secretary to the Council of the Twelve, also became President Smith's personal secretary, assistant and traveling companion, in January of 1970, and continued as such until President Smith's death. Francis "Frank" Gibbons became secretary to the presidency. Shortly thereafter, he was also sustained as president of Bonneville Stake, with President Smith's son Douglas as first counselor.

Upon accepting the job as the president's secretary and assistant, Brother Haycock recalled an experience he had had with President Smith a few years earlier: He said that one day as he was approaching the side door to the Church Office Building President Smith was ahead of him, unlocking the door. It is necessary to enter this door by key, and few people have a key. Arthur hurried up the stairs, two or three at a time, to get his foot in the door before it closed. He barely made it. As he got inside the

President Joseph Fielding Smith with his personal secretary, D. Arthur Haycock.

building he hurried again to catch up with President Smith to walk to the elevator with him. He commented to him, "I hope I can be that lucky to squeeze into heaven through the door you open." President Smith did not reply and Brother Haycock thought, "Well, I guess I blew that." As they reached the elevator President Smith said, with a twinkle in his eye, "Now, brother, don't ever count on that!"

Upon becoming president it was appropriate that Joseph Fielding relinquish the office of Church Historian and Recorder, a position he had held for half a century. It was a job he had enjoyed and one he disliked leaving. He appointed Howard W. Hunter of the Council of the Twelve as his successor. Elder Hunter was also head of the Genealogical Society, a position President Smith had long occupied. By January of 1972, however, the decision was reached to release members of the Council of the Twelve from other specific assignments, so Theodore M.

Burton, an assistant to the Twelve and number two man in the Genealogical Society, became president in Elder Hunter's place, in May, 1972, and Leonard J. Arrington of Utah State University was appointed church historian in Elder Hunter's place, with Earl E. Olson as church archivist and Donald T. Schmidt as church librarian.

For years prior to Ernest Wilkinson's term as president of Brigham Young University there had been a church commissioner of education, with Franklin L. West as the last man in the job. After nearly a quarter of a century this position was reactivated by President Smith, with Neal Maxwell being appointed to it. Under Maxwell three new college presidents were appointed within a short time: Dallin H. Oaks at BYU, Henry B. Eyring Jr. at Ricks College in Rexburg, Idaho, and Stephen L. Brower at Church College of Hawaii. Wilkinson remained on the BYU staff to help establish a law school there. Plans were made to establish some elementary and secondary schools among church members in Latin America and perhaps other places.

President Smith ordained several new temple presidents: Myrthus W. Evans in Los Angeles, C. Bryant Whiting in Mesa, Arizona, Fred W. Schwendiman in Salt Lake for the New Zealand Temple, and Charles Lloyd Walch in Salt Lake for the Hawaiian Temple, Cecil E. Hart for the Idaho Falls Temple, and Reed Whipple for the St. George Temple. He dedicated a new temple in Ogden and presided at the dedication of a new temple in Provo.

During his presidency the Church magazines were revamped with Doyle L. Green as editor-in-chief over all of them. The names, The Improvement Era, The Instructor, The Relief Society Magazine, The Children's Friend were dropped; also the seminary system's Impact. These magazines were changed into three, one for adults, one for youth, and one for children, and named respectively, The Ensign, The New Era, and The Friend. President Smith and his two counselors were listed as editors of these publications and took turns writing editorials for them. R- and X-rated movie ads were dropped from the Church's daily newspaper, the Deseret News.

The Deseret Sunday School Union was reorganized and renamed the Sunday School of The Church of Jesus Christ of Latter-day Saints. Upon receiving his call to preside over the Eastern States Mission, David Lawrence McKay, eldest son of President David O. McKay, was released as superintendent, and Russell M. Nelson was appointed in his place, with the new title of president. The general Sunday School board membership was considerably reduced.

The Church Social Services Department was reorganized with Marvin J. Ashton as chairman, and a church commissioner of health services, Dr. James O. Mason, was appointed. A Department of Internal Communications and a Department of External Communications were organized with J. Thomas Fyans and Wendell J. Ashton as managing directors, respectively. The Church took specific steps to aid Negroes, Indians and other minority groups, both inside and outside the Church, through various programs.

Emphasis was given to the Church's home teaching and family home evening programs, in a continuing effort to strengthen family solidarity. President Smith though in advanced age continued to set an example to the Church by meeting in family home evenings with his children and grandchildren.

A new training program for bishops was inaugurated to aid them in their duties and responsibilities. The Teacher Development Program for all prospective church teachers, inservice teachers, and their supervisors was enhanced on a church-wide basis with training for general authorities, stake, and ward priesthood leaders included.

A new program was instituted to bring the Aaronic Priesthood and MIA leaders into closer cooperation for the benefit of the growth of the Church. The Scouting program was correlated, with the Presiding Bishopric serving as the chairmen of the General Boy Scout Committee of the Church. A new Personal Achievement Program for youth was inaugurated which permits the young people to set their own goals under the supervision of leaders and ward bishops or branch presidents. Stress was placed on priesthood quorum activities, particularly the elders quorums, resulting in a more unified spirit of activity. One of the chief objectives of President Smith's was to unify the priesthood to enable its members to take their rightful place in the Church's future.

The next general area conference was announced to be held in Mexico City in August 1972.

In the two and a half years Joseph Fielding served as president 14 additional missions were created, some by a division of previously existing missions, bringing the total at the time of his death to 101. During the same period an additional 82 stakes were organized, bringing the total at the time of his death to 581. Total Church membership increased from 2,930,810 in January of 1970 to 3,170,000 in July of 1972.

In June, 1972, less than a week before his death, 70 new church regions were created, with mission fields as well as stakes to be included in the regions; 35 additional regional representatives were appointed, and 29 mission representatives were called to assist the general authorities in directing missionary work.

The church building program continued at a rapid pace, with hundreds of chapels, schools, and other buildings being constructed. A 31-story Church office building east of the Salt Lake Temple was nearing completion at the time of his death. Its dedication had been scheduled for December 1972. Here would be housed the various church auxiliary organizations and service departments in one magnificent center.

Two general authorities, Thorpe B. Isaacson and Richard L. Evans, and also President David O. McKay's widow, Emma Rae Riggs McKay, as well as his own wife Jessie, preceded President Smith in death during his term of office. President Isaacson, who had suffered a paralytic stroke a few months following his appointment to the church presidency, died November 9, 1970. Sister McKay died less than a week later, November 14. Elder Evans, a member of the Council of the Twelve and long-time neighbor of the Smiths, died a year later, November 1, 1971. President Smith was a speaker at each of these three funeral services.

To the vacancy in the Council of the Twelve created by the death of Elder Evans, President Smith appointed Marvin J. Ashton, an assistant to the Twelve and son of the late Marvin O. Ashton, who had been a counselor in the presiding bishopric years earlier.

Victor L. Brown, who had been serving as second counselor in the presiding bishopric, was appointed as presiding bishop in April, 1972, with H. Burke Peterson and Vaughn J. Featherstone as his counselors. Bishop John H. Vandenberg, and his first counselor, Robert L. Simpson, were named assistants to the Twelve.

On May 31, 1971 President Smith presided at the dedication of a new visitor center in Independence, Missouri, the cornerstone for which he had laid two years earlier. Nearly 5,000 persons, traveling as far as 600 miles, attended the dedication of the visitor center at Independence. The program was held out-of-doors, under threatening skies, and midway through President Smith's address there was a flash of lightning followed by a loud clap of thunder. Unruffled, President Smith paused in his talk only long enough to comment, "I hardly expected to have to fight the devil here today!" It was here at Independence, in Jackson County, Missouri, that the Saints had sought to build up their new Zion, only to be rudely ejected by ruffian mobs. But Jackson County would yet be an important site in the program of the restored gospel. The world was finally recognizing the importance of the man rejected here:

"Because of the part which Jackson County, Missouri, has played and will yet play in the glorious work of restoration in this dispensation, I desire to call attention to two great truths," said President Smith: "First, that Jesus Christ is the Son of God, and second, that Joseph Smith is a prophet. I mention the first, which is one of the greatest truths ever revealed to man, as a prelude to bearing testimony of the second. . . .

"Joseph Smith is the revealer of the knowledge of Christ and of salvation to the world for this day and generation. . . . I, for one, want to be numbered forever among those who seek counsel and authority and blessings as they have come from this great prophet whom the Lord raised up to commence the restoration of all things in this final, glorious gospel dispensation.

"And I am pleased to testify that as the years pass, people in all nations, from one end of the earth to the other, are increasingly turning to Joseph Smith and the gospel restored through his instrumentality in order to find peace in this life and gain a hope of eternal life in the world to come. Joseph Smith is the one to whom all men must look in this day to learn the truth about Christ and his gospel. . . ."

A visitor center was also opened in Nauvoo, Illinois, two months later, on July 31, 1971. Unfortunately President Smith was unable to attend, for his wife Jessie was critically ill.

President Smith had spent his 95th birthday anniversary, July 19, sitting at her bedside in the Salt Lake Latter-day Saint Hospital. After transferring to an apartment in Hotel Utah she died a few days later, on August 3, 1971, at the age of 68, four months following their 33rd wedding anniversary. So for the third time President Smith had the sorrow of burying a wife.

Despite his sorrow and loneliness and old age, President Smith later that month, on August 27-29, presided over the Church's first area general conference, conducted in Manchester, England, with several thousand attending. "All of the presidents of the Church except the Prophet Joseph Smith have performed missionary service in this great nation," he reminded the British saints. "I served as a young missionary here over 70 years ago."

To the Church members in England he also proclaimed, "We are members of a world church, a church that has the plan of life and salvation, a church set up by the Lord himself in these last days to carry his message of salvation to all his children in all the earth.

In attendance at conference at Manchester, England, were, left to right, Derek A. Cuthbert, regional representative; Douglas A. Smith, President Joseph Fielding Smith, D. Arthur Haycock, and Dr. Donald E. Smith.

"The day is long since past when informed people think of us as a peculiar group in the tops of the Rocky Mountains in America. It is true that the church headquarters are in Salt Lake City, and that the Lord's house has been erected there to which people have come from many nations to learn the law of the Lord and to walk in his paths.

"But now we are coming of age as a church and as a people. We have attained the stature and strength that are enabling us to fulfill the commission given us by the Lord through the Prophet Joseph Smith, that we should carry the glad tidings of the restoration to every nation and to all people. And not only shall we preach the gospel in every nation before the second coming of the Son of Man, but we shall make converts and establish congregations of Saints among them. We are and shall be a world church. This is our destiny. It is part of the Lord's program."

Indeed, so world renown had The Church of Jesus

Christ of Latter-day Saints become by 1970 that there was a constant stream of visiting dignitaries to 47 East South Temple Street in Salt Lake City to meet the president of the Church—men and women from nearly every part of the world. The Church's attraction for so many VIP's, its ability and willingness to be a host of hosts, reminds one of the Prophet Joseph Smith's joyous aspirations in seeking to build the Nauvoo House in the early 1840's. "And let the name of that house," advised a revelation to the Church, "be called Nauvoo House; and let it be a delightful habitation for man, and a resting place for the weary traveler, that he may contemplate the glory of Zion, and the glory of this, the corner-stone thereof. . . ."

Some of President Smith's visitors in Salt Lake City, in order of their visits, were: 1970—General William C. Westmoreland, U.S. Army Chief of Staff; Rogers Morton, chairman of the Republican National Committee; Felix Schnyder, Swiss Ambassador to the United States; Afioga Afoafouvale Misimoa, Secretary General of the South Pacific Commission; President Richard M. Nixon, Mrs. Nixon, and daughter Tricia; George Romney, U.S. Secretary of Housing and Urban Development; David M. Kennedy, U.S. Secretary of the Treasury; Ramon Nobel, director of music in the Mexican National Ministry of Culture; James D. Hodgson, U.S. Secretary of Labor; Malcolm R. Lovell, Jr., Assistant Secretary of Labor for Manpower; Jerome M. Rosow, Assistant Secretary of Labor for Policy, Evaluation and Research; Vice President Spiro T. Agnew; Robert H. Finch, U.S. Secretary of Health and Welfare; Per W. Frellesvig, Consul General of Denmark; Congressman K. Gunn McKay; Pedro Eduardo Real, Ambassador from Argentina and Mrs. Real; Glenn M. Miller, Exalted Ruler of the Elks; Clyde M. Clark, new director of the "Relationships" Division of the National Council, Boy Scouts of America.

1971—Dr. Theodore C. Marrs, Deputy Assistant Secretary of Defense for Reserve Affairs; Senator Henry M. Jackson, Washington D.C.; Astronauts of Apollo 15,

Col. David R. Scott, Col. James B. Irwin, Lt. Col. Alfred
M. Worden; Mrs. Katherine Pearce, president of the Na-
tional Retired Teachers Association; Fred Faassen, presi-
dent of the American Association of Retired Persons;
governors from Japan—Gov. and Mrs. Gonichiro Nishi-
zawa, Gov. Tokichi Abiko, Gov. Hiroshi Kuroki, Gov.
Yasunobu Takeichi, Gov. Kinichiro Nozaki, Gov. and Mrs.
Kunio Tanabe, Gov. and Mrs. Kokichi Nakada, Gov.
Tokitada Sakai, Rev. Nikkyo Niwano of the Buddhist
Church, Japan; His Eminence Archbishop Iakovos, Pri-
mate of the Greek Orthodox Church of North and South
America.

1972—Dr. Thor Heyerdahl, Norwegian anthropolo-
gist and famed explorer of Kon-Tiki and the Ra Expedi-
tions; Rear Admiral Francis L. Garrett, Chief of Navy
Chaplains; Alden G. Barber, Chief Scout Executive, Boy
Scouts of America; Col. Hampton Price of Colorado
Springs, Colo.; Dr. Howard Hansen, eminent composer
and conductor; Frank E. Fitzsimmons, president of the
Teamsters Union; Rep. Carl B. Albert, Speaker of the
House of Representatives, Washington, D.C.; Devere
Baker, Lehi Raft Expeditions; Nobihiko Ushiba, Japanese
Ambassador to the United States; Dr. Joseph Ginat, deputy
advisor on Arab affairs to the Prime Minister of Israel,
and Hon. Jacob Barmore, Israel's Ambassador to the
United Nations, New York.

A few of the visitors from the entertainment world
were: Pat Boone and family; Osmond Brothers; Johnny
Whitaker, who plays Jody in television program "Family
Affair"; Johny Jordaan, and "Tante" Leen, famous recording stars from Holland.

In the two and a half years of his presidency, Joseph
Fielding presided at five annual and semi-annual general
conferences of the Church, and accepted an amazing
number of invitations to speak, especially to youth
groups. He spoke at Brigham Young University, Church
College of Hawaii, Ricks College, Utah State University,
Weber State College, College of Southern Utah, University of Utah, Snow College—to name a few. He even ad-

President Joseph Fielding Smith, with the aid of translator, Tatsui Sato, greets eight Japanese governors in Church Office Building.

dressed several stake conferences, mostly in Salt Lake City. He served both years, 1970 and 1971, as grand marshal of Salt Lake City's Days of '47 Parade. And he received numerous awards and recognitions from Brigham Young University and other Church organizations, so many that he was hard pressed for a place to put them.

At a press conference the day following his appointment as president of the Church he had expressed amazement at all the "fuss" being made over him. As the months wore on he had cause to feel even more amazed. One minor recognition that caught his fancy, however, was that he was the holder of the oldest savings deposit account in the Zion's Savings Bank (now Zion's First National Bank). His father had opened an account there in his name when he was born in 1876, just three years after the bank was begun. And the account remained intact until his death in 1972. President Smith was always

Thor Heyerdahl, famous Norwegian adventurer and author of Kon Tiki, *and other books of particular interest to Latter-day Saints, visited President Smith, January 1, 1972.*

President Joseph Fielding Smith and his wife, Jessie, enjoying ride in grand marshal's car in Days of '47 Parade.

Zion's Savings Bank as it appeared when Joseph Fielding Smith's savings account was opened by his father.

President Joseph Fielding Smith, whose savings account had been in continuous service since 1876, looks over old bank signature book.

a strong believer in thrift and the savings account was symbolic of that thrift.

He took all the honors and recognition in good stride, for he was a modest man. As he addressed the saints assembled in conference in April 1970, when he was sustained as president of the Church, he declared, "I stand before you today in humility and thanksgiving, grateful for the blessings which the Lord has poured out upon me, upon my family, upon you, and upon all his people. I know we are engaged in the work of the Lord and that he raises up men to do his work in every time and age of the earth's history. . . . I desire to say that no man of himself can lead this church. It is the Church of the Lord Jesus Christ; he is at the head. . . . Men are only instruments in the Lord's hands, and the honor and glory for all that his servants accomplish is and should be ascribed unto him forever. . . . I rejoice in the work of the Lord and glory in the sure knowledge I have in my soul of its truth and divinity!"

Although President Smith became a bit feeble with age, his hearing, eyesight, and other faculties remained good right to the last moment of life. He was truly remarkable that way—greatly blessed. And to the end he retained his sense of humor:

When appointed president of the Church he kept staying on in the same office room he had occupied for over 50 years, rather than moving to the president's office, which he called "the cubby hole." One day Rubie Egbert, his secretary, asked him again when he was going to move to the president's office. His emphatic reply was, "Not until the president of the Church tells me I have to!"

The night he returned home from London following the British conference late in August 1971, he and his two traveling companions, his son Douglas and his nephew Don Smith, who was his personal physician, were sitting in the airport waiting for a plane that had been delayed by fog. Douglas and Don sat eating some nuts. President Smith finally said to them, "When you boys have finished your nuts, perhaps we could be on our way."

Douglas explained to him, "We can't leave because of the fog."

"Then we will walk," said President Smith.

"Across the water?" asked Douglas.

"It's been done before," said President Smith. Then after a pause, "But, perhaps this isn't our night for it."

In December 1971, four months after Jessie's death, President Smith fell, cracked three ribs and broke a piece of bone off his hip. He limped around in pain for ten days before finally agreeing to have X-rays taken to see what had happened. His doctor then recommended that he use a wheelchair as much as possible to help the hip mend. Reluctantly he did so for two or three days, but grew restless and decided to discontinue using it. After all, why should a man only 95 years old be confined to a wheelchair? At the end of the day's work, as his assistant, Arthur Haycock, pushed the wheelchair toward him at his desk, President Smith waved it away, declaring, "I can walk! My hip feels all right."

"Yes," persisted Brother Haycock, "your hip is beginning to heal, and we want to keep it that way."

"Well, hip, hip hooray!" exclaimed President Smith. For those last six months of his life he did not use the wheelchair.

One day in March, 1972, as his son Joseph called at his office to take him home they met Asahel D. Woodruff, an acquaintance, in the hallway of the Church Office Building. President Smith asked, "Asahel, what are you doing here?"

"I'm serving as a guide here today," explained Brother Woodruff.

"Then," said President Smith, "come and guide us to the front door."

Chapter 20

*"Those that die in me shall
not taste of death . . ."*

His Death

He had signed his last letter, saw that his desk was neat and clean, and all things in good order. Then as Joseph Fielding Smith left his office on Friday afternoon, June 30, 1972, in company with his assistant, Arthur Haycock, he felt a nostalgic urge to visit the Church Historian's Office, up on the third floor, where he had labored for more than six decades.

With Brother Haycock at his side he walked through the Historian's Office, greeting the employees there as he used to do when in charge of that office. Then after taking the elevator to the basement of the Church Office Building where his car was parked in the underground lot, he stopped to greet the telephone operators on duty at the switchboard. He just wanted to express appreciation for their service.

It was his last visit to the Church Office Building. Sunday morning he rested at home, at the home of his daughter Amelia and son-in-law Bruce McConkie, with whom he had lived since shortly after the death of his wife Jessie in August, 1971. The McConkies live up near Ensign Peak, high above the State Capitol Building, affording an excellent view of the Salt Lake Valley. It was a view that President Smith enjoyed. He often mused upon the contrast in the appearance of the city and valley now with their teeming population and the rural Salt Lake that he knew as a boy.

Sunday afternoon he desired to attend sacrament service—fast and testimony meeting—in his home Eighteenth Ward near First Avenue and A Street. So Amelia took him to church, at 2 p.m. As usual, his presence prompted a special feeling among the congregation. One young mother brought her small child to him and asked, "President Smith, would you please touch my baby?" He smiled and lovingly patted the child. A young man took hold of his arm to help him down the steps, calling his attention to the fact that there were two steps. With a twinkle in his eye President Smith asked, "Do you think I can jump them?"

It was the weekend preceding the Fourth of July, and the chorister announced that as a closing hymn the congregation would sing the national anthem. President Smith was one of the first to arise, and tears welled in his eyes as he joined with the others in singing "The Star Spangled Banner." He had been born in the centennial year and month of the founding of the American Republic, on July 19, 1876. And now plans were well underway for the nation's bicentennial celebration. Would he live to see it? In 17 days he would be 96 years old.

Sunday following church he enjoyed hearing Bruce McConkie and Bruce's daughter Sarah read to each other and discuss chapters 5 through 12 of the Book of First Nephi in the Book of Mormon. No matter how often he heard or read the book, it was always a pleasure to hear it once again.

Later Sunday afternoon his son Reynolds called and took him for a ride out to his oldest daughter's, Josephine Reinhardt, at Bountiful. Joseph Fielding generally avoided any travel on Sunday, but he felt this short trip was all right because they were going out to make plans to hold a family home evening service at Josephine's place the following evening. He, Reynolds, and another son, Douglas, and their families would meet together with Josephine, who had been a widow for many years. It was a pleasant visit with Josephine Sunday afternoon, sitting in her garden and taking light refreshments. He thought back to the day that Josephine had been born to his first wife Louie, in 1902. What a joy she had been to him through the years.

Reynolds delivered him back to his home at the McConkies a few minutes after 7 p.m., and shortly afterward his oldest son Joseph Fielding had phoned to say that his cousin, President Smith's niece, Macksene Rux, director of the Mormon Miracle Pageant at Manti, had phoned to inquire whether her Uncle Joseph would like to come down and see the pageant this year. Amelia had answered the phone call from Joseph and called to her father to inquire whether he would like to go. Yes, he said he would enjoy that. He had heard some good reports about the pageant and looked forward to seeing it. It was good in life to always have something pleasant to look forward to. Yes, he would like to go to Manti and see the pageant. Macksene was a daughter of his oldest brother, Apostle Hyrum Mack Smith, who had died in 1918, followed in death a few months later by his wife, leaving five little children orphaned. Joseph Fielding had done what he could to help the sorrowing youngsters, becoming almost as a second father to them.

President Smith ate a light supper with the McConkies at 7:30 p.m. Then he relaxed in his favorite chair, a large comfortable black vinyl recliner that had been brought from his apartment especially for his enjoyment. It was the chair that Jessie had been sitting in when she died 11 months ago. Oh, what a lonely 11 months that had been without her. How terribly he missed her. And how he missed Louie and Ethel, and his son Lewis and other loved ones who had departed this life. And yet, how fortunate he was to have such good devoted children to look after him and comfort and help him in his old age and loneliness. Each week his children living in the Salt Lake area had taken turns coming to the McConkie home to spend a night a week with him: Douglas on Monday nights, Naomi on Tuesdays, Reynolds on Wednesdays, Joseph on Thursdays, Milton on Fridays, Emily on Saturdays, and Josephine on all the spare afternoons or evenings when others were not available. It was thoughtful and good of them, and he appreciated it.

Amelia and Bruce and their youngsters had done all possible to make him feel welcome in their home. They had brought not only his favorite chair and some other pieces of furniture up for his use, but a collection of his favorite books. As he conversed Sunday evening with Amelia he again expressed his love and appreciation for her.

As he sat meditating, President Smith also thought back over the past week. It had been a busy and thus a satisfying week for him. On Sunday, the first day of the week, June 25, he had addressed the closing general session of the Mutual Improvement Association conference, in the Salt Lake Tabernacle. He had been at his office part of each day Monday through Friday answering correspondence, conversing with his associates and visitors. Tuesday he had met with his two counselors in a weekly meeting of the church presidency. Thursday he had addressed a seminar for new mission presidents, introducing to them a revised program in which the First Council of Seventy would assume a greater leadership role in missionary work and in which regional representatives and mission representatives would be appointed to strengthen the mission program of the Church. As usual his talk had been brief and to the point. "You have been called to serve in the most important work in the world," he had concluded. Friday evening he had attended a dinner for the mission presidents. It had, indeed, been a busy week for a man nearly 96 years old. . . .

While visiting with her father Amelia was also writing a letter to one of her children. At about 9:20 p.m. she left the living room for a minute or two to get an address she needed.

"When Amelia returned," reported Bruce, "she found her father in what seemed to be a state of shock. She called to me, and within moments, not more than a few seconds at most, we were giving him oxygen—to no avail. It was apparent his time had come and that the tenement of clay no longer housed the eternal spirit.

"His passing was as sweet and easy, as calm and as peaceful as though he had fallen asleep, which in fact he had. . . . Truly when the Lord took his prophet, there was no sting. President Smith did not taste of death. . . ."

Amelia immediately phoned her oldest brother Joseph and told him to "come quickly," and to call the other brothers and sisters. Joseph phoned his brother Reynolds then asked his wife Zella to call the others, and he and his son Lane, a medical doctor who happened to be visiting at his home, left immediately for the McConkies, each driving a different car. When they arrived, about 9:35, and found President Smith dead they with Bruce laid his body upon the couch, and then Joseph phoned President Harold B. Lee and told him, "Father has passed away." President Lee was greatly shocked by the news. At Joseph's request he in turn phoned President N. Eldon Tanner. These two men who had served as counselors in the Church presidency reached the McConkie home about half an hour later. Upon seeing President Smith's lifeless body President Lee dropped to his knees by the couch and held to President Smith's hands for several minutes. It was as though he sought some final word, some final communication from him.

Other members of the family had soon reached the McConkie home, and it was decided that they would meet the following morning with a committee of the Council of the Twelve to plan jointly the funeral service. The committee appointed by President Lee was comprised of Ezra Taft Benson, Mark E. Petersen and Delbert L. Stapley. Meanwhile, news of his death was flashed around the world via the mass media, and letters and telegrams of condolences began pouring in from men of many faiths and many countries. One of the most esteemed of these was from President Richard Nixon, then at the western White House in San Clemente, California—in the confines of the same LDS ward as the vacation home of the president of the Church. President Nixon, who also sent a floral wreath, declared:

"Mrs. Nixon and I were deeply saddened to learn of the death of Joseph Fielding Smith, and on behalf of all Americans, we send our sincere sympathy. . . . For over 70 years—from his first days as a missionary, then as a leading religious scholar, and finally as the tenth president of The Church of Jesus Christ of Latter-day Saints —Joseph Fielding Smith gave enormously to others, helping them to find greater fulfillment in their relationship to God. As son of another president of the Church and grand nephew of its first president, he received a rich heritage from the past. Perhaps his greatest accomplishment was the way he carried forward and enriched that legacy for the future.

"I had the privilege of enjoying the friendship of Joseph Fielding Smith in the closing years of his life. This was a profound experience for me, and I know that men and women everywhere have lost a devoted and inspirational leader. . . ."

When Joseph Fielding Smith had been appointed to the Council of the Twelve in 1910, *The Salt Lake Tribune* had been abusive in its editorial comment, criticizing his father, President Joseph F. Smith, for making the appointment. But now on the morning of the Fourth of July the *Tribune* devoted its lead editorial to praise of the life of Joseph Fielding Smith, concluding with this statement, "Joseph Fielding Smith, a man stern in devotion to his creed, yet tender in regard for essential needs of people everywhere, gave wise counsel to his associates, loving care to his family and exalted leadership to his church responsibilities. He will be missed, but remembered with special esteem."

President Smith's body lay in state in the rotunda of the Church Office Building all day Wednesday and Thursday morning, as thousands filed past the coffin to get a final glimpse of the body of a prophet they loved and respected.

It was not surprising that in his last will and testament, prepared June 2, 1971, he bequeathed to the Church "all of the books and papers belonging to me, wheresoever they are located, [also] the 'Hyrum Smith chair' as well as all other items of equipment belonging to me in or pertaining to my office in my home or in or pertaining to my office in the Church Office Building in Salt Lake City, Utah, such books, papers, and other items to be housed and used under the direction of the First Presidency of the Church." These are to be placed in an exhibit room in the new Church Office Building, along with mementos of other church presidents.

Funeral services were conducted on Thursday, July 6, in the Salt Lake Tabernacle, with President Lee conducting. The Tabernacle was crowded with mourners, and the services were heard and seen by additional thousands via radio and television. Extensive coverage was also given by many newspapers. Several Salt Lake City business firms, including non-LDS ones, remained closed throughout the day. Speakers at the services were President Bruce R. McConkie, President Tanner, and President Lee. Family prayer at the mortuary was offered by Joseph Fielding Jr., the invocation at the services by Elder Ezra Taft Benson, and the benediction by Bishop LaMar S. Williams of the Eighteenth Ward. Music was provided by the Tabernacle Choir under the direction of Richard P. Condie. A medley of hymns including "I Need Thee Every Hour" was played as prelude music by Alexander Schreiner. The choir sang "Does the Journey Seem Long?" with words written by President Smith; "I Know that My Redeemer Lives," and "O My Father." Honorary pallbearers were all general authorities and the Ensign Stake presidency. Pallbearers were grandsons and a great-grandson representing various branches of the family.

"As we, President Tanner and I, have been associated with President Smith the past two years," said President Lee in his sermon, "we have marveled at the clarity of his mind, the health of his body, the fact that he could speak well and walk well without difficulty, when most men his age could not have done either."

This remarkable state of mental and physical health that President Smith enjoyed right to the last moment of

General authorities, friends, and family assembled in the Tabernacle for President Smith's funeral services.

mortal life was literal fulfillment of the patriarchal blessing pronounced upon his head in 1913 in Scipio by Patriarch Joseph D. Smith who had declared, "I bless you with wisdom to use the knowledge that God will give you in the furtherance of his work in the earth, and in the preserving of your body until you have completed all you have been sent to do."

Calling attention to the rich heritage that was President Smith's and also the faithfulness of President Smith's children and grandchildren, President Lee further commented that "Four generations of the Smith leaders now have shown their metal by the strength of their presidency and their great leadership in the Church."

President Tanner observed that President Smith's life span "covered the period from the covered wagon to the jet and space age. . . . He served with four presidents of the Church, and was the last of the general authorities to bridge the gap between the days of Brigham Young and the present generation. Since he became a member of the Twelve, the number of stakes in the Church has increased from 62 to 581; the number of members from 393,000 to 3,090,953; the number of missions from about a dozen to 101. He has attended dedications of 11 of the 13 temples, including the St. George and the Salt Lake. . . . He took keen satisfaction in recounting the fact that as a boy he watched the quarrying, stone cutting, and transporting of the huge granite stones used in the building of the [Salt Lake] temple. . . ."

President Smith's family of 11 children, 59 grandchildren and 99 great-grandchildren, totaling 169 direct descendants, President Tanner noted, was "more than twice the total population of the whole House of Israel in the day Jacob took his family into Egypt."

In conclusion President Tanner quoted from President Smith's last general conference address, in April, 1972, which included these admonitions to the world and to the Church: "And so we invite all our Father's children, everywhere, to believe in Christ, to receive him as he is revealed by living prophets, and to join The

Church of Jesus Christ of Latter-day Saints. We call upon the world to repent, to worship that God who made them, and to believe the words of these whom he hath sent in this day to proclaim his gospel.

"To those who have received the gospel we say: Keep the commandments. Walk in the light. Endure to the end. Be true to every covenant and obligation, and the Lord will bless you beyond your fondest dreams. As it was said by one of old, 'Let us hear the conclusion of the whole matter: Fear God, and keep his commandments; for this is the whole duty of man.' "

In the conclusion of his funeral sermon President McConkie also quoted from a recent conference address of President Smith's, this one delivered at the closing session of the October, 1971 conference:

"I have sought all my days to keep the commandments and do those things which will please the Lord, and I desire to bear testimony of his goodness to me and to all his saints.

"As I stand now, in the twilight of life, with the realization that in a not far distant day I shall be called upon to give an account of my mortal stewardship, I bear testimony again of the truth and divinity of this great work."

As the funeral service ended and the cortege moved slowly east on South Temple street en route to the Salt Lake City Cemetery, the bells tolled in the Catholic Cathedral of the Madeleine, at Third East and South Temple, even as they had done for another President Joseph Fielding Smith 54 years earlier. At N Street the procession turned north and up the steep avenue to the city cemetery. Here on a beautiful green hillside close to the graves of loved ones, his grave was dedicated by his secretary, D. Arthur Haycock, who had served him faithfully and well during his two and a half years as church president. And so his mortal remains were laid to rest. As President Tanner had observed to a friend, "His death was in the nature of a noble benediction at the end of another day of peace and service."

A few days following the funeral service the children of Joseph Fielding Smith received the following letter from President Harold B. Lee:

"My dear Ones:

"Now that the adulation, the commendation, and the well-deserved tributes have been made and we move to carry on in the footsteps of your great patriarch and our great leader, Joseph Fielding Smith, I wanted to take this opportunity of making a few comments in addition to what I have said publicly.

"From the first time I heard your father, when, as a young boy I sat in the old opera house at Preston, Idaho, and heard one of the youngest apostles bear his testimony, and to preach doctrinal sermons, I have leaned upon and listened to his counsel and interpretations of the gospel principles, as an authority on so many points of doctrine about which there might have been misunderstandings.

"Knowing as I have been told many times by him, that he was tutored by his father Joseph F. Smith, I have realized that through his father and his forebears generally, of the generations that have passed, he has had the constant guiding inspiration from Joseph Smith Sr. through Hyrum Smith and his father Joseph F. Smith, and to him personally. We who are the recipients of that kind of inspiration are now humbly grateful and I personally, that I can now dip into the treasure house of what he has left us and there be more certain than I otherwise could be in the responsibilities which now are mine.

"Truly the greatest monument to him is the great posterity which he has given to the world. I speak honestly and with much thoughtful appraisal of other families when I say that I believe that the Joseph Fielding Smith family, linked with the Smith generations before, have been one of the greatest, if not the greatest, family that has lived upon the earth. I have no doubt but that now he has been welcomed into the company of those who have preceded him and is now finding the joy that one like he is worthy and entitled to receive.

"His passing to me was as near a translation from life unto death as I think we will see in our lifetime experience. He died as he lived and has demonstrated to all of us how one can be so honored and so privileged when he has lived so close to the Lord as has your noble patriarch and father, Joseph Fielding Smith.

"To you of his immediate family who have stood by him, and particularly during this last year when his third wife was taken from him, I pay my deep respect and assurance of my full comprehension of what it has meant to him and to you. I have never seen him happier, and I believe, as I have observed, never has his family been closer to him than in this last year of his life. . . ."

It is pleasant to contemplate the happy reunion that President Smith enjoyed in Paradise that Sunday evening, with a host of family members and friends to greet him. There would be his beloved father, whom he had not seen in 54 years, and his dear mother, who had been gone for 38 years. There was his son Lewis, whom he had had no opportunity to bid goodbye 28 years ago. There were brothers and sisters, aunts and uncles, and the brethren with whom he had been so closely associated through the years, such as his predecessor, President David O. McKay, who also had arrived on a Sabbath day, two and a half years earlier. There were those noble relatives whom he knew so well by reputation: His grandfather Hyrum, his grand-uncle the Prophet Joseph, their father Joseph Sr., and others whose names he had honored upon the earth. They would all be there to greet him.

Surely none could have been more anxious to welcome him home than three lovely women who had borne his name upon earth and who were sealed to him for eternity: Louie, Ethel, and Jessie, each one Sister Joseph Fielding Smith. It was 64 long years since he and Louie had said goodbye. What a glorious moment to be once again in her presence. And Ethel. It was 35 years since he had bid Ethel farewell. But now he was again with her. And Jessie. Only 11 months had passed since her departure, yet what a long and lonely 11 months it had been.

President Harold B. Lee conducts graveside services for President Joseph Fielding Smith.

In January, 1938, as he anticipated marrying Jessie, he had written to his son Lewis, who was then on a mission in Switzerland, "No one can take your mother's place, nor Aunt Louie's place. The place of each is secure, if I will do my part faithfully, through all eternity. I am certainly grateful for this knowledge which I have. Aunt Jessie will take her own place, and it too will be secure and hers forever, if I will remain faithful and true, which I humbly hope and pray I will do to the end. Thank the Lord for the knowledge of the eternity of the family, and the privilege to obtain these blessings, which I have taken steps to do in the case of Aunt Louie and your mother, and which I expect to do once again. . . . I feel with perfect assurance that I have the approval of the wives that have been given me, in what I am doing now. I feel that to be the case. With love, Father."

And now on this Sunday evening, July 2, 1972, here

385

suddenly they were all together: Joseph Fielding Smith who wrote the letter, Lewis Warren Smith who received and accepted it, and the three lovely women who were the subject of the letter. And it all seemed natural and proper as it should be. Although he had had the sorrow of burying three wives, he also had the joy of having three devoted, talented women in his life as wives. By mortal view it seemed incredible that one man living in monogamy could have three wives in this life for as long as Joseph Fielding did: Louie for 10 years, then Ethel for 29 years, and finally Jessie Ella for 33 years. But such was the case, and even those years become in length of time insignificant when compared to the eternity of time that lies ahead.

If one believed in numerology he might find significance in the fact that each of Joseph Fielding's three wives had married him in a year ending in the figure 8: Louie in 1898, Ethel in 1908, and Jessie in 1938. At least it is an interesting coincidence. And it is interesting to note that the figure 8 is formed by two circles, and the circle, as the Prophet Joseph Smith illustrated with his ring, symbolizes the eternal, having no beginning and no end. It is difficult for the human mind to comprehend the concept of no beginning, and just a little easier to think of no end. Yet the ring, the circle, does suggest the possibility of each. Perhaps that is one reason people enjoy wearing a wedding ring on their finger. Such a ring Joseph Fielding enjoyed wearing: a gold wedding band with a diamond inset that Jessie gave to him. But symbols are of this life, and that which is but symbolic in this life becomes reality in eternal life.

The moment of arrival and reunion on that Sabbath evening was one that Joseph Fielding Smith had often contemplated, looking forward to with keen anticipation. His hopes, his desires, and his gratitude had been expressed often, but perhaps never more poignantly than in a letter written to his son Douglas, who was then on a church mission in Juneau, Alaska, with a copy also to his son Milton, then on a mission in Argentina; on July

18, 1948, the day before Joseph Fielding's 72nd birthday anniversary:

"Thank you for your birthday card. I want you to know, son, that I greatly appreciate it. I am proud of my sons, even if they may not know it. I wonder, at times, if they really appreciate just how I feel towards them. I am very thankful that the Lord gave me good children. At times I wish some of them would be a little better, but they are all good and I do not think I am deceived. I greatly appreciate your kind sentiments, and it makes me happy to know that you feel as you do about your heritage. It is, son, a good one. Be true to it. There is none better. I am not speaking of myself, for I too am proud of my heritage. I had a noble father, and grandfather, and great-grandfather, and I *must not* fail them. I am duty bound, for their sakes, as well as for my own, to be faithful and true to the Church, the mission of the Prophet Joseph Smith and above all, to our Redeemer.

"I sit and reflect at times, and in my reading of the scriptures, I think of the mission of our Lord, what he did for *me*, and when these feelings come upon me I say to myself, I cannot be untrue to him. He loved me with a perfect love, as he has done for all men, especially those who serve him, and I *must* love him with all the love I can, even if it is imperfect, which it should not be. It is wonderful. I did not live in the days of our Savior; he has not come to me in person. I have not beheld him. His Father and he have not felt it necessary to grant me such a great blessing as this. But it is not necessary. I have felt his presence. I know that the Holy Spirit has enlightened my mind and *revealed him unto me*, so that I do love my Redeemer, I hope, and feel it is true, better than everything else in this life. I would not have it otherwise. I want to be true to him. I know he died for me, for you and all mankind that we might live again through the resurrection. I know that he died that I might be forgiven my follies, my sins, and be cleansed from them. How wonderful is this love. How can I, knowing this, do anything else but love him, my Redeemer. I want my boys in the mission fields to feel this same way. I want my children and my grandchildren to feel that way, and never stray from the path of truth and righteousness.

"I know the truth! I am not deceived, and I know if I continue in faithfulness to the end, keeping the covenants which I have made, and the commandments the Lord has given, that I will be worthy of a place in the celestial kingdom. I want to take with me all that is mine! My wives and children. And the Lord has blessed me. The mother of Josephine and Julina is mine. She was in life one of the noble souls, full of faith and devotion. Your mother, that is the mother of my other children, was just as true and faithful. Both of these have earned a just reward. They are entitled to a place in the celestial kingdom. They belong to me, if I continue to the end, forever. Our present mother, we call Aunt Jessie, is also a noble soul. Do you think for one moment, I want to give any one of those good women up? Verily no. And, thanks to the gospel, I do not have to if I am true.

"Tomorrow is my birth anniversary. When I think of my age, I have to realize that I am getting old, but I do not feel it; I do not realize it, but evidently it is true. So, in the course of a few years, I will have to take my departure as those have done before me, but I want to feel that I am leaving here my family determined to be faithful and true. This life is temporary; the life to come is permanent. How glorious it will be, when we can all meet again in peace, love and perfection. This is our privilege if we will continue steadfast in the truth."

Authors' Notes on Materials and Preparation of the Book

Thousands of hours have been devoted to the preparation of this biography, in gathering material, writing the book, and proofreading it. The authors were fortunate in having been able to work as a team, the one primarily responsible for the researching and compiling of material and the other for the writing, but each sharing in all aspects of its preparation, from the beginning of the planning for it to the final checking of page proofs. For them it has been a labor of love, sharing as they do the highest esteem for President Joseph Fielding Smith.

Although the actual writing of the book was not begun until a year prior to its publication in October 1972, the gathering of material for it was begun several years earlier, with the thought that the book would be published shortly after his death. This was the time schedule developed by the authors and William James Mortimer, manager of Deseret Book Company. In discussions regarding it President Smith indicated that he did not wish a biography published until after his death.

The authors and publisher decided against the use of footnotes in the book, for these tend to distract the reader and thus are more of a nuisance than a benefit to most readers. Recognizing that some readers would like information on source material, however, and also to give due acknowledgment for material used, the following bibliographic notes are included:

Much of the information in the book is from firsthand knowledge and acquaintance of the authors, one of whom is the eldest son of President Smith and the other a friend. The authors were fortunate also in having the use of President Smith's personal daily journals, letters and other documents. A large portion of the quoted material in the book is from these primary sources, which afford a far more intimate view of the man than could be had through any other material. Some quotes have been drawn from President Smith's own books, particularly from his biography of his father, the *Life of Joseph F. Smith*. President Smith's other children, three of his sisters and other relatives and friends shared with the authors letters they had received from him or/and memories of their associations with him. There was quite a complete file of his several dozen letters to his sons while they were on their missions or in the armed forces. In 1963 his son Douglas tape-recorded an interview with him and this was a helpful reference. Counselors, assistants, secretaries and other close associates of President Smith also provided material. Through the years several articles on him had been published in the church periodicals, particularly *The Improvement Era* and its successor *The Ensign*. The standard works of the Church and the *Documentary History of the Church* afforded some useful references. In President Smith's files were some pertinent clippings from early 1900 editions of *The Deseret News*, *The Salt Lake Tribune* and other Salt Lake City and Ogden newspapers. Several unpublished documents in the Church Historian's Office were also useful.

It was the pleasure of the authors to not only visit with President Smith, his wife Jessie, and others close to him, but to visit in the houses, apartment, and offices where he had lived and worked. It was interesting, for instance, to look through the old Joseph F. Smith home, now abandoned, where Joseph Fielding Smith was born and spent his childhood and young manhood, including his first year or two of married life: likewise, the house that he had built on Second West Street, where he and Louie and then Ethel reared their family. In his apartment on South Temple and State Street could be seen many interesting items that helped reflect the life of Joseph Fielding Smith: the portrait of his father, the shelves of books, the grand piano, the mementos from his travels, his typewriter and typetable, the sword that had been carried by his grandfather Hyrum Smith, the letters that his father had written as a lonely 15-year-old orphaned missionary on the Hawaiian Islands. Such visits helped immeasurably in the attempt to write about this man Joseph Fielding Smith.

Chapter by chapter, bibliographic and other notes include the following:

Chapter 1. No written sources here except one journal entry. Based largely upon personal acquaintance and interviews. This chapter was originally prepared as a magazine article; thus the use of the first person "I" of the writer.

Chapter 2. Life of Joseph F. Smith was the chief reference.

Chapter 3. Life of Joseph F. Smith plus some unpublished autobiographical documents in the Smith family.

Chapter 4. Some genealogical data regarding Louie Shurtliff Smith were provided by Warren N. Shurtliff of Ogden and Wallace V. Shurtliff of Fort Bridger, Wyoming, and a copy of the university commencement program and list of graduates was provided by the University of Utah. Remembrances of his sisters.

Chapter 5. His missionary journals and letters to and from his wife and parents. The pressed flowers he and Louie sent to each other are still in the envelopes.

Chapter 6. His journals and early pamphlets.

Chapter 7. His journals. The scriptural quotes are from Genesis 3:19 and Job 1:21.

Chapter 8. His journals, and one letter to Ethel, written April 16, 1925, from Great Falls, Montana.

Chapter 9. His journals and his interview with Douglas. The *Tribune* editorial is from the April 7, 1910 edition.

Chapter 10. His journals, letters to Ethel, and interview with Douglas: remembrances of his sisters and older children; his *Life of Joseph F. Smith.*

Chapter 11. His journals and letters; remembrances of his children, some of which were expressed in letters to the authors. His interview with Douglas.

Chapter 12. His journals and his letters to and from Ethel. Her tribute to him was published in the June 1932 issue of *The Improvement Era* as part of a biographical sketch on him by Bryant S. Hinckley.

Chapter 13. His journals, and letters to his son Lewis, then serving a mission to Switzerland; also Salt Lake newspapers of 1938.

Chapter 14. His journals and his letters to his son Lewis in Switzerland; also a journal Jessie Evans Smith kept on the European tour.

Chapter 15. His journals, and his letters to his sons while they were on Church missions or in the armed forces; his folder of documents on his son Lewis.

Chapter 16. His journals and letters, and the journals Jessie kept of their mission tours; also reports he prepared on the tours, and published accounts in the *Church News* and *The Improvement Era.*

Chapter 17. His journals, his letter from President McKay, and a report that Alvin R. Dyer prepared, entitled, *Journal Record of the Visit of President David O. McKay to Adam-ondi-Ahman. The Improvement Era* article by Doyle L. Green, editor, is in the July, 1966, issue.

Chapter 18. Letters by his children and family records.

Chapter 19. Heslop's and Van Orden's *A Prophet Among the People;* issues of *The Improvement Era* and *The Ensign* for this period;

several unpublished church documents. Remembrances of his secretaries and other associates.

Chapter 20. Copies of the funeral services and sermons; his letters to his sons Lewis and Milton; President Lee's letter to the family.

Photographs were obtained from Joseph Fielding Smith Jr.'s private collection and from the *Deseret News,* courtesy of J M. Heslop.

INDEX